Desiring
the Kingdom

Desiring the Kingdom

WORSHIP, WORLDVIEW, AND CULTURAL FORMATION

Volume 1 of Cultural Liturgies

James K. A. Smith

Baker Academic

a division of Baker Publishing Group

Grand Rapids, Michigan

© 2009 by James K. A. Smith

Published by Baker Academic
a division of Baker Publishing Group
P.O. Box 6287, Grand Rapids, MI 49516-6287
www.bakeracademic.com

Printed in the United States of America

Library of Congress Cataloging-in-Publication Data
Smith, James K. A., 1970–
  Desiring the kingdom : worship, worldview, and cultural formation / James K. A. Smith.
      p.   cm. — (Cultural liturgies ; v. 1)
  Includes bibliographical references and indexes.
  ISBN 978-0-8010-3577-7 (pbk.)
  1. Liturgics. 2. Christianity and culture. 3. Liturgical adaptation. 4. Christianity—Philoso-
phy. I. Title.
BV178.S63 2009
264.001—dc22   2009009315

16   9

For Madison:
That little glint in your eye is,
for me,
a sure sign that the kingdom
is a kingdom of love.

Delight yourself in the Lord,
and he will give you the desires of your heart.

Psalm 37:4 NIV

Reason: I, Reason, am in minds as the power of looking is in the eyes. Having eyes is not the same thing as looking, and looking is not the same as seeing. The soul therefore needs three things: eyes which it can use aright, looking, and seeing. . . . It is impossible to show God to a mind vitiated and sick. Only the healthy mind can see him. But if the mind does not believe that only thus will it attain vision, it will not seek healing. Even if it believes that this is true, and that only so will it attain the vision, but at the same time despairs of healing, will it not abandon the quest and refuse to obey the precepts of the physician?

Augustine: Most assuredly, especially because the disease must have sharp remedies.

Reason: So to faith must be added hope. [But] suppose it believes all this is true and hopes that healing is possible, but does not love and desire the promised light, and thinks it must be meantime content with its darkness which through habit has become pleasant, will it not, no less, spurn the physician?

Augustine: Perfectly true.

Reason: Therefore a third thing is necessary, *love*.

Augustine, *Soliloquies* 1.6.12

The boy sat tottering. The man watched him that he not topple into the flames. He kicked holes in the sand for the boy's hips and shoulders where he would sleep and he sat holding him while he tousled his hair before the fire to dry it. All of this like some ancient anointing. So be it. Evoke the forms. Where you've nothing else construct ceremonies out of the air and breathe upon them.

Cormac McCarthy, *The Road*

Contents

Sidebars and Figures

Sidebars

Picturing This

To Think About

Figures

Preface

This book has a primary target, but it's also hoping for some collateral impact. The genesis of the project was a desire to communicate to students (and faculty) a vision of what authentic, integral Christian learning looks like, emphasizing how learning is connected to worship and how, together, these constitute practices of formation and discipleship. Instead of focusing on what Christians *think*, distilling Christian faith into an intellectual summary formula (a "worldview"), this book focuses on what Christians *do*, articulating the shape of a Christian "social imaginary" as it is embedded in the practices of Christian worship. (Alexander Schmemann's *For the Life of the World* was an inspiring, working model here—though I don't pretend to have approached the compact majesty of that marvelous little book.) In short, the goal is to push down through worldview to worship as the matrix from which a Christian worldview is born—and to consider what that means for the task of Christian education and the shape of Christian worship. This doesn't require rejecting worldview-talk, only situating it in relation to Christian practices, particularly the practices of Christian worship. Thus I envision the book as a companion volume to classroom texts on worldview such as Walsh and Middleton's *Transforming Vision*, Wolters's *Creation Regained*, or Plantinga's *Engaging God's World*.

As I was working on the project over the past several years and had opportunity to field-test the ideas in various contexts, it was suggested to me that the book's argument might be of interest to a couple of further audiences. First, because it articulates the formative importance of worship and the vision of the world implicit in the practices of Christian worship, the book may be of interest to pastors, campus ministers, worship leaders, and others responsible for the shape of Christian worship in local congregations. It would be an honor and pleasure for me if this book could be a catalyst for inviting evangelical and Reformed communities to further intentional reflection on what we do as a people gathered by worship. Second, fellow scholars who heard or read early drafts of the project suggested that some of the issues and themes engaged here might also be breaking new ground and striking some new paths for Christian thought, and so might be of interest to scholars (philosophers, theologians, social scientists, and others). However, I didn't want to abandon the pedagogical intentions of the project and write a scholarly book. So scholars might read this volume as a précis or abstract of a larger project—a bit of a promissory note.

I hope to keep those promises in two follow-up monographs that will constitute volumes 2 and 3 of Cultural Liturgies. The second volume will specifically focus on the philosophical anthropology sketched in chapters 1 and 2, with particular attention to the emerging dialogue between phenomenology, cognitive science, and social-scientific reflection on practiced formation. The third volume will address current debates in political theology, both in the particular orbit of the Reformed tradition (Mouw, Wolterstorff, and others) as well as the current debate between Jeffrey Stout's vision of a traditioned democracy and "new traditionalist" critiques of liberalism (MacIntyre, Hauerwas, Milbank). This first volume provides hints of the sorts of contributions I want to make to these discussions. But in order to keep the book focused on its core audience (students and teachers), I have kept these scholarly trajectories rather chastened, largely pushing those hints into footnotes.

Acknowledgments

This book owes its original impetus to the vision and energy of John Witvliet, director of the Calvin Institute of Christian Worship. As a liturgical theologian, John sensed and saw the importance of reconnecting worship and worldview and invited me to tackle the task. His prompting birthed an entire research agenda and was really an occasion for me to do some stocktaking of my work and its future, and to retool my interests in order to more intentionally let philosophical and theological reflection serve the church. He can't be blamed for what follows, but I am grateful for his catalytic vision. I am also grateful for a research grant from the Calvin Institute of Christian Worship in 2005–6, with funds from the Lilly Endowment, Inc., which got this project off the ground. I also owe a debt to Shirley Roels, director of the Lilly Vocation Project at Calvin College, for a course reduction while I was a Lilly Vocation Fellow in the same year. This was followed by a Vocation Venture Fund grant in fall 2007 that brought together some valued colleagues for a reading retreat focused on a first draft of this book. That group included Claudia Beversluis, Jeff Bouman, Ronald Feenstra, Shirley Roels, Kurt Schaefer, David Smith, Bill VanGroningen, and John Witvliet, to whom I'm grateful for their time and insights.

My thinking on these matters developed and matured in no small way because of conversations I've enjoyed as part of a working group on philosophy and liturgy, also funded by the Calvin Institute of Christian Worship, which I have had the pleasure of directing with Nick Wolterstorff and John Witvliet. This group has been one of the intellectual highlights of my career, and I am very grateful to Sarah Coakley, Terence Cuneo, Reinhard Hütter, Peter Ochs, Nick, and John for such wise and stimulating conversations.

The book started to take shape when I had occasions to give lectures and talks in various contexts. Several opportunities in particular provided congenial environments for deepening my thinking on these issues. In the spring of 2006 I once again visited L'Abri in Huémoz, Switzerland, and presented two lectures based on this project. It was in conversations with the workers and students at L'Abri that I first got a sense of how much more deeply I could explore these issues, which transformed the project from a single, small volume to a more robust and systematic trilogy unpacking a philosophical theology of culture. My special thanks to Greg Laughery, Richard Bradford, and all the good folks at L'Abri for continuing to sustain one of the most unique and energizing environments for Christian reflection that I have ever experienced. Shortly after returning from L'Abri, I had opportunity to speak to the national conference of the Christian Reformed Campus Ministers Association at the University of Illinois-Champaign. Because they inhabit a provocative space between the university and the church, conversation with these chaplains helped me expand my vision and imagine how this project might hit the ground outside the classroom. I also presented versions of several chapters to college-wide audiences at King's University College in Edmonton, Alberta, and Redeemer University College in Ancaster, Ontario. It was a special treat to discuss these issues with colleagues and students at these sister institutions. Their confirmation and critique undoubtedly improved the argument. My thanks to Roy Berkenbosch at King's and Syd Hielema at Redeemer for the invitations, and to both communities for their gracious (Canadian!) hospitality. Finally, I had a unique opportunity to think about these matters with respect to K–12 education due to a felicitous invitation from Linda Boersma to speak at a faculty retreat of the Langley Christian Schools in British Columbia. My thanks to those teachers for warmly receiving an egghead philosopher and teaching me so much in the process.

The book's argument owes so much to so many influences that I can't hope to enumerate them here; the footnotes will have to serve that purpose to some extent. In particular, my thinking on these matters has been deeply shaped by recent friendships fostered by the Ekklesia Project. Those familiar with the work of Stanley Hauerwas, William Cavanaugh, D. Stephen Long, Mike Budde, Dan Bell, Brent Laytham, Sam Wells, Therese Lysaught, David Matzko McCarthy, and others will find much here that is familiar, though perhaps somewhat remixed because of conversations I have enjoyed in a different orbit with Rich Mouw, Jim Bratt, Hans Boersma, Nicholas Wolterstorff, John Witvliet, John Bolt, Cheryl Brandsen, Jeff Bouman, and other Reformed folk. My thinking is a result of the chemical reaction that results from being in these Catholic and Reformed conversations; indeed, this book is my attempt to articulate the Reformed tradition as an Augustinian renewal movement within the church catholic. My little project is not novel in any significant way. It is already anticipated in works such as Schmemann's *For the Life of the World*, Yoder's *Body Politics*, and others. What's unique is perhaps a contemporary articulation from within the Reformed tradition, with a view of reaching an audience that is both catholic and evangelical—as well as the specific focus here on the shape and task of Christian higher education.

We continue to call Grand Rapids home because it's where our friends live. I am grateful to be part of the Calvin College community, which nourishes and sustains a rich intellectual environment and provides the space for collaboration with wise friends. The Christian publishers that call Grand Rapids home also contribute to the intellectual life of the city. It's a particular treat to have my editor, Bob Hosack, just a few blocks away and to count him a friend. Thanks especially to Bob for his gracious patience on this project. We are also grateful to the friends who have become our family here: Mark and Dawn Mulder (thanks for Wednesday Night Wine and loving us even in our "comfy clothes") and Matt and Lisa Walhout ("We'll always have Mexico!") have welcomed and embraced the Smith clan with all our warts and blemishes. We're also grateful to the saints at Neland Avenue CRC for welcoming us into the fold. In many ways, I didn't know how to write chapter 5 until being shaped by worship at Neland.

This book has been like a seventh member of our family over the past several years—an increasingly disruptive member more recently. I'm grateful to my family for making room for this interloper, showing it (and me) gracious hospitality. Finally, this book argues that we human creatures are lovers before and above all else, and that the people of God is a community marked by a love and desire for the kingdom of God. Everything I know of love I have learned in the "school" that is marriage to Deanna, a school from which I hope never to graduate. She has been a patient teacher. I hope this book is some small testimony of the romantic vision of the world she embodies.

Given that this book has been gestating so long, the sound track has grown to a multidisc set, including selections from Patty Griffin's *Children Running Through*; Nickel Creek's *Why Should the Fire Die?*; Bach's *St. Matthew Passion*; the Indigo Girls' *All That We Let In*; Uncle Tupelo's *March 16–20, 1992*; *The Historical Conquests of Josh Ritter*; and Romantica's *It's Your Weakness That I Want* and *America*. Perhaps you'll hear them in the background.

Introduction

What is education *for*? And more specifically, what is at stake in a distinctively Christian education? What does the qualifier *Christian* mean when appended to education? It is usually understood that education is about ideas and information (though it is also too often routinely reduced to credentialing for a career and viewed as a ticket to a job). And so distinctively *Christian* education is understood to be about Christian ideas—which usually requires a defense of the importance of "the life of the mind."[1] On this account, the goal of a Christian education is the development of a Christian perspective, or more commonly now, a Christian *worldview*, which is taken to be a system of Christian beliefs, ideas, and doctrines.

But what if this line of thinking gets off on the wrong foot? What if education, including higher education, is not primarily[2] about the absorption

1. This defense is necessary because many North American Christians have an understanding of faith that prizes concern with eternity and personal salvation over "worldly" activities like engaging in research and gaining knowledge of this world. According to this dualistic picture, Christians should be spending their time and energy in missions and evangelism, not cancer research and art history. Thus many articulations of the ideals of Christian higher education begin back on their heels and have to first justify why Christians should be concerned with "the life of the mind." See, for example, Clifford Williams, *The Life of the Mind: A Christian Perspective* (Grand Rapids: Baker Academic, 2002).

2. I ask the reader who might be worried that my proposal amounts to a newfangled form of anti-intellectualism to especially note the adverbial qualifiers in this paragraph (*primarily, fundamentally, first and foremost*, etc.). I am not advocating a new form of pious dichotomy that would force us to choose between *either* the heart *or* the mind. Rather, I will sketch an account of the priority of affectivity that undergirds and makes

of ideas and information, but about the *formation* of hearts and desires? What if we began by appreciating how education not only gets into our head but also (and more fundamentally) grabs us by the gut—what the New Testament refers to as *kardia*, "the heart"? What if education was primarily concerned with shaping our hopes and passions—our visions of "the good life"—and not merely about the dissemination of data and information as inputs to our thinking? What if the primary work of education was the transforming of our imagination rather than the saturation of our intellect? And what if this had as much to do with our bodies as with our minds?

What if education wasn't first and foremost about what we know, but about what we love?

That actually is the wager of this book: It is an invitation to re-vision Christian education as a formative rather than just an informative project.[3] It is an invitation to what we'll call an "adventure in philosophical anthropology"; its root conviction is that how we think about education is inextricably linked to how we think about human persons. Too much of our thinking about education (including much recent talk about worldviews) sees education as a matter of disseminating information precisely because it assumes that human beings are primarily thinking things, or maybe believing animals. But I think both of these models give us a stunted, flattened picture of the rich complexity of being human.

There are (at least) two important implications that follow from this— such that the stakes of my argument spill beyond the walls of the school and university. On the one hand, this will obviously have implications for how we think about Christian education and, in particular, how we think about the mission and task of Christian schools, colleges, and universities. Based on the alternative model I will sketch in this book, how we think about distinctly Christian education would not be primarily a matter of sorting out which Christian ideas to drop into eager and willing mind-receptacles; rather, it would become a matter of thinking about how a Christian education shapes us, forms us, molds us to be a certain kind of people whose hearts and passions and desires are aimed at the kingdom of God. And that will require sustained attention to the practices that effect such transformation. In short, it's going to require that Christian educa-

---

possible the work of the intellect. In short, I'm not arguing that we love, and therefore we need not know; rather, we love *in order to* know. In this respect I hope I'm echoing an ancient theme we find in Augustine and Maximus the Confessor. For related discussion, see Aristotle Papanikolaou, "Liberating Eros: Confession and Desire," *Journal of the Society of Christian Ethics* 26 (2006): 115–36.

3. My primary focus in this book will be Christian higher education. However, I think almost everything I have to say here also has implications for Christian education at the K–12 level.

tion find its font and foundation in the practices of Christian worship. On the other hand, I think we'll also have to broaden our sense about the "spaces" of education. If education is primarily *form*ation—and more specifically, the formation of our desires—then that means education is happening all over the place (for good and ill). Education as formation isn't the sort of thing that stays neatly within the walls of the school or college or university. If education is about formation, then we need to be attentive to all the formative work that is happening outside the university: in homes and at the mall; in football stadiums and at Fourth of July parades; in worship and at work.

Perhaps above all, this book is out to raise the stakes of Christian education, which will also mean raising the stakes of Christian worship. The goal is to get us to appreciate what's at stake in both—nothing less than the formation of radical disciples who desire the kingdom of God. But in order for this stake-raising to take place, we need to become attentive to our environment and our habits, to see them with new eyes, as if for the first time. To do that, let's consider a little case study.

Making the Familiar Strange: A Phenomenology of Cultural Liturgies

I would like to invite you for a tour of one of the most important religious sites in our metropolitan area. It is the kind of place that may be quite familiar to many of you, but my task here is actually to try to make this place strange. I will try to invite you to see it with new eyes, which will require trying to shake off the scales of mundane familiarity. This will require focused attention to detail; like a Tarkovsky film, imagine your attention focused by the slow, patient, observant gaze of the camera frame. We'll turn that camera gaze and let it hang on something you see all the time, but perhaps without *seeing* it. So you might imagine that we are Martian anthropologists who have come to this strange world of twenty-first-century North America in order to gather data on the rituals and religious habits of its inhabitants. Having made our way from Mars, equipped with the tools of ethnographic description, we are going to venture to one of this culture's most common religious sites and observe it with eyes that are focused on the religious aspects of its rituals. So join me in the approach to this site.

As we're still off at a distance, I want you to notice the sheer popularity of the site as indicated by the colorful sea of parking that surrounds the building. The site is throbbing with pilgrims every day of the week as thousands and thousands make the pilgrimage. In order to provide a hospitable environment and absorb the daily influx of the faithful, the site provides an ocean of parking. But the monotony of black tarmac is covered by dots of color from cars and SUVs lined up, row by row, patiently waiting as the pilgrims devote themselves to the rituals inside. Indeed, the parking lot constitutes a kind of moat around the building since there are no sidewalks that lead to the site. Religious sites of this kind almost inevitably emerge on the suburban edges of cities—areas planned around the automobile and generally suspicious of pedestrians. The sacred building even provides a sanctuary from this incessant culture of automobility, as some pilgrims make their way to this sanctuary—especially in winter— just for the space to walk.

We've now made our way into this glistening sea of black and color and found a haven for our vehicle, still quite a distance from the sanctuary. However, already the hospitality of this community extends itself: waiting for us is a train-like cart to convey our family across the parking lot. Other pilgrims board the conveyance, and we begin to wend our way toward the building that sprawls in both directions and seems to be rising from the horizon—a dazzling array of glass and concrete with recognizable ornamentation. Indeed, because this particular religious site is part of an international, yea "catholic," network of religious communities, the architecture of the building has a recognizable code that makes us feel at home in any city. The large glass atriums at the entrances are framed by banners and flags; familiar texts and symbols on the exterior walls help foreign faithful to quickly and easily identify what's inside; and the sprawling layout of the building is anchored by larger pavilions or sanctuaries akin to the vestibules of medieval cathedrals.

Our train ride has brought us to one of several grandiose entrees to the building, channeling us through a colonnade of chromed arches to the towering glass face, with doors lining its base. As we enter the space, we are ushered into a narthex of sorts intended for receiving, orienting, and channeling new seekers as well as providing a bit of a decompression space for the regular faithful to "enter in" to the spirit of the space. For the seeker, there is a large map—a kind of worship aid—to give the novice an orientation to the location of various spiritual offerings and provide direction into the labyrinth that organizes and channels the ritual observance of the pilgrims. (One can readily recognize the "regulars," the faithful, who enter the space with a sense of achieved familiarity, who know the rhythms by heart because of habit-forming repetition.)

The design of the interior is inviting to an almost excessive degree, sucking us into the enclosed interior spaces, with windows on the ceiling open to the sky but none on the walls open to the surrounding automotive moat. This conveys a sense of vertical and transcendent openness that at the same time shuts off the clamor and distractions of the horizontal, mundane world. This architectural mode of enclosure and enfolding offers a feeling of sanctuary, retreat, and escape. From the narthex entry one is invited to lose oneself in this space, which channels the pilgrim into a labyrinth of octagons and circles, inviting a wandering that seems to escape from the driven, goal-oriented ways we inhabit the "outside" world. The pilgrim is also invited to escape from mundane ticking and counting of clock time and to inhabit a space governed by a different time, one almost timeless. With few windows and a curious baroque manipulation of light, it almost seems as if the sun stands still in here, or we lose consciousness of time's passing and so lose ourselves in the rituals for which we've come. However, while daily clock time is suspended, the worship space is very much governed by a kind of liturgical, festal calendar, variously draped in the colors, symbols, and images of an unending litany of holidays and festivals—to which new ones are regularly added, since the establishment of each new festival translates into greater numbers of pilgrims joining the processions to the sanctuary and engaging in worship.

The layout of this temple has architectural echoes that hark back to medieval cathedrals—mammoth religious spaces that can absorb all kinds of different religious activities all at one time. And so one might say that this religious building has a winding labyrinth for contemplation, alongside of which are innumerable chapels devoted to various saints. As we wander the labyrinth in contemplation, preparing to enter one of the chapels, we'll be struck by the rich iconography that lines the walls and interior spaces. Unlike the flattened depictions of saints one might find in stained-glass windows, here is an array of three-dimensional icons adorned in garb that—as with all iconography—inspires us to be imitators of these exemplars. These statutes and icons embody for us concrete images of "the good life." Here is a religious proclamation that does not traffic in abstracted ideals or rules or doctrines, but rather offers to the imagination pictures and statues and moving images. While other religions are promising salvation through the thin, dry media of books and messages, this new global religion is offering embodied pictures of the redeemed that invite us to imagine ourselves in their shoes—to imagine ourselves otherwise, and thus to willingly submit to the disciplines that produce the saints evoked in the icons.

Here again, we need to appreciate the catholicity of this iconography: these same icons of the good life are found in such temples across the country and around the world. The symbols and colors and images associated with their religious life are readily recognized the world over. The wide circulation of these icons through various mediums even outside the sanctuary invites us to make the pilgrimage in the first place. This temple—like countless others now emerging around the world—offers a rich, embodied visual mode of evangelism that attracts us. This is a gospel whose power is *beauty*, which speaks to our deepest desires and compels us to come not with dire moralisms but rather with a winsome invitation to share in this envisioned good life. (Yet one should note that it has its own modes of exclusivity too; because of its overwhelming success in converting the nations, it is increasingly difficult to be an infidel.) And it is a mode of evangelism buoyed by a transnational network of evangelists and outreach, all speaking a kind of unified message that puts other, fractured religions to shame. If unity is a testimony to a religion's truth and power, it will be hard to find a more powerful religion than this catholic faith.

As we pause to reflect on some of the icons on the outside of one of the chapels, we are thereby invited to consider what's happening within the chapel—invited to enter into the act of worship more properly, invited to taste and see. We are greeted by a welcoming acolyte who offers to shepherd us through the experience, but also has the wisdom to allow us to explore on our own terms. Sometimes we will enter cautiously, curiously, tentatively making our way through this labyrinth within the labyrinth, having a vague sense of need but unsure of how it will be fulfilled, and so are open to surprise—to that moment when the spirit leads us to an experience we couldn't have anticipated. Having a sense of our need, we come looking, not sure what for, but expectant, knowing that what we need must be here. And then we hit upon it: combing through the racks, we find that experience and offering that will provide fulfillment. At other times our worship is intentional, directed, and resolute: we have come prepared for just this moment, knowing exactly why we're here, in search of exactly what we need.

In either case, after time spent focused and searching in what the faithful call "the racks," with our newfound holy object in hand, we proceed to the altar, which is the consummation of worship. While acolytes and other worship assistants have helped us navigate our experience, behind the altar is the priest who presides over the consummating transaction. And this is a religion of transaction, of exchange and communion. When invited to worship here, we are not only invited to give; we are also invited to take. We don't leave this transformative experience with just good feelings or pious generalities, but rather with something concrete and tangible, with newly minted relics, as it were, that are themselves the means to the good life embodied in the icons who invited us into this participatory moment in the first place. And so we make our sacrifice, leave our donation, but in return receive something with solidity that is wrapped in the colors and symbols of the saints and the season. Released by the priest with a benediction, we make our way out of the chapel in a kind of denouement—not necessarily to leave (our awareness of time has been muted), but rather to continue contemplation and be invited into another chapel. Who could resist the tangible realities of the good life so abundantly and invitingly offered?

You've no doubt suspected that my phenomenology of this "religious" site is tongue in cheek, but I would resist the charge. Perhaps we need to confirm the identity of this religious site: as most of you have by now guessed, it is embodied in your local mall. Any generic, suburban mall will do, since the catholicity of this religion means that one will find an overwhelmingly uniform gospel preached at all of them. But I want to adamantly contend that describing the mall as a religious site is *not* merely a metaphor or an analogy. I'm not out to be merely playful or irreverent; rather, my goal is to try to make strange what is so familiar to us precisely in order to help us see what is at stake in formative practices that are part of the mall experience. The description is meant to be apocalyptic, in a sense, unveiling the real character of what presents itself as benign.[4] The description is meant to shift our attention and perspective in order for us to recognize the charged, *religious* nature of cultural institutions that we all tend to inhabit as if they were neutral sites. Looking at the mall through the eyes of worship and liturgy, with attention to the concrete material practices that are part of the experience, gives us an angle on this cultural institution such that we can see that the mall has its own pedagogy, an interest in the education of desire. If it's not quite *The Education of Henry Adams*, we might think of it as *The Education of Hannah Montana*.[5] So we can at once appreciate that the mall is a religious institution because it is a *liturgical* institution, and that it is a pedagogical institution because it is a *formative* institution.

Seeing the mall as a liturgical and pedagogical institution helps us to see what's at stake in its practices; at the same time, and for just this reason, I think this phenomenology of the mall's liturgy points out the limits of a worldview approach. It's hard to think of the mall in terms of worldview, as a place where ideas are proffered (quite the opposite!); but if we look at it from the perspective of love and practice, we become attentive to what's at stake and begin to notice things we hadn't seen before. Worldview approaches regularly (and rightly) make the claim that all human beings are inherently religious, that all human beings at root are *believers* who are committed to and oriented by a fundamental constellation of beliefs that,

4. This notion of an "apocalyptic" reading of culture will be pursued in more detail in chapter 3.

5. See Mark Schwehn's reflections on *The Education of Henry Adams* in *Exiles from Eden: Religion and the Academic Vocation in America* (New York: Oxford University Press, 1993), 94–126. There is an interesting literary history found in works concerned with "The Education of . . . ," such as Erasmus's *Education of a Prince* (1516); Schiller's *Letters upon the Aesthetic Education of Man* (1794); Marie, the Grand Duchess of Russia, in her memoir *The Education of a Princess* (1890); and most famously, *The Education of Henry Adams*. This literary tradition tends to exhibit a more holistic understanding of education as the formation of an identity and the forging of character—education as the creation of a *kind* of person.

even if not reflected upon, govern and control our being and our doing—
what James Olthuis calls our "visions *of* and *for* life."[6] Worldview-thinking
also seeks to discern how such worldviews orient not just persons, but also
communities, institutions, and systems.[7] However, while worldview-talk
(which I don't want to entirely abandon) is critical of rationalist accounts
of the human person that would reduce us to thinking machines, it still
tends to exhibit a fairly "heady" or cognitive picture of the human person,
and thus still thinks that the site of contestation between worldviews or
ground-motives is located in the realm of ideas.

But I think we run up against the limits of this approach when we try to
make sense of the mall (to pick just one important cultural institution; we
could also consider the university, the state, etc.). While with some hard
work and some intellectual acrobatics one could make the case that what's
at stake at the mall is ideas or beliefs, I don't think the faithful pilgrims
to Hollister will find this very convincing. Indeed, the genius of mall religion is that actually it operates with a more holistic, affective, embodied
anthropology (or theory of the human person) than the Christian church
tends to assume! Because worldview-thinking still tends to focus on ideas
and beliefs, the formative cultural impact of sites like the mall tends to
not show up on our radar. Such a heady approach, focused on beliefs, is
not really calibrated to see the quasi-liturgical practices at work in a site
like the mall. An idea-centric or belief-centric approach will fail to see
the pedagogy at work in the mall, and thus will also fail to articulate a
critique and counter-pedagogy. In order to recognize the religious power
and formative force of the mall, we need to adopt a paradigm of cultural
critique and discernment that thinks even deeper than beliefs or worldviews
and takes seriously the central role of formative practices—or what I'll
describe in this book as *liturgies*.

If many configurations of cultural practices function as quasi-liturgies,
as formative pedagogies of desire that are trying to make us a certain kind
of person, we need to ask ourselves: Is there a place that could form us
otherwise—a space of counter-formation? Given the kinds of creatures we
are—affective, desiring, liturgical animals—this can't be addressed merely
with new ideas or even Christian perspectives. The pedagogy of the mall
does not primarily take hold of the head, so to speak; it aims for the heart,
for our guts, our *kardia*. It is a pedagogy of desire that gets hold of us
through the body. So what would it take to resist the alluring formation
of our desire—and hence our identity—that is offered by the market and
the mall? If the mall and its "parachurch" extensions in television and

6. James Olthuis, "On Worldviews," *Christian Scholar's Review* 14.2 (1985): 153–64.
7. E.g., Herman Dooyeweerd, *Roots of Western Culture*, trans. John Kraay (Toronto:
Wedge, 1979).

advertising offer a daily liturgy for the formation of the heart, what might be the church's counter-measures? What if the church unwittingly adopts the same liturgical practices as the market and the mall? Will it then really be a site of counter-formation? What would the church's practices have to look like if they're going to form us as the kind of people who desire something entirely different—who desire the kingdom? What would be the shape of an alternative pedagogy of desire?

Because our hearts are oriented primarily by desire, by what we love, and because those desires are shaped and molded by the habit-forming practices in which we participate, it is the rituals and practices of the mall—the liturgies of mall and market—that shape our imaginations and how we orient ourselves to the world. Embedded in them is a common set of assumptions about the shape of human flourishing, which becomes an implicit *telos*, or goal, of our own desires and actions. That is, the visions of the good life embedded in these practices become surreptitiously embedded in us through our participation in the rituals and rhythms of these institutions. These quasi-liturgies effect an education of desire, a pedagogy of the heart. But if the church is complicit with this sort of formation, where could we look for an alternative education of desire?

The core claim of this book is that liturgies[8]—whether "sacred" or "secular"—shape and constitute our identities by forming our most fundamental desires and our most basic attunement to the world. In short, liturgies make us certain kinds of people, and what defines us is what we *love*. They do this because we are the sorts of animals whose orientation to the world is shaped from the body up more than from the head down. Liturgies aim our love to different ends precisely by training our hearts through our bodies. They prime us to approach the world in a certain way, to value certain things, to aim for certain goals, to pursue certain dreams, to work together on certain projects. In short, every liturgy constitutes a pedagogy that teaches us, in all sorts of precognitive ways, to be a certain kind of person. Hence every liturgy is an education, and embedded in every liturgy is an implicit worldview or "understanding" of the world.[9] And by this I don't mean that implanted in the liturgies are all kind of ideas to be culled from them; rather, implicit in them is an understanding of the world that is pretheoretical, that is on a different register than ideas. That

8. Throughout this book, I simply use the term *liturgy* as a synonym for *worship*. In the word *liturgy*, readers should not hear the valorization of any particular form or style; at the same time, I hope those readers who associate negative connotations with the word *liturgy* will suspend judgment and simply hear the word as a shorthand for naming worship practices of all kinds. I discuss this further at the end of chapter 4.

9. In the next section, and chapters 1 and 2, we'll nuance this claim a bit, drawing on Heidegger's notion of "understanding" (*Verstehen*) as developed in Charles Taylor's notion of "social imaginaries."

is why the education of desire requires a project that aims below the head; it requires the pedagogical formation of our imagination, which, we might say, lies closer to our gut (*kardia*) than our head.

Now, in the same way that I've tried to raise the stakes of what's going on in the mall, I also want to raise the stakes of what's happening in Christian worship, whether in the storefront chapel or the metropolitan cathedral. What sorts of habits are going to be fostered by these rhythms and rituals? What sort of education of desire is taking place for those immersed in these sorts of worship contexts? Can we exegete the worldview implicit in these practices—these liturgies? An exegesis of several secular liturgies is the focus of chapter 3; a full exegesis of the practices of Christian worship is the task of chapters 4 and 5.

But what does this have to do with Christian education? What does liturgy have to do with learning? What does the church have to do with the Christian college? In this introduction, our concern is merely to get some issues and questions on the table, to open a space to consider a couple of key themes that will orient the book: first, I have tried to get us thinking about education, or pedagogy, in terms of practices or even rituals. In particular, I've been suggesting that education is not primarily a heady project concerned with providing *information*; rather, education is most fundamentally a matter of *formation*, a task of shaping and creating a certain kind of people. What makes them a distinctive kind of people is what they love or desire—what they envision as "the good life" or the ideal picture of human flourishing. An education, then, is a constellation of practices, rituals, and routines that inculcates a particular vision of the good life by inscribing or infusing that vision into the heart (the gut) by means of material, embodied practices. And this will be true even of the most instrumentalist, pragmatic programs of education (such as those that now tend to dominate public schools and universities bent on churning out "skilled workers") that see their task primarily as providing *informa*tion, because behind this is a vision of the good life that understands human flourishing primarily in terms of production and consumption. Behind the veneer of a "value-free" education concerned with providing skills, knowledge, and information is an educational vision that remains formative. There is no neutral, nonformative education; in short, there is no such thing as a "secular" education.

This is why I have also suggested a second, related theme: that the sorts of practices that form us—that form our core or ultimate identities—constitute liturgies. While this claim will be further unpacked in chapters 1 and 2, here let me just briefly explain: Because I think that we are primarily desiring animals rather than merely thinking things, I also think that what constitutes our ultimate identities—what makes us who we are, the kind of people we are—is what we love. More specifically, our identity is shaped by what we ultimately love or what we love *as* ultimate—what, at the end of the day, gives us a sense of meaning, purpose, understanding, and orientation to our being-in-the-world. What we desire or love ultimately is a (largely implicit) vision of what we hope for, what we think the good life looks like. This vision of the good life shapes all kinds of actions and decisions and habits that we undertake, often without our thinking about it. So when I say that love defines us, I don't mean our love for the Chicago Cubs or chocolate chip scones, but rather our desire for a way of life. This element of ultimacy, I'll suggest, is fundamentally *religious*. But *religion* here refers primarily not to a set of beliefs or doctrines but rather to a way of life. What's at stake is not primarily ideas but love, which functions on a different register. Our ultimate love/desire is shaped by practices, not ideas that are merely communicated to us. This is why I describe the formative "civic pedagogies" of both the church and the mall as liturgies. This is a way of raising the stakes of what's happening in both. Thinking about such formative pedagogies as liturgies will help us appreciate that these constitute an education that is primarily formative rather than merely informative, and that such formation is about matters of ultimate concern.

So, "What does this have to do with education?" I hear someone ask. What does the Christian college have to do with these worship contexts? Are you saying we should quit college and stick to church? I want to note, up front, that this has two important implications (we'll discuss further implications in chapter 6). First, this model should push us to ask: Just what is a "Christian" education *for*? What is the aim, or *telos*, of a Christian education? Second, this should prompt us to rethink a common mantra in Christian schools and colleges, namely, that a Christian education is concerned with providing a Christian worldview. If we think about learning in terms of liturgy—pedagogy *as* liturgy—then I think we need a rearticulation of the end of Christian education, which will require a reconsideration of worldview-talk[10] as it has come to dominate conceptions of Christian education.

The End of Christian Education: From Worldview to Worship (and Back Again)

Let me suggest an axiom: behind every pedagogy is a philosophical anthropology. In more pedestrian terms, behind every constellation of educational practices is a set of assumptions about the nature of human persons—about

---

10. When I use this phrase throughout the book, I'm playing off Mary Ann Glendon, *Rights Talk: The Impoverishment of Political Discourse* (New York: Free Press, 1993).

the kinds of creatures we are. Thus a pedagogy that thinks about education as primarily a matter of disseminating information tends to assume that human beings are primarily "thinking things" and cognitive machines. Ideas and concepts are at the heart of such pedagogies because they are aimed primarily at the head. Because of the intellectualist philosophical anthropology that is operative here, the body tends to drop out of the picture. There is little attention to the nitty-gritty details of material practices and the role that they play in education. In contrast, a pedagogy that understands education as formation usually assumes that human beings are a different kind of animal. It's not that we don't think, but rather that our thinking and cognition arise from a more fundamental, precognitive orientation to the world.[11] And that precognitive or prerational orientation to the world is shaped and primed by very material, embodied practices. Thus such a pedagogy is much more attuned to the formative role of ritual.

Picturing Education as Formation in Orwell's *Road to Wigan Pier*

We are so prone to associating education with the cognitive stuff of ideas that it's difficult for us to imagine education as a more formative, affective matter. Our imaginations get stuck in a rut, and it becomes difficult to get out of them to imagine things differently.[12] When that happens, theoretical dissertations aren't effective in

11. I continue to find it difficult to come up with a lexicon that can address these distinctions in a neat and tidy way, particularly since the same terms can mean very different things in different disciplines. Wrestling with this challenge will be a core project of volume 2. To this point, I tend to use the word *cognitive* as a shorthand for describing a reflective, propositional way of intending the world that traffics in thinking and ideas. I will then tend to distinguish this from what I'll call the *affective*, by which I mean a prereflective, imaginative "attunement" to the world that precedes the articulation of ideas and even beliefs. (Indeed, I have in mind something like Heidegger's account of *Befindlichkeit*, "attunement" or "affectedness.") If it's not too cute, I would suggest this distinction (which is *not* an opposition) is akin to the distinction between reading the newspaper or a textbook and reading a poem or a novel. Both have content, but they activate very different comportments to the world, drawing on different parts of us, as it were.

12. This is an example of the way that particular configurations of the "social imaginary" can become so dominant that we fail to see them as a particular, contingent construal. Instead, these ingrained habits of perception are taken to just be "the way things are." Thus Charles Taylor contends that the "modern" social imaginary "has now become so self-evident to us that we have trouble seeing it as one possible conception among others" (*Modern Social Imaginaries* [Durham, NC: Duke University Press, 2004], 2). In a similar way, Christian Smith suggests that the ubiquity of "liberal democratic capitalism" in the modern West is what also secures its transparency: "Its suppositional beliefs, its deeply trusted assumptions, its elemental cultural ontology have become nearly invisible to us precisely because it has become ubiquitous and dominant" (*Moral, Believing Animals* [Oxford: Oxford University Press, 2003], 60). In short, the ubiquity and dominance of this social imaginary make it almost impossible to imagine anything other. Both education and

destabilizing these habits of imagination: providing an argument for education as formation—the sort of thing that targets our cognitive head—often fails to touch our more ingrained imagination, whose center of gravity is closer to our bodies. To jolt the imagination, we need more affective pictures. So throughout this book I will occasionally try to picture my claims by drawing on the imaginative reservoirs of literature and film. The goal is to draw on more affective modes of expression in order not only to convince us of these things at a cognitive level but also to persuade us of them at a more affective level.[13]

For instance, I have been claiming that an education—whether acknowledged or not—is a formation of the desires and imagination that creates a certain kind of person who is part of a certain kind of people. The facts and information learned as part of the process are always situated and embedded in something deeper that is being learned all along: a particular vision of the good life. A rather ugly instance of this is pictured in George Orwell's *Road to Wigan Pier*, a work commissioned as a tract that would unveil the plight of the English working class in the coal-mining cities of the industrial North. To do so, Orwell spent time in the dilapidated slums that were so-called home to the underfed and underpaid miners and their families, whose work undergirded everything else that happened in the remnants of the British Empire. Orwell is particularly interested to remind his readers of this fact, readers from the South, members of the "intellectual Left" who would be reading Orwell's book in the comfort of heated homes with electric light and inside bathrooms—all things foreign to the miners' existence. How important to remember, then, that

> our civilisation, *pace Chesterton*, *is* founded on coal, more completely than one realizes until one stops to think about it. The machines that keep us alive, and the machines that make the machines, are all directly or indirectly dependent upon coal. In the metabolism of the Western world the coal-miner is second in importance only to the man who ploughs the soil. He is a sort of grimy caryatid upon whose shoulders nearly everything that is *not* grimy is supported.[14]

The first half of the book is Orwell at his finest as an investigate journalist, filling in the picture of the plight of the working class from firsthand immersion. It is a harrowing account of malnutrition, illness, and the debilitating psychological effects of persistent unemployment and poverty. But in the second half of the book, Orwell takes a surprising turn: he takes on the supposed middle-class champions of the working

---

worship should be practices that precisely loosen up and stretch our imaginations such that we can begin to imagine things otherwise. We will discuss this further in chapters 1 and 2.

13. I have in mind here something like the account of "persuasion" at work in Milbank's *Theology and Social Theory* and David Bentley Hart's *Beauty of the Infinite*. Persuasion is a more aesthetic mode than demonstration. For a discussion, see James K. A. Smith, "Questions about the Perception of 'Christian Truth': On the Affective Effects of Sin," *New Blackfriars* 88 (September 2007): 585–93.

14. George Orwell, *The Road to Wigan Pier* (London: Penguin, 2001), 18.

class, the intellectual Left, and challenges their sympathies. In particular, he questions whether they're really ready to jettison the class structure that they renounce in the parlors and lecture halls of London.

It is in this context that he provides a powerful portrayal of the effects of education. Orwell captures the odious nature of this caste system by seizing upon an axiom that eludes simple propositional articulation. As he puts it, "The real secret of class distinctions in the West" can be "summed up in four frightful words" that are often left unuttered: *The lower classes smell.*[15] The statement itself is pungent to our ears (to mix senses). But Orwell's point is that the root of class distinctions in England is not intellectual; it's olfactory. The habits and rhythms of the system are not so much cerebral as visceral; they are rooted in a bodily orientation to the world that eludes theoretical articulation, which is why theoretical tirades also fail to displace it. Thus Orwell notes that we run up against "an impassable barrier": "For no feeling of like or dislike is quite so fundamental as a *physical* feeling." Almost every other kind of discrimination could be countered theoretically, with the weapons of facts, ideas, and information, "but physical repulsion cannot."[16]

But then, how does such a physical visceral stance get embedded in the middle and upper classes? It is a matter of formation ("in my childhood we were brought up to believe that they were dirty"), and more specifically, education. Thus Orwell recounts:

> When I was fourteen or fifteen I was an odious little snob, but no worse than other boys of my own age and class. I suppose there is no place in the world where snobbery is quite so ever-present or where it is cultivated in such refined and subtle forms as in an English public school.[17] Here at least one cannot say that English "education" fails to do its job. You forget your Latin and Greek within a few months of leaving school—I studied Greek for eight or ten years, and now, at thirty-three, I cannot even repeat the Greek alphabet—but your snobbishness, unless you persistently root it out like the bindweed it is, sticks by you till your grave.[18]

The information that the public schools provided—like Latin and Greek—didn't really take root. What did get inscribed into the pupils, however, was an entire comportment to the world and society, a training in "snobbishness" that could not be easily overturned or undone by new facts or data or information. What would be required to "root out" such a visceral orientation is an equally visceral and physical education or counter-formation. Thus Orwell, somewhat in reverse, illustrates our core intuition that education is an embodied formation that captures our very being and shapes our orientation to the world. This may help us picture what it means to

15. Ibid., 119.
16. Ibid.
17. North American readers should note that "public" schools in Britain are elite "private" schools in American parlance.
18. Orwell, *Road to Wigan Pier*, 128.

talk about education as formation. But it might also be an occasion to ask whether a Christian education could have the same odious effects as a public school education. Could we offer a Christian education that is loaded with all sorts of Christian ideas and information—and yet be offering a formation that runs counter to that vision?

If we consider these two very different understandings of education (the informative and the formative), and the different understandings of the human person that are at work behind them, I suggest that, over the past decades, institutions of Christian education have unwittingly absorbed the former and eschewed the latter. Many Christian schools, colleges, and universities—particularly in the Protestant tradition—have taken on board a picture of the human person that owes more to modernity and the Enlightenment than it does to the holistic, biblical vision of human persons. In particular, Christian education has absorbed a philosophical anthropology that sees human persons as primarily thinking things. The result has been an understanding of education largely in terms of *in*formation; more specifically, the end of Christian education has been seen to be the dissemination and communication of Christian ideas rather than the formation of a peculiar people. This can be seen most acutely, I think, in how visions of Christian education have been articulated in terms of "a Christian worldview."

Over the past couple of decades, the growth of Christian colleges and universities has been attended by expanded discussions of their mission as "the integration of faith and learning."[19] It is then commonly claimed that students at Christian colleges and universities will learn a "Christian worldview"; or they will learn what everyone else learns but "from a Christian perspective" or a "Christian point of view." However, "a Christian worldview" is identified primarily as a set of doctrines or a system of beliefs. Consider, for instance, Francis Beckwith's definition of *worldview* in a recent collection:

> What we mean is that the Christian faith is a philosophical tapestry of interdependent ideas, principles and metaphysical claims that are derived from the Hebrew-Christian Scriptures as well as the creeds, theologies, communities, ethical norms and institutions that have flourished under the authority of these writings. These beliefs are not mere utterances of private religious devotion but are propositions whose proponents claim accurately

19. I will not focus on "integration" talk here. For my criticisms, see James K. A. Smith, *Introducing Radical Orthodoxy: Mapping a Post-secular Theology* (Grand Rapids: Baker Academic, 2004), 143–79.

instruct us on the nature of the universe, human persons, our relationship with God, human communities and the moral life.[20]

This is echoed in more popular usages of worldview that advocate "thinking 'worldview-ishly'" and the importance of "worldview-thinking" by putting the Christian "belief-system" at the center of our cognition because "how a person *thinks* significantly influences his [*sic*] *actions.*"[21] A worldview is construed as a set of implicit ideas.

Such construals of worldview belie an understanding of Christian faith that is dualistic and thus reductionistic: It reduces Christian faith primarily to a set of ideas, principles, claims, and propositions that are known and believed. The goal of all this is "correct" thinking. But this makes it sound as if we are essentially the sorts of things that Descartes described us to be: thinking things that are containers for ideas. What if that is actually only a small slice of who we are? And what if that's not even the most important part? In the rationalist picture, we are not only reduced to primarily thinking things; we are also seen as things whose bodies are nonessential (and rather regrettable) containers for our minds. This is why such construals of a Christian worldview are also dualistic: they tend to assume a distinction between our souls and our bodies—and then tend to ignore our embodiment (or wish it weren't there). But what if our bodies are essential to our identities? Weren't we created *as* embodied creatures? What if the core of our identity is located more in the body than the mind?

In chapter 1, I want to suggest that worldview-talk has misconstrued the nature and task of Christian education because the operative notion of worldview at work there has been tied to a stunted, rationalist picture of the human person; in short, "worldview" has gotten hitched to the wagon of a misguided philosophical anthropology. Granted, I think this represents a distortion of a richer, more nuanced understanding of worldview in the Reformed tradition; but given how worldview-talk is generally understood, the concern of chapters 1 and 2 is a retooling of our understanding of the human person in order to push us beyond and under worldview to consider the central, formative role of worship. Being a disciple of Jesus is not primarily a matter of getting the right ideas and doctrines and beliefs into your head in order to guarantee proper behavior; rather, it's a matter of being the kind of person who *loves* rightly—who loves God

20. Francis Beckwith, introduction to *To Everyone an Answer: A Case for the Christian Worldview*, ed. Francis Beckwith, William Lane Craig, and J. P. Moreland (Downers Grove, IL: InterVarsity, 2004), 14.

21. Kenneth Richard Samples, *A World of Difference: Putting Christian Truth-Claims to the Worldview Test* (Grand Rapids: Baker Books, 2007), 15. For other popular accounts along these rationalist lines, see "The Truth Project" from Focus on the Family (www.thetruthproject.org).

> ## To Think About: The Shape of Christian Education
>
> Consider the following as points for discussion:
>
> - Because Christian education is conceived primarily in terms of *in*formation, assuming the philosophical anthropology behind that, it should be no surprise to find that Christian faith doesn't touch our pedagogical commitments. Instead, we adopt the pedagogies of rationalist modernity and drop Christian ideas into the machine. But that's a bit like taking a pizza crust, putting kidney and mushy peas on top, and then describing it as British cuisine. We need to think further about how a Christian understanding of human persons should also shape *how* we teach, not just *what* we teach.
> - Further, we need to think more about how the Christian story should shape why we teach and why we want to learn. What is the goal of Christian education? To produce honest, cheerful, grateful, and pious producers and consumers? Or does the Christian story narrated in the practices of Christian worship paint a very different picture of human flourishing? Shouldn't Christian education be about that? And if so, how would our schools, colleges, and universities look different?
> - Third, the distorted understanding of worldview that dominates current models assumes a rationalist, intellectualist, cognitivist model of the human person; as a result, it fails to honor the fact that we are embodied, material, fundamentally *desiring* animals who are, whether we recognize it or not (and perhaps most when we don't recognize it), every day being formed by the material liturgies of other pedagogies—at the mall, at the stadium, on television, and so forth. As such, Christian education becomes a missed opportunity because it fails to actually counter the cultural liturgies that are forming us every day. An important part of revisioning Christian education is to see it as a mode of counter-formation.
> - Finally, dualistic models of Christian education are a missed opportunity in a second sense: they fail to form us for the kingdom precisely because they are inattentive to the centrality of embodied, material, liturgical practice for such formation. While Hollister and Starbucks have taken hold of our heart with tangible, material liturgies, Christian schools are "fighting back" by giving young people Christian *ideas*. We hand young people (and old people!) a "Christian worldview" and then tell them, "There, that should fix it." But such strategies are aimed at the head and thus miss the real target: our hearts, our loves, our desires. Christian education as formation needs to be a pedagogy of *desire*.

and neighbor and is oriented to the world by the primacy of that love. We are made to be such people by our immersion in the material practices of Christian worship—through affective impact, over time, of sights and smell in water and wine.

The liturgy is a "hearts and minds" strategy, a pedagogy that trains us as disciples precisely by putting our bodies through a regimen of repeated practices that get hold of our heart and "aim" our love toward the kingdom of God. Before we articulate a worldview, we worship. Before we put into words the lineaments of an ontology or an epistemology, we pray for God's healing and illumination. Before we theorize the nature of God, we sing his praises. Before we express moral principles, we receive forgiveness. Before we codify the doctrine of Christ's two natures, we receive the body of Christ in the Eucharist. Before we think, we pray. That's the kind of animals we are, first and foremost: loving, desiring, affective, liturgical animals who, for the most part, don't inhabit the world as thinkers or cognitive machines. In chapter 4, I'll describe this as the primacy of worship to worldview or the priority of liturgy to doctrines. However, the point is fundamentally a reassertion and gloss on the classical axiom *lex orandi, lex credendi*: what the church prays is what the church believes. My contention is that given the sorts of animals we are, we pray *before* we believe, we worship before we know—or rather, we worship *in order to* know.

And this, I'm going to argue, should make a difference for how we think about the nature and task of Christian education—and thus what's at stake at a Christian college. The goal of chapter 6 is to rearticulate the *end* of Christian education by re-visioning both the *telos* and the practice of Christian education. With respect to its *telos*, or goal, in light of what we've suggested above about the nature of education as formative pedagogy, I will propose that the primary goal of Christian education is the formation of a peculiar people—a people who desire the kingdom of God and thus undertake their vocations as an expression of that desire. The task of a Christian school, college, or university is not to just provide a "safe" place for the dissemination of information that one can get at the public or state school down the street. Nor is it merely to provide a "Christian perspective" on what the world thinks counts as knowledge in order to become successful and productive citizens of a disordered society. Rather, the Christian college's mission is more radical than that: in some significant way, it involves the formation of disciples. In short, the Christian college is a *form*ative institution that constitutes part of the teaching mission of the church.

With respect to practice, I will suggest that this vision of the mission of Christian education requires a correlate pedagogy that honors the formative role of material practices. Thus, I will argue that education at Christian colleges must be understood as liturgical in more than an analogical or metaphorical sense. Or perhaps to put it more starkly, I will suggest that we need to move from the model of "Christian universities," identified as sites for transmitting Christian ideas, to "ecclesial colleges," understood to be institutions intimately linked to the church and thus an extension of its practices. If Christian learning is nourished by a Christian worldview, and if that worldview is first and foremost embedded in the understanding that is implicit in the practices of Christian worship, then the Christian college classroom is parasitic upon the worship of the church—it lives off the capital of Christian worship.

Elements of a Theology of Culture: Pedagogy, Liturgy, and the Church

Before moving from this overview of the project to a more substantive unpacking of its components in the chapters that follow, let me also note that much of what I'll articulate here is not only of concern for students and professors, but also for pastors and parishioners. Indeed, many of the failures that I have noted with respect to stunted, dualistic visions of Christian education apply equally to how, over the past decades, we have come to "do church." The core intuitions I'll unpack in this book are germane to the task of discipleship broadly conceived. In that sense, *Desiring the Kingdom* can be understood as a "theology of culture" (or, more generally, a Christian cultural theory) that

- Understands human persons as *embodied actors* rather than merely thinking things.
- Prioritizes *practices* rather than ideas as the site of challenge and resistance.
- Looks at cultural practices and institutions through the lens of worship or liturgy.
- Retains a robust sense of *antithesis* without being simply "anti-cultural."

My concern is to develop a cultural theory that has a radar, so to speak, attuned not primarily to ideas but to practices, and more specifically, to identity-forming practices that I'll describe as liturgies. The goal is a theology of culture that gives space to a certain ambivalence—a theological account of culture that is nimble, can recognize and account for complexity, but also has an ecclesial center of gravity, we might say. By looking at cultural institutions through the lens of worship and liturgy, I hope to raise the stakes of what it means for us to be immersed in such cultural rituals. And as a result, I also hope to give us a new appreciation for what is at stake in the practices of Christian worship as an alternative cultural formation.

Desiring, Imaginative Animals

WE ARE WHAT WE LOVE

In the introduction, I suggested an axiom: Behind every pedagogy is a philosophical anthropology; that is, implicit in every constellation of educational practices there is a set of assumptions about the nature of human persons. In order to articulate a vision of Christian worship as a pedagogy of desire, and a correlate picture of Christian education as a kind of liturgical formation, it's important first to articulate the understanding of the human person that informs this vision. The overall goal of part 1 is to sketch a formal account of education as the formation of the imagination by affective practices. Chapter 1 articulates a philosophical anthropology that understands human persons as defined by love—as desiring agents and liturgical animals whose primary mode of intending the world is love, which in turn shapes the imagination. Chapter 2 then outlines how our love/desire is shaped and directed by material, embodied practices. In chapter 3, we'll undertake an exegesis of "secular" liturgies in order to discern why and how they function as liturgies.

1

Homo Liturgicus

THE HUMAN PERSON AS LOVER

I am inviting us to rethink the relationship between worship and worldview by thinking about the connection between liturgy, learning, and formation. This task is motivated by two different sorts of questions that represent two different ways of coming to the same issues. On the one hand, we are concerned about the nature and task of Christian higher education: Why are we studying at a Christian college? What are we teaching at a Christian college? Why do we even have Christian colleges? So we're asking: What is the connection between the task of Christian education and the cadences of the church's liturgical life? On the other hand, concerned with articulating a theology of culture and an understanding of worship as cultural formation, we're asking: In what ways do other cultural practices constitute (competing) liturgies that are at the same time pedagogies? And in what way does Christian worship function (or fail to function) as an alternative pedagogy that forms us otherwise? At stake in both of these questions is the matter of pedagogy and formation: in both cases and from both angles we're interested in discerning how material practices constitute pedagogies for the education of desire that shape our very identity. On this account, education is not something that traffics primarily in abstract, disembodied ideas; rather, education is a holistic endeavor that involves the whole person, including our bodies, in a process of formation that aims our desires, primes our imagination, and orients us to the world—all before we ever start *thinking* about it. This is why educational strategies that traffic only in ideas often fail to actually educate; that is, they fail to *form* people. Given this link between formation and embodiment, we might say that education is a "meatier" task than we often assume.

Before we can consider just how this works, we need to consider why this works. Why is it that embodied rituals and material practices are so effective in shaping our identities and forming our desires? So before considering how material practices train us in this way (chapter 2), and before we can give attention to the different ends to which these different liturgies are directed (chapter 3), we first need to follow up on an axiom suggested in the introduction: that behind every pedagogy is a philosophical anthropology, a model or picture of the human person. The focus of this chapter is the elucidation of a philosophical anthropology that recognizes that we are, ultimately, *liturgical animals*[1] because we are fundamentally desiring creatures. We are what we love, and our love is shaped, primed, and aimed by liturgical practices that take hold of our gut and aim our heart to certain ends. So we are not primarily *homo rationale* or *homo faber* or *homo economicus*; we are not even generically *homo religiosis*. We are more concretely *homo liturgicus*; humans are those animals that are religious animals not because we are primarily believing animals but because we are liturgical animals—embodied, practicing creatures whose love/desire is aimed at something ultimate. If a pedagogy presumes a philosophical anthropology, then the articulation of a distinctly Christian education requires that we first unpack the elements of a Christian philosophical anthropology. We'll do this by first considering some common (but reductionistic) models of the human person and then unpack the alternative understanding of human persons as loving, liturgical animals.

From Thinking Things to Liturgical Animals

At stake in how we think about this strange beast, the Christian university—and thus how we think about the relation between church and university—is an even deeper question about what human beings are. For too long we have tried to think of the relationship between the church and the university,

---

1. The use of the term *animals* here, as will become clear below, is not merely accidental or metaphorical. The philosophical anthropology outlined in this chapter will emphasize what Alasdair MacIntyre rightly describes as "our animal condition" or our "human animality." See MacIntyre, *Dependent, Rational Animals* (Chicago: Open Court, 1999), 5. In this respect, my project—like MacIntyre's, I think (see ibid., 8)—is unapologetically "assimilationist" according to Robert Brandom's use of the term (more on this below). My title for part 1, "Desiring, Imaginative Animals," is offered as something of a play on both MacIntyre's *Dependent, Rational Animals* and Christian Smith's *Moral, Believing Animals*.

as well as the hybrid beast, the Christian college, in terms of *ideas*. So we tend to think about this as a matter of relating the sacred and the secular, or how to integrate faith and learning, or we tend to organize the discussion around a clash of worldviews—and imagine the difference between the university and the church primarily in terms of *thinking* and *believing*. But I think the relation—and the challenge—is deeper than that. And I think this is the case precisely because human persons are not primarily or for the most part thinkers, or even believers. Instead, human persons are—fundamentally and primordially—lovers. I want to make sense of that claim by a brief tour of options in philosophical anthropology. Here the key questions are these: What are human beings? What kinds of creatures are we? And what are we called to be? There are different, competing models of the human person that we can see throughout the history of philosophy and theology.

"I Think, Therefore I Am": The Human Person as Thinker

A dominant model, as old as Plato but rebirthed by Descartes and cultivated throughout modernity, sees the human person as fundamentally a thinking thing. Recall Descartes' basic project as outlined in *Discourse on Method* and his later *Meditations*. Racked with anxiety because his prior certainties have become shipwrecked on the shores of later doubt, Descartes finds himself in an existential crisis: If things that have seemed so certain to him can later be unveiled as false, then how can he be certain about anything?

Trying to tackle this angst head-on, Descartes retreats to isolation in a room for several days, simply in order to *think* his way through the problem. (How different would the world be if Descartes could have just gotten a date?!) You probably know the rough-and-ready outline of the story: meditating on the conditions for knowledge, Descartes sets about to discover if anything can be known with certainty. After writing off the senses and the body as sources of deception and doubt, and even the realm of mathematical truths, Descartes despairs whether anything is certain. While I might think that 2 + 2 = 4 is a certain truth, it is at least possible that God is an evil demon, toying with me, and deceiving me into thinking that's obviously true, when in fact it is not. Almost swallowed by this sea of raging doubt, Descartes catches a glimpse of hope—a sort of intellectual beacon that promises solid ground. For, he reasons, even if I'm being deceived about what seems most certain, it must be the case that, in order for me to be deceived, I must exist. And so, in the *Meditations*, Descartes' famous maxim "I think, therefore I am" takes on an even starker form: "I'm deceived, therefore I am"—because even if I am being deceived, I would have to exist in order to be deceived. With this insight, Descartes' battered vessel in search of certainty finally reaches a shore.[2]

So, with certainty, Descartes concludes *that* I am. But this raises the next question: *What* am I? Just what is the nature of this "I" that most certainly exists? Having cast aside the senses and the body already in his meditations, Descartes concludes that "I" am "a thinking thing." In other words, *what* I am is an essentially immaterial mind or consciousness—occasionally and temporarily embodied, but not essentially.[3] This bequeaths to us a dominant and powerful picture of the human person as fundamentally a thinking thing—a cognitive machine defined, above all, by thought and rational operations. We might call this a broadly "rationalist" or "intellectualist" picture of the human person, and it has both a long pedigree (back to Plato) and a large progeny (through Kant and into the present). It entails a sense that persons are defined by thinking and is often allied with a sense of functional disembodiment (that is, the person as thinking thing is only contingently related to a body). As such, what nourishes or fuels the "I" is a steady diet of ideas, fed somewhat intravenously into the mind through the lines of propositions and information.

While this model of the person as thinking thing assumed different forms throughout modernity (e.g., in Kant, Hegel), this rationalist picture was absorbed particularly by Protestant Christianity (whether liberal or conservative), which tends to operate with an overly cognitivist picture of the human person and thus tends to foster an overly intellectualist account of what it means to be or become a Christian[4]—which helps explain the rationalist distortions of "worldview" discussed above. It is just this adoption of a rationalist, cognitivist anthropology that accounts for the shape of so much Protestant worship as a heady affair fixated on "messages" that disseminate Christian ideas and abstract values (easily summarized on PowerPoint slides).[5] The result is a talking-head version of Christianity that is fixated on doctrines and ideas, even if it is also paradoxically allied with a certain kind of anti-intellecutalism. We could describe this as "bobble head" Christianity, so

2. There is a more complicated version of this that, looking at Meditation III, sees the "I think" cast back into doubt. I'm going to bracket consideration of that more nuanced, contested reading for the moment.

3. Recall that half of Descartes' interest in the *Meditations* was to demonstrate the immortality of the soul (see his "Prefatory letter to the Sorbonne"). The same sort of focus of human identity in the rational, immaterial soul was articulated much earlier in Plato's *Phaedo*.

4. See Stanley Hauerwas, "How Risky Is *The Risk of Education?*" in *The State of the University: Academic Knowledges and the Knowledge of God* (Oxford: Blackwell, 2007), 50–51.

5. For my criticism of this "rationalist worship," see James K. A. Smith, *Who's Afraid of Postmodernism? Taking Derrida, Lyotard, and Foucault to Church* (Grand Rapids: Baker Academic, 2006), 140–41.

fixated on the cognitive that it assumes a picture of human beings that look like bobble heads: mammoth heads that dwarf an almost nonexistent body. In sum, because the church buys into a cognitivist anthropology, it adopts a stunted pedagogy that is fixated on the mind. So rather than calling into question this reductionistic picture of the human person, the church simply tries to feed different ideas through the same intellectual IV.

"I Believe in order to Understand": The Human Person as Believer

Now, this rationalist or cognitivist picture of the human person as a "thinking thing" has been contested, especially within the Reformed tradition, as a reductionistic account that fails to honor the richness and complexity of the human person and also naively imagines that thinking constitutes a neutral or objective base. Instead, the criticism goes, we need to recognize the degree to which thinking operates on the basis of *faith*, that thought is not a neutral, objective activity but rather a particular way of seeing the world that is itself based on prior faith or trust. So before we are thinkers, we are believers; before we can offer our rational explanations of the world, we have already assumed a whole constellation of beliefs—a *worldview*—that governs and conditions our perception of the world. Our primordial orientation or comportment to the world is not as thinkers but as believers. Beliefs, we might say, are more "basic" than ideas.[6] In this alternative anthropology, human persons are understood not as fundamentally thinking machines but rather as believing animals, or essentially religious creatures, defined by a worldview that is pre-rational or supra-rational.[7] What defines us is not what we think—not the set of ideas we assent to—but rather what we *believe*, the commitments and trusts that orient our being-in-the-world. This moves the essence of the human person from the more abstract, disembodied world of ideas to a prerational level of commitments that are more ingrained in the human person. Before we are thinkers, we are believers. Thus this line of worldview-thinking generated by the Reformed tradition developed precisely as a critique of more rationalistic construals of Christianity that have now hijacked worldview-talk to rationalistic ends.

This critique of rationalism—and especially Christianized rationalism—is laudable and important. The Reformed emphasis on a more holistic sense of our identity as believers contests the reductionistic rationalisms

---

6. Thus Alvin Plantinga speaks of "properly basic beliefs" and Nicholas Wolterstorff of "control beliefs."

7. For a more technical discussion of this point, see Herman Dooyeweerd, *In the Twilight of Western Thought: Studies in the Pretended Autonomy of Theoretical Thought*, ed. James K. A. Smith, Collected Works B/4 (Lewiston, NY: Edwin Mellen, 1999).

that continue to dominate both the academy and public consciousness.[8] It also contests an important feature that attends such rationalist accounts of the human person, namely, claims regarding the "objectivity" of reason that engender a secularization of the "public" sphere, including the public sphere of the university—just the sort of boundary marking that makes the "Christian university" sound like an oxymoron.[9] By contesting this, the Reformed emphasis on humans as fundamentally and inescapably *believing* animals pushes back on the logic of secularity and thus carves out a space to articulate a rationale for distinctly Christian education.[10] However, while I affirm much of this critique, I have two reservations about this faith-based (rather than rationalist) anthropology:

1. While it contests a narrow, naive focus on ideas, this model of the human person seems just to move the clash of ideas down a level to a clash of beliefs. Those beliefs often still look like the propositions and ideas of the rationalist model; they've just been given the status of *Ur*-ideas—the originary beliefs that undergird all ideas. Such beliefs still feel like the sort of thing that can be formulated as P or P′ on a register that is not qualitatively different from the rationalist register on which we would map ideas. Does such a (merely seman-tic?) shift really honor the richness of the human person? Again, I think this manifests itself in how this model shapes our thinking about the relationship between faith and the university. While we might not reduce it to a matter of ideas, the worldview model still tends to think about the difference and relation primarily in terms of beliefs. Once that step down is made—from ideas to the worldview commitments that undergird those ideas—the discussion looks a lot like the discussion in the person-as-thinker model.

2. I find that the person-as-believer model still tends to operate with a very disembodied, individualistic picture of the human person. The beliefs that orient me still seem quite disconnected from my body,

8. This is also the burden of Christian Smith's methodological manifesto for the social sciences, *Moral, Believing Animals* (Oxford: Oxford University Press, 2003), in which he argues that regnant paradigms in the social sciences continue to reflect a reductionistic picture of human beings as merely rational machines (or, alternatively, as only biologi-cal machines). Thus Smith calls for social theory that begins from a richer, more holistic understanding of human persons as *believing* and *narratological* animals. With respect to the former, he draws specifically on the work of Wolterstorff and thus can be somewhat situated within the tradition I'm describing here.

9. I have discussed this in much more detail in James K. A. Smith, *Introducing Radical Orthodoxy: Mapping a Post-secular Theology* (Grand Rapids: Baker Academic, 2004), particularly chapter 5.

10. Articulated with verve in George Marsden, *The Outrageous Idea of Christian Schol-arship* (New York: Oxford University Press, 1997).

and with little or no attachment to the things I do *as* a body, and so with little attachment to the others that my body bumps into, embraces, hugs, and touches. While this model tries to articulate a more integral relationship between faith and reason, believing and knowing, it tends to do so in ways that imagine the individual Christian as a believer who knows on the basis of this individual belief. Hence, discussions of how to relate faith and learning are usually articulated in terms of connecting Christianity or Christian faith to the disciplines or to the college. One will find little if any discussion of the church. Instead, given this disembodied, individualist picture of the person-as-believer, such a model fosters a focus on developing "Christian perspectives" on X, Y, and Z. Both the materiality of the body (along with attendant bodily practices) and the specificity of the church drop out of this picture. As Hauerwas rightly notes, when Christianity is turned into "a belief system," it is reduced to something "available without mediation by the church."[11] So while in the person-as-believer model, the human person is not a "brain in a vat," she still seems like an isolated, disembodied island of beliefs. In this model, the "believer" feels like a chastened rationalist: beliefs still seem to be the sorts of things that are more commensurate with thinking. Or to put it otherwise, if I bump into a "thinking thing" and a "believing thing" on the street, I don't think I'd notice much difference.

Taken together, these criticisms suggest that the person-as-believer model still gives us a somewhat reductionistic account of the human person—one that is still a tad bit heady and quasi-cognitive. And that is significant because of the pedagogy it yields. Recalling our working axiom—that every pedagogy assumes and expresses an anthropology—we need to ask, Is the "believing" pedagogy really going to look much different from the "rationalist" pedagogy? Insofar as the former still doesn't seem very attentive to embodiment and formation by practice, it seems to me that the "believing" pedagogy will simply be a tweaked version of the *in*formative paradigm. And I think that's just what we find in the curricula and practices of Christian schools and universities across the continent. While the Reformed tradition of worldview-thinking generates a radical critique of rationalism and its attendant claims to objectivity and secularity, the critique still feels reductionistic insofar as it fails to accord a central role to embodiment and practice. Because of this blind spot, it continues to yield a quasi-rationalist pedagogy.

11. Hauerwas, "How Risky?" 51.

Now, these criticisms do not constitute a rejection of the worldview model per se. I think the claims vis-à-vis rationalism are correct: that our knowing is governed and conditioned by constellations of belief that are more primordial than our ideas. So the criticism is not a rejection; rather, the point is that the emphasis on belief does not go far enough. We might say that this Reformed worldview emphasis on the person as believer is a step in the right direction, but that it is insufficiently Augustinian. We still get a somewhat stunted anthropology that fails to appreciate that our primordial orientation to the world is not knowledge, or even belief, but *love*.[12] Thus, in contrast to both the person-as-thinker and the person-as-believer models, I want to articulate a more robustly Augustinian anthropology that sees humans as most fundamentally oriented and identified by love. Only such a robust anthropology—which accords a more central, formative place to embodiment—can yield a truly alternative understanding of pedagogy. And such an alternative pedagogy will have two important outcomes: first, it will make us attentive to the ways in which all sorts of cultural practices actually constitute pedagogies of desire, thus heightening our sense of what is at stake in seemingly banal cultural institutions. Second, it will help us envision a more integral and radical understanding of distinctively Christian education.

"I Am What I Love": The Human Person as Lover

I have described both the person-as-thinker and the person-as-believer models as reductionistic; by that I mean that they fail to honor the complexity and richness of human persons and instead reduce us and our core identities to something less than they should be. There are at least a couple of ways to account for this reductionism. In one sense, such models are too narrow; they are focused on only a slice of being human and so tend to be blind to other, more significant factors that constitute human identity. Instead, they take the slice to be the whole and thus absolutize just one aspect of the human person. In particular, both of these models remain narrowly focused on the cognitive aspect of our nature and tend to reduce us to that aspect (whether in terms of thoughts or beliefs). As a result, significant parts of who we are—in particular, our noncognitive ways of being-in-the-world that are more closely tethered to our embodiment or animality—tend to drop off the radar or are treated as nonessential. In another sense, we could say such models are too static; they tend to treat the human person as the sort of thing that can be captured in a snapshot. In the same way that our

12. Recall that what distinguishes Augustine's two cities (the earthly city and the city of God) is not ideas or beliefs but *love*. See Augustine, *City of God* 19.24.

embodiment drops out of the picture, so too does our temporality: if humans are conceived almost as beings without bodies, then they also are portrayed as creatures without histories, without any sense of unfolding and development over time. So these models are too narrow in the sense that they ignore our embodiment and too static in the sense that they ignore our temporality.

In contrast, we need a nonreductionistic understanding of human persons as embodied agents of desire or love. This Augustinian model of human persons resists the rationalism and quasi-rationalism of the earlier models by shifting the center of gravity of human identity, as it were, down from the heady regions of mind closer to the central regions of our bodies, in particular, our *kardia*—our gut or heart. The point is to emphasize that the way we inhabit the world is not primarily as thinkers, or even believers, but as more affective, embodied creatures who make our way in the world more by feeling our way around it. Like the blind men pictured in Rembrandt's sketches, for the most part we make our way in the world with hands outstretched, in an almost tactile groping with our bodies.[13] One might say that in our everyday, mundane being-in-the-world, we don't lead with our head, so to speak; we lead out with our heart and hands. This model of the person as desiring creature also contests the earlier models by articulating a more dynamic sense of human identity as both unfolding and developing over time (a process of formation), something characterized by a kind of dynamic flow. The human person is the sort of creature who can never be captured in a snapshot; we need video in order to do justice to this dynamism.

In order to articulate and unpack this alternative model, let me first provide a diagram that attempts to outline the key features of this anthropology (see figure 1). I will then explain each of the features.

1. INTENTIONALITY: LOVE'S AIM

This model begins from what we'll call an *intentional* account of human persons. Rather than thinking about human persons as static containers for ideas or beliefs, this way of thinking about humans as intentional[14] em-

---

13. For a discussion of this, see Jacques Derrida, *Memoirs of the Blind: The Self-Portrait and Other Ruins*, trans. Pascale-Anne Brault and Michael Naas (Chicago: University of Chicago Press, 1993). See also my commentary in "Is Deconstruction an Augustinian Science? Augustine, Derrida, and Caputo on the Commitments of Philosophy," in *Religion with/out Religion: The Prayers and Tears of John D. Caputo*, ed. James H. Olthuis (London: Routledge, 2001), 50–61.

14. Whether in the more ancient accents of Augustine and Aquinas or the more phenomenological mode of Husserl and Heidegger. These two ways of talking about "intentionality" are not unrelated; the Augustinian model was an influence on both Husserl and Heidegger's "phenomenological" account. For a discussion, see James K. A. Smith, "Confessions of an Existentialist: Reading Augustine after Heidegger," in *The Influence*

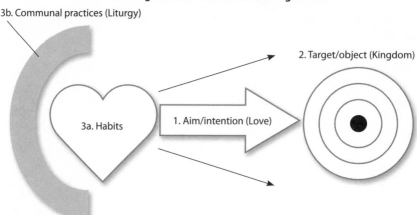

FIGURE 1
Homo Liturgicus: The Human as Desiring Animal

phasizes that our being-in-the-world is always characterized by a dynamic, "ek-static" orientation that "intends" the world or "aims at" the world as an object of consciousness. The Latin *intentio* can be translated as "aim"; thus when we describe the human person or consciousness as *intentional*, we mean that it is always "aimed at" something: it *intends* something as an object. This is a central maxim in Husserl's phenomenology: consciousness is always consciousness *of* . . . Contrary to Descartes, I can never just "think"; I will necessarily be thinking *of* . . . something. To confirm this, try a little experiment. Take a few moments and just think. Ready? Put down the book, close your eyes, and just think. . . . OK, how did you do? Were you able to just think? Or was it rather the case that you found yourself thinking *about* something? Granted, you might have been thinking about thinking, or thinking about whether it's possible to just think, or you might have been thinking about deep-fried Twinkies (in which case coming back to this book is going to be a big disappointment). But in any case, my wager is that the exercise confirmed that when you're thinking, you're always and necessarily thinking *of* something. That is simply what we mean by saying that human consciousness is *intentional*. So the human person is not the sort of creature that can be diagramed with a dot or an "X marks the spot"; rather, because of this dynamic, intentional nature of our being, the first move is to sketch the human person as an arrow that intends the world or aims at the world.

However, that is just a first step. To say that we are intentional is not really saying that much (yet), though it does already get us away from the

---

of Augustine on Heidegger: The Emergence of an Augustinian Phenomenology, ed. Craig J. N. DePaulo (Lewiston, NY: Edwin Mellen, 2006), 221–57.

more static models of the person we saw earlier. But to say that we intend the world or aim at the world does not yet tell us much about *how* we do that. The phenomenological tradition—which, anachronistically, we might say reaches back to Augustine—recognizes that there are different ways of being conscious; there are many different ways to intend the world. For instance, we might *think* about our friend Theodore, or we might *perceive* him. We might also *remember* him or *hope* for him. In some strange circumstance, we might even be *afraid* of him. Or we might *love* him. All of these (and others) are different ways of intending the world, different *modes* of intentionality. Here we enter the terrain of a key debate in phenomenology between Husserl and Heidegger regarding which mode was most fundamental or basic to being human. Primarily and for the most part, do we *think* about the world? Or do we most of the time intend the world in some other way? Heidegger argued that Husserl—in Cartesian fashion[15]—tended to see humans as primarily cognitive or rational animals, as if we fundamentally and for the most part intended the world in the mode of thinking or perception. Heidegger thought that Husserl's account of intentionality was reductionist in a way not unlike our critique of the models above: Husserl tended to reduce the richness and complexity of our lived experience to mere perception or cognition, thus reducing the texture of the world to a collection of "objects"—as if we went around all day *perceiving* chairs and *perceiving* our friends, rather than sitting on chairs and embracing our friends while engaged in much more interesting ways of inhabiting the world.

In contrast, Heidegger argued that primarily and for the most part, we don't *think* about a world of objects; rather, we are *involved* with the world as traditioned actors. The world is the environment in which we swim, not a picture that we look at as distanced observers.[16] Thus, rather than suggesting that perception or mere cognition is the fundamental mode of intentional consciousness, Heidegger argued that *care* is the most primordial way that we "intend" the world.[17] With this, Heidegger made a critical move: he shifted the center of gravity of the human person from the cognitive to the noncognitive—from the head to something like

---

15. In *Being and Time*, whenever Heidegger really wants to take a shot at his teacher Husserl, he lays the charge at the feet of Descartes (thus suggesting a fundamental continuity between Descartes' rationalism and Husserl's particular, overly cognitivist version of phenomenology). But it didn't take much for Husserl to figure out that he was the intended target here; on his edition of *Being and Time*, Husserl scribbled: "Plato's a friend, but truth is a greater friend."

16. I have unpacked this in more detail in James K. A. Smith, *Speech and Theology: Language and the Logic of Incarnation* (London: Routledge, 2002), 67–82.

17. See Martin Heidegger, *Being and Time*, trans. John Macquarrie and Edward Robinson (New York: Harper & Row, 1966), §§41–42.

the heart, from the cerebral regions of mind to the more affective region of the body.[18] For Heidegger, we might say that I don't *think* my way through the world, I *feel* my way around it. With this shift, Heidegger both signaled the influence of Augustine (and a later Augustinian, Pascal) and began to articulate an anthropology that was an alternative to the cognitivist paradigms that had dominated the scene up to that point (and that remain operative in the person-as-thinker and person-as-believer models noted above).

So our model of the person as lover begins from an affirmation of our intentional nature; further, with Heidegger, we would affirm that our most fundamental way of intending the world is not cognitive but noncognitive. Our primary or default mode of intending the world is not reflective or theoretical; we don't go around all day *thinking* about how to get to the classroom or *thinking* about how to brush our teeth or *perceiving* our friends. Most of the day, we are simply involved in the world. We navigate our way and orient ourselves for the most part without thinking about it—like driving home from work by a route so familiar that we can do it without even being "conscious," and thus sometimes find ourselves in the driveway unable to remember driving home. Our default way of intending the world is noncognitive and prereflective: it is an affective mode of "feeling our way around" the world—what Heidegger called our "attunement" to the world. However, we need to push this one step further. Augustine—to whom Heidegger owed no small debt in his phenomenology of *care*—would articulate this slightly differently, and in doing so would challenge Heidegger in a way analogous to Heidegger's critique of Husserl. Rather than settling for the more generic notion of "care" or "concern" as the most primordial mode of intentionality, Augustine would argue that the most fundamental way that we intend the world is *love*.[19]

The "desiring" model of the human person begins from our nature as intentional beings who first and foremost (and ultimately) intend the world in the mode of *love*. We are primordially and essentially agents of love, which takes the structure of desire or longing.[20] We are essentially and

18. Even in *Being and Time*, which is his rather "secularized" (formalized) account, Heidegger specifically refers to Augustine on this point: "Our existential analytic of Dasein toward 'care' occurred to the author in connection with attempts at an interpretation of Augustinian, that is, Greek and Christian, anthropology" (ibid., 405n7).

19. See Augustine, *Teaching Christianity*, trans. Edmund Hill (New York: New City, 1996), 1.26.27–1.29.30; and for a commentary , see Smith, "Confessions of an Existentialist." Volume 2 of the present project will provide space to explore these themes in much more detail, particularly in dialogue with Merleau-Ponty. I hope to articulate the claim that worship is something like an "existentiale."

20. See Augustine, *Homilies on I John* 4.6, "The whole life of the good Christian is a holy longing. . . . That is our life, to be trained by longing; and our training through

ultimately desiring animals, which is simply to say that we are essentially and ultimately lovers. To be human is to love, and it is what we love that defines who we are. Our (ultimate) love is constitutive of our identity.[21] So we're not talking about trivial loves, like when we say we "love" pizza or the Boston Red Sox; we're not even quite talking about significant loves, like when we say we "love" our parents or we "love" a spouse (though these will be wrapped up in the sort of love we're concerned with). Rather, we are talking about *ultimate* loves—that to which we are fundamentally oriented, what ultimately governs our vision of the good life, what shapes and molds our being-in-the-world—in other words, what we desire above all else, the ultimate desire that shapes and positions and makes sense of all our penultimate desires and actions.

This sort of ultimate love could also be described as that to which we ultimately pledge allegiance; or, to evoke language that is both religious and ancient, our ultimate love is what we *worship*. The reason we emphasize that this is a matter of love is to signify that our orientation to what's ultimate is not primarily on the order of thinking. It's not what I think that shapes my life from the bottom up; it's what I desire, what I love, that animates my passion. To be human is to be the kind of creature who is oriented by this kind of primal, ultimate love—even if we never really reflect on it. In fact, sometimes this subterranean, prereflective desire governs us most powerfully precisely when we don't reflect on it (which, as we'll discuss below, can be a problem).

So this love or desire is a structural feature of being human. It is not just a characteristic of passionate people or romantic people or even specifically religious people. To be human is to be just such a lover—a creature whose orientation and form of life is most primordially shaped by what one loves as ultimate, which constitutes an affective, gut-like orientation to the world that is prior to reflection and even eludes conceptual articulation. To say that humans are, at root, lovers is to emphasize that we are the sorts of animals for whom things *matter* in ways that we often don't (and can't) articulate. There is a sort of drive (or pull, depending on the

the holy longing advances in the measure that our longings are severed from the love of this world" (in *Augustine: Later Works*, ed. John Burnaby [Philadelphia: Westminster, 1955], 290). For a qualification of the meaning of "this world" in this context, see chapter 5 below. In this book, I basically make no distinction between *love* and *desire*, eschewing any distinction between *eros* and *agapē*. As will become clear below, *agapē* is rightly directed *eros*. Here the Augustinian distinction between *caritas* and *cupiditas* can be helpful, though I tend to think of both as directional modes of *dilectatio*. Whether that is properly Augustinian, I'll let others judge. For a helpful discussion, see John von Heyking, *Augustine and Politics as Longing in the World* (Columbia: University of Missouri Press, 2001).

21. For discussion, see James H. Olthuis, *The Beautiful Risk: A New Psychology of Loving and Being Loved* (Grand Rapids: Zondervan, 2001), 68–70.

metaphor) that pushes (or pulls) us to act in certain ways, develop certain relationships, pursue certain goods, make certain sacrifices, enjoy certain things. And at the end of the day, if asked why we do this, ultimately we run up against the limits of articulation even though we "know" why we do it: it's because of what we love.

However, that does not mean that we all love the same thing. The structure of love can take different directions, which means that such love can also be misdirected.[22] It depends upon how our love is aimed. What distinguishes us (as individuals, but also as "peoples")[23] is not *whether* we love, but *what* we love. At the heart of our being is a kind of "love pump"[24] that can never be turned off—not even by sin or the Fall; rather, the effect of sin on our love pump is to knock it off kilter, misdirecting it and getting it aimed at the wrong things.[25] Our love can be aimed at different ends or pointed in different directions, and these differences are what define us as individuals and as communities. This brings us to the second element of the "desiring" model (recall figure 1 earlier in this chapter).

2. TELEOLOGY: LOVE'S END

To say that we are dynamic, intentional creatures entails a second characteristic: we are *teleological* creatures. We are the sorts of animals whose love is aimed at different ends or goals (Greek: *teloi*). As intentional, love always has a target, something that it intends or aims at. So as we inhabit the world primarily in a noncognitive, affective mode of intentionality, implicit in that love is an end, or *telos*. In other words, what we love is a specific vision of the good life, an implicit picture of what we think human flourishing looks like.[26] Such a picture of human flourishing will have all sorts of components: implicit in it will be assumptions about what good relationships look like, what a just economy and distribution of resources look like, what sorts of recreation and play we value, how we ought to relate

22. I'm drawing on the structure/direction distinction so helpfully articulated and developed by Albert Wolters, *Creation Regained* (Grand Rapids: Eerdmans, 1985), 72–95.

23. See Augustine, *City of God* 19.24–26.

24. Compare John Piper's notion of the heart as a "desire factory" in *Future Grace* (Sisters, OR: Multnomah, 1995), 277–79. My thanks to Norris and Lois Aalsma for pointing me to Piper's picture.

25. Augustine would say that the effect of sin on our love is not that we stop loving but that our love becomes disordered. It gets aimed at the wrong ends and finds "enjoyment" in what it should merely be "using." Or, in other words, instead of being *caritas*, our love becomes *cupiditas*. See Augustine, *Teaching Christianity* 1.26.27–1.27.28.

26. Compare Charles Taylor, *A Secular Age* (Cambridge, MA: Harvard University Press, 2007), 16: "Every person, and every society, lives with or by some conception(s) of what human flourishing is: What constitutes a fulfilled life? What makes life really worth living? What would we most admire people for?"

to nature and the nonhuman environment, what sorts of work count as good work, what flourishing families look like, and much more. (Perhaps it is most important, at this point, to emphasize that this is a *social* vision. This is not a picture of just what it looks like for me to be "saved"; rather, a vision of human flourishing—even an *individualist* vision—includes some account of human intersubjectivity and social institutions.) Our ultimate love is oriented by and to a picture of what we think it looks like for us to live well, and that picture then governs, shapes, and motivates our decisions and actions.

It is important to emphasize that this is a *picture*. This is why I have emphasized that we are fundamentally noncognitive, affective creatures. The *telos* to which our love is aimed is not a list of ideas or propositions or doctrines; it is not a list of abstract, disembodied concepts or values. Rather, the reason that this vision of the good life moves us is because it is a more affective, sensible, even aesthetic *picture* of what the good life looks like. A vision of the good life captures our hearts and imaginations not by providing a set of rules or ideas, but by painting a picture of what it looks like for us to flourish and live well. This is why such pictures are communicated most powerfully in stories, legends, myths, plays, novels, and films rather than dissertations, messages, and monographs.[27] Because we are affective before we are cognitive (and even *while* we are cognitive),[28] visions of the good get inscribed in us by means that are commensurate with our primarily affective, imaginative nature. This isn't to say that the cognitive or propositional is a completely foreign register for us (if it were, this book would be an exercise in futility!); however, it doesn't get into our (noncognitive) bones in the same way or with the same effect.[29] The

27. See Stanley Hauerwas, "A Story-Formed Community: Reflections on *Watership Down*," in *The Hauerwas Reader*, ed. John Berkman and Michael Cartwright (Durham, NC: Duke University Press, 2001), 171–99. This is also why it is important that Christian worship function on this affective register, *picturing the story*. Many of our imaginative genres that currently function in this way (plays, novels, etc.) actually constitute a certain secularizing of embodied Christian worship. For a discussion of drama as a secularization of the Eucharist, see Graham Greene, "Dramatists," in Elizabeth Bowen et al., *The Heritage of British Literature* (London: Thames & Hudson, 1983), 67–107. For an account of opera in the same vein, see Jean-Luc Marion, *The Crossing of the Visible*, trans. James K. A. Smith (Stanford, CA: Stanford University Press, 2004), 64–65.

28. This is one of the points regularly emphasized by MacIntyre in *Dependent Rational Animals*: even when humans engage in cognitive reflection, we don't *cease* to be noncognitive animals. As he puts it, "Human identity is primarily, even if not only, bodily" (8). Thus the "prelinguistic" (what I've been calling noncognitive or affective) is not just a "stage of our early lives" that we grow out of; it remains functional (and primary) "throughout our lives" (36). We'll explore this further in the next section.

29. Graham Ward helpfully analyzes this dynamic in "Narrative and Ethics: The Stuctures of Believing and the Practices of Hope," *Literature and Theology* 20 (2006): 438–61. Intending to supplement the narrative theology of Hauerwas and Loughlin, Ward is con-

cognitive and propositional is easily reduced and marginalized as just more "blah-blah-blah" when our hearts and imaginations are captured by a more compelling *picture* of the good life—the way it's hard to listen to someone talking when the television is on, with its blinking images functioning as magnets for our attention.

Our ultimate love moves and motivates us because we are lured by this picture of human flourishing. Rather than being pushed by beliefs, we are pulled by a *telos* that we desire. It's not so much that we're intellectually convinced and then muster the willpower to pursue what we ought; rather, at a precognitive level, we are attracted to a vision of the good life that has been painted for us in stories and myths, images and icons. It is not primarily our minds that are captivated but rather our *imaginations* that are captured, and when our imagination is hooked, *we're* hooked (and sometimes our imaginations can be hooked by very different visions than what we're feeding into our minds). Those visions of the good life that capture our heart have thereby captured our selves and begin to draw us toward them, however implicitly or tacitly. The goods and aspects of human flourishing painted by these alluring pictures of the good life begin to seep into the fiber of our (everyday, noncognitive) being (i.e., our hearts) and thus govern and shape our decisions, actions, and habits. Thus we become certain kinds of people; we begin to emulate, mimic, and mirror the particular vision that we desire. Attracted by it and moved toward it, we begin to live into this vision of the good life and start to look like citizens who inhabit the world that we picture as the good life. We become little microcosms of that envisioned world as we try to embody it in the here and now. So many of the penultimate decisions, actions, and paths we undertake are implicitly and ultimately aimed at trying to live out the vision of the good life that we love and thus *want* to pursue.

This is just to say that to be human is to desire "the kingdom," *some* version of the kingdom, which is the aim of our quest. Every one of us is on a kind of Arthurian quest for "the Holy Grail," that hoped-for, longed-for, dreamed-of picture of the good life—the realm of human flourishing—that we pursue without ceasing. Implicitly and tacitly, it is such visions of the kingdom that pull us to get up in the morning and suit up for the quest.

However, to say that all humans desire the kingdom does not mean that we all desire the *same* kingdom. Structurally, we are lovers, and that "love pump" can't be turned off; and because love is intentional and teleological,

cerned to show that *all* narratives—whether the Gospels or Proust—"structure emotions, desires and hopes that impact upon what we believe and how we come to value certain acts" (439). He concludes that "the narrative economy, in engaging our expectant emotions, opens up a transcendent horizon that configures our sense of what is real and what is valuable" (455–56).

our love is always aimed at *some* particular vision of the good life that has been pictured for us.[30] But because the structure of love can be misdirected, there can be many different *teloi*. In other words, there are very different visions of what "the kingdom" looks like. The shape of the kingdom is contested, generating very different stories and thus different kinds of peoples, citizens who see themselves as subjects of rival kings. There are many roundtables. One of the core tasks of cultural discernment will be to "read" the particular configuration of the kingdom that is assumed by different cultural institutions and narratives.[31]

3A. HABITS: LOVE'S FULCRUM

The anthropology we've sketched has emphasized that we are fundamentally creatures of desire or love and that our love is always already oriented to an ultimate vision of the good life, a picture of the kingdom that embodies a particular image of human flourishing. We further suggested that these pictures—these affective icons of the good life—get into our bones and our hearts and thus shape our character by aiming our desire to a particular end. But this raises important questions: Just *how* does that happen? How does our love get aimed in different directions? Does this happen by some kind of magic or alchemy? Does it happen by the dissemination of ideas and propositions that convince us to pursue this vision? What are the mechanisms by which particular visions of the good life get infused in our hearts such that they could motivate and govern a way of life (decisions, actions, pursuits, relationships)?

This brings us to the third element of figure 1: a desire for and orientation to a particular vision of the good life (the kingdom) becomes operative in us (motivating actions, decisions, etc.) by becoming an integral part of the fabric of our *dispositions*—our precognitive tendencies to act in certain ways and toward certain ends. Philosophers like Aristotle, Aquinas, and MacIntyre describe such dispositions as "habits." Good habits, for instance,

---

30. I recognize that things aren't quite this neat and tidy: that we are often fragmented, "split" selves who might be simultaneously captivated by *competing* visions of the good. Few of us inhabit enclaves where only one story is dominant; rather, we find ourselves in spaces where competing stories are told. As Ward rightly observes, "Christians, like any other human beings, are shaped by and implicated in more than one community; they have social and even psychological spaces with those who may be far removed from Christian narratives" ("Narrative and Ethics," 439). And precisely because these stories and visions function affectively and prereflectively, we can be quite taken with stories that cognitively we might criticize. I will return to this layer of complexity below (in chapters 2 and 5); for the moment, in this first sketch, I will keep things simpler.

31. Such cultural exegesis will be the task of chapter 3, which will exegete the particular visions of the kingdom embedded in the market, the stadium, and the university; but it will also be the focus of chapter 5, which will exegete the particular vision of the kingdom that is embedded in the practices of Christian worship.

are "virtues," whereas bad habits are "vices." These habits constitute a kind of "second nature": while they are learned (and thus not simply biological instincts), they can become so intricately woven into the fiber of our being that they function *as if* they were natural or biological.[32] They represent our default tendencies and our quasi-automatic dispositions to act in certain ways, to pursue certain goods, to value certain things, to cherish certain relationships, and so forth. So the virtuous person is someone who has an almost automatic disposition to do the right thing "without thinking about it." Our habits incline us to act in certain ways without having to kick into a mode of reflection; for the most part we are driven by an engine that purrs under the hood with little attention from us. This precognitive engine is the product of long development and formation—it's *made*, not some kind of "hard wiring"—but it functions in a way that doesn't require our reflection or cognition.

Our habits thus constitute the *fulcrum* of our desire: they are the hinge that "turns" our heart, our love, such that it is predisposed to be aimed in certain directions. For the most part this takes place under the radar, so to speak. We don't wake up each day *thinking* about a vision of the good life and then consciously, reflectively make discrete decisions about "what we'll do today" as penultimate means to our ultimate ends. That would be quite a strange morning, like waking up but still being in a kind of Cartesian dream where we constantly function as cognitive machines (not a great way to start the day!).[33] Instead, because for the most part we are desiring, imaginative, noncognitive animals, our desire for the kingdom is inscribed in our dispositions and habits and functions quite apart from our conscious reflection.[34] So when we say that to be human is to love, to

32. Once again MacIntyre emphasizes the continuity and relation of dependence between the two: "For it is of the first importance that what we thereby become are redirected and remade animals and not something else. Our second culturally formed language-using nature is a set of partial, but only partial transformation of our first animal nature" (*Dependent Rational Animals*, 49).

33. One can imagine a sequel to the film *Memento* (compare my discussion of the real *Memento* in *Who's Afraid of Postmodernism?* chapter 2) where Leonard, instead of lacking memory, actually lacks any capacity for noncognitive habits or dispositions. He can live only on the basis of conscious reflection and intentional focus on propositional content. So beside his bed he has to pin up stated propositions to orient him each morning. He has propositions plastered all over the house, in his car, and keeps a laminated card with key propositions in his wallet. The most important propositions are tattooed on his body. Timothy Wilson documents a case not unlike this, the case of Mr. D (in honor of Descartes), who has to consciously focus in order to manage any bodily functions. See Timothy D. Wilson, *Strangers to Ourselves: Discovering the Adaptive Unconscious* (Cambridge, MA: Harvard University Press, 2002), 18–22.

34. I don't mean to suggest that conscious reflection is either impossible or bad. It will be important for us to step back and critically reflect on our dispositions and habits (MacIntyre actually emphasizes that it is this reflexivity that is unique to *human* animals

desire the kingdom, we're suggesting that this vision of the kingdom's good life becomes inscribed and infused in our habits and dispositions and thus woven into our precognitive (second) nature.

That, however, only half answers our question. If our love or desire is aimed by the fulcrum of our habits, then we've just pushed the questions back: How do habits become inscribed in us? How are these dispositions formed? Where do these inclinations come from?

3b. Practices: Love's Formation

Here's where the emphasis on our embodiment becomes crucial. Alongside emphasizing that we are affective, noncognitive, desiring animals, I have also emphasized that we are *embodied* creatures. We've even suggested that the picture of human persons as creatures of desire requires shifting the center of gravity of human identity from the head (or more specifically, a disembodied mind) to the heart, which is more closely tethered to our sensible, affective nature. Thus I've been suggesting that a *Message*-like translation of *kardia* (heart), one that will shock us out of our familiarity, is "gut"—which captures both a sense of this bowel-level center of gravity of our identity, as well as the grittiness of its embodiment. We feel our way around our world more than we think our way through it. Our worldview is more a matter of the imagination than the intellect, and the imagination runs off the fuel of images that are channeled by the senses.[35] So our affective, noncognitive disposition is an aspect of our animal, bodily nature. The result is a much more holistic (and less dualistic) picture of human persons as essentially embodied. Hence, it should be no surprise that the way to our hearts is our stomach; or, if not specifically

---

and thus an obligation for humans [*Dependent Rational Animals*, 66–69]). However, I think it is also important to recognize two things: (1) Such reflection does not come first; in fact, such reflection presupposes prereflective ("animal") dispositions as the object of reflection (ibid., 56); (2) Such reflection is not sustainable; at best, it is sporadic. Even the philosopher only inhabits a small part of any particular day engaged in conscious reflection. The rest of the time she's making her way in the world as a noncognitive animal like everyone else. And so it is crucial that we consider the kinds of precognitive dispositions that orient her being-in-the-world. (My thanks to Jeff Dudiak for pressing me on these matters.) An important outcome of such a reorientation is, I think, a way of honoring the way that mentally challenged persons inhabit the world. While they are not, perhaps, adept at being thinkers or theorists, they nonetheless inhabit the world as lovers. For relevant discussions, see ibid., 73–74; and Amos Yong, *Theology and Down Syndrome: Reimagining Disability in Late Modernity* (Waco: Baylor University Press, 2007), 188–91. Further, I think this model also better honors what Martin Marty describes as "the mystery of the child" and can better grasp just why children—who aren't given to theoretical, cognitive reflection—might nonetheless have a better grasp on the kingdom. See Marty, *The Mystery of the Child* (Grand Rapids: Eerdmans, 2007).

35. Cf. Thomas Aquinas, *Summa theologica* Ia.76.

To Think About: Nabokov on Reading with Our Spines

Given this role of the imagination, we might suggest that liturgy is like literature: it gets hold of us through the body. In that connection, consider Vladimir Nabokov's comment on reading Dickens's *Bleak House*:

All we have to do when reading *Bleak House* is to relax and let our spines take over. Although we read with our minds, the seat of artistic delight is between the shoulder blades. That little shiver behind is quite certainly the highest form of emotion that humanity has attained when evolving pure art and pure science. Let us worship the spine and its tingle. Let us be proud of our being vertebrates, for we are vertebrates tipped at the head with a divine flame. The brain only continues the spine: the wick really goes through the whole length of the candle. If we are not capable of enjoying that shiver, if we cannot enjoy literature, then let us give up the whole thing and concentrate on our comics, our videos, our books-of-the-week. But I think Dickens will prove stronger. (Vladimir Nabokov, *Lectures on Literature* [New York: Harvest, 2002], 56)

our stomachs, the way to our hearts is through our bodies. We can see this in at least two ways.

First, as we've already suggested, an orientation toward a particular vision of the good life becomes embedded in our dispositions or "adaptive unconscious" by being *pictured* in concrete, alluring ways that attract us at a noncognitive level (recall the description of "icons" in our opening analysis of the mall). By "pictures" of the good life I mean aesthetic articulations of human flourishing as found in images, stories, and films (as well as advertisements, commercials, and sitcoms). Such pictures appeal to our adaptive unconscious because they traffic in the stuff of embodiment and affectivity. Stories seep into us—and stay there and haunt us—more than a report on the facts. A film like *Crash* gets hold of our hearts and minds and moves us in ways that textbooks on racism never could. This is because it is a medium that traffics in affective images, and such affective articulations are received by us on a wavelength, as it were, that is closer to the core of our being. Such compelling visions, over time, seep into and shape our desire and thus fuel dispositions toward them.

In addition, habits are inscribed in our heart through bodily practices and rituals that train the heart, as it were, to desire certain ends. This is a noncognitive sort of training, a kind of education that is shaping us often without our realization. Different kinds of material practices infuse noncognitive dispositions and skills in us through ritual and repetition precisely because our hearts (site of habits) are so closely tethered to our bodies. The senses are portals to the heart, and thus the body is a channel to our core dispositions and identity. Over time, ritual practices—often in tandem with aesthetic phenomena like pictures stories—mold and shape our precognitive disposition to the world, training our desires. It's as if our appendages function as a conduit to our adaptive unconscious: the motions and rhythms of embodied routines train our minds and hearts so that we develop habits—sort of attitudinal reflexes—that make us tend to act in certain ways toward certain ends. Consider a couple of trivial examples: First, our body knows its way around a keyboard the way our conscious mind does not. So if I ask you, "What letter is to the left of F on a keyboard?" it's going to take you a second or two—or maybe longer—to sort that one out. This will probably involve you putting your hands on the table and working through a little imaginary exercise to reconnect what your fingers "know" with what your mind can say. Well, how did your hands get to "know" this? Through rituals, routines, and exercises that trained your adaptive unconscious. These exercises put your body through the motions over and over again until this know-how became lodged in a part of your brain that you don't often call to mind—which is why the question is a kind of shock to the system.

We might think of such training as a mundane example of how our hearts are trained through our bodies. Consider an example highlighted by *New York Times* columnist David Brooks (drawing on the work of Timothy Wilson and Jeff Hawkins): playing baseball. Whether six or sixty, a baseball game is almost inevitably preceded by a series of drills—quasi-rituals—that are meant not only to get the blood flowing but also to train the body (including the brain) to respond and react in an automatic way to various scenarios. So the classic "pepper" drill in infield practice hammers balls into the ground at different speeds and places in order to train the player to react to different hops and bounces, seizing the ball and firing it to first base. When a "hot" ball is making its way down the third-base line, the player doesn't want to have to think about what to do: the player has been doing these drills for years precisely so that she or he *doesn't* have to think about it; instead, the person—body and mind—has been trained and primed to respond and act "automatically." Thus Brooks comments, "Over the decades, the institution of baseball has figured out how to instruct the unconscious mind, to make it better at what it does. As we know the automatic brain only by the behavior it produces, so we can instruct it only by forcing it to repeat certain actions. Jeff Kent is practicing covering first after all these years because the patterns of the automatic brain have to be constantly and repetitively reinforced."[36] It is the bodily practices (drills)

36. David Brooks, "Your Brain on Baseball," *New York Times*, March 18, 2007, available at http://select.nytimes.com/2007/03/18/opinion/18brooks.html.

that train the body (including the brain) to develop habits or dispositions to respond automatically in certain situations and environments. Our desire is trained in the same way.

These claims regarding the material, bodily formation of our noncognitive dispositions are as old as Aristotle. At times it has been criticized as speculative, idealistic, and perhaps tinged with behaviorism.[37] However, such ancient claims are now receiving support and evidence from contemporary neuroscience and cognitive science.[38] I have been emphasizing that the "desiring" model of the human person accords a primacy and primordiality to our noncognitive "understanding" of the world rather than a cognitive "knowledge" of the world (to adopt a distinction from Heidegger). The point is that, for the most part, we make our way in the world by means of under-the-radar intuition and attunement—that we live not so much by what we know but instead by know-*how*. Being desiring, imaginative animals, our primary orientation to the world is visceral, not cerebral—which is also why our attunement and behavior is so profoundly shaped by bodily practices that connect with us on this visceral register.

It turns out that recent research in cognitive psychology and neuroscience is filling in this picture. As Timothy Wilson summarizes, psychology's rejection of behaviorism (particularly Skinnerian versions of it so popularized in widespread knowledge of Pavlov's dogs) ushered in the age of "cognitivism" in psychology, which required new attention to what was going on "inside our heads." However, this renewed focus on interior mental life was linked to a discomfort with, even rejection of, the notion of the "unconscious" (which smacked of Freudian psychoanalysis and thus lacked "scientific" rigor). The result was a focus on mental life as always "on"—always conscious, active, and "intentional" in a narrow sense. "But as cognitive and social psychology flourished," Wilson wryly notes, "a funny thing happened. It became clear that people could not verbalize many of the cognitive processes that psychologists assumed

37. For a contemporary criticism somewhat in this vein, see Christian Scharen's critique of Hauerwas in *Public Worship and Public Work: Character and Commitment in Local Congregational Life* (Collegeville, MN: Liturgical Press, 2004), 19–40. This echoes a common critique of theology from the social sciences, namely, that the claims regarding formation made by theologians are empirically unverified (and likely unverifiable). I agree with Scharen that theologians need to own up to the fact that they are making empirical claims of some sort. In volume 2, I hope to address these concerns by suggesting that contemporary work in cognitive science and "neuroplasticity" provide some empirical backing for this long-standing philosophical and theological intuition. In addition, we will need a more complex and nuanced account of how we inhabit multiple "liturgies."

38. Timothy Wilson explicitly picks up this Aristotelian thread in *Strangers to Ourselves*, 211–16.

were occurring inside their heads."[39] Thus psychologists were gradually pressed to concede that something like the "unconscious" (still tinged with Freudian overtones) not only remained operative but also perhaps accounted for the majority of our attunement to the world. The field now recognizes this crucial influence of "nonconscious" or "automatic" operations.[40] Wilson, conceding the problems with Freud's concept of the unconscious, especially notes Freud's failure to appreciate the scope of the unconscious:

> When [Freud] says (following Gustav Fechner, an early experimental psychologist) that consciousness is the tip of the mental iceberg, he was short of the mark by quite a bit—it may be more the size of a snowball on top of that iceberg. The mind operates most efficiently by relegating a good deal of high-level, sophisticated thinking to the unconscious, just as a modern jumbo jetliner is able to fly on automatic pilot with little or no input from the human, "conscious" pilot. The adaptive unconscious does an excellent job of sizing up the world, warning people of danger, setting goals, and initiating action in a sophisticated and efficient manner.[41]

The sorts of operations Wilson says are delegated to the unconscious include some of the operations I have associated with desire above. Our love or desire—aimed at a vision of the good life that moves and motivates us—is operative, I suggest, on a largely nonconscious level. Further, some of the sorts of functions often associated with a worldview are also functional at the level of the adaptive unconscious—operations such as interpretation, evaluation, and goal-setting.[42] In other words, I'm suggesting that the sort of orientation that has commonly been described as a "worldview" is actually, for the most part, operative on this nonconscious level. If Christian education is, in some significant sense, about the formation of a Christian worldview, then we need to consider how the unconscious is shaped and formed. The work of Wilson and others points to the "tactile" ways that the adaptive unconscious learns over time.[43]

39. Ibid., 4.

40. Compare John A. Bargh and Tanya L. Chartrand, "The Unbearable Automaticity of Being," *American Psychologist* 54 (1999): 462–79.

41. Wilson, *Strangers to Ourselves*, 6–7. One of the key differences between the "new" unconscious and the Freudian unconscious is that the "new" account attributes the unconscious not to repression but rather to efficiency. Operations are not forced down into the unconscious as "defense mechanisms" to help us cope with trauma but rather serve to maximize our capacities (8–9).

42. Ibid., 27–35.

43. Wilson cites the case of an amnesiac encountered by Edouard Claparède. The woman's amnesia meant that she lacked the ability to retain conscious memory; that is, each time he visited, she had no recollection of having met him before. "One day, Claparède

The intimate link between bodily practices and our adaptive unconscious is a testament to the holistic character of human persons. We are not conscious minds or souls "housed" in meaty containers; we are selves who *are* our bodies; thus the training of desire requires bodily practices in which a particular *telos* is embedded.[44]

We will circle back to a more detailed consideration of practices in chapter 2. At this point, in sketching the components of an anthropology of desire, I note just two more features: first, practices are *communal* or social. There are no "private" practices; rather, practices are social products that come to have an institutional base and expression. Practices don't float in society; rather, they find expression and articulation in concrete sites and institutions—which is also how and why they actually shape embodied persons. There are no practices without institutions. Second, a *telos* is always already embedded in these practices and institutions. That is, there is an intimate and inextricable link between the *telos* to which we are being oriented and the practices that are shaping us in that direction. The practices "carry" the *telos* in them. Just as we desiring animals are intentional and teleological, so the practices themselves are teleological. They are essentially loaded with a particular vision of the good life—a specific vision of a *telos*—which is then communicated or transmitted to our desire through the practice.

So we don't just "naturally" desire particular configurations of the kingdom; we are formed or trained to be aimed at particular configurations of the good life. But where does such training take place? Are there particular educational institutions that do this? Yes—but they're everywhere! We'll return to this with concrete analyses in chapter 3.

Summary

We have now articulated an alternative to the person-as-thinker and person-as-believer models in the person-as-lover model. We have highlighted four key elements of this model: Human persons are intentional creatures whose fundamental way of "intending" the world is love or desire. This love or desire—which is unconscious or noncognitive—is

---

reached out and shook her hand, as usual, but this time he concealed a pin in his hand. The woman withdrew her hand quickly, surprised at the painful prick. The next time Claparède visited the woman, she showed no sign of recognizing him, and so he reintroduced himself and held out his hand. This time, however, she refused to shake his hand. She had no conscious recollection of ever having met Claparède but somehow 'knew' that she shook this man's hand at her own risk" (ibid., 25). She exhibited a similar ability to learn the way to the dining hall, though she could not articulate how to get there. These are cases of what Wilson describes as the "implicit" learning that forms the unconscious (24–27).

44. Much more needs to be said here; these themes will be further developed in volume 2.

always aimed at some vision of the good life, some particular articulation of the kingdom. What primes us to be so oriented—and act accordingly—is a set of habits or dispositions that are formed in us through affective, bodily means, especially bodily practices, routines, or rituals that grab hold of our hearts through our imagination, which is closely linked to our bodily senses.

This represents something of a paradigm shift with respect to how we tend to think about both education and worldview within the context of Christian higher education. In order to consider the implications of this in more detail, we'll consider an alternative to worldview-talk that might be better suited to the complexities of human identity that we've articulated in the "desiring" model.

From Worldviews to Social Imaginaries

Several times I have suggested that the model of the human person as lover shifts the center of gravity of human identity away from a fixation on thinking, ideas, and doctrines and locates it lower, at it were, in the region of our affective, nonconscious operations.[45] We might picture it as outlined in figure 2 (see next page).

What does this have to do with worldview-talk? My concern is that worldview-talk—particularly in its recently distorted form, but also perhaps even at its best moments—still retains a picture of the human person that situates the center of gravity of human identity in the cognitive regions of the mind rather than the affective regions of the gut/heart/body. While it rejects thinking-thing-ism, it is prone to fall prey to believing-thing-ism, where "beliefs" are still treated as quasi-ideas, propositions that require assent. In short, it still retains an emphasis on the cognitive and often remains blind to the significance of the affective and bodily center of who we are. The result is a narrow, reductionistic understanding of the human person that fails to appreciate the primarily affective, noncognitive way that we negotiate being-in-the-world. One of the significant implications of such cognitive-centric notions of the human person is the model of education that results from it. The scope and focus of education remains fixated on the heady realm of ideas, beliefs, and "perspectives." Of course, ideas and beliefs are an important part of any education, but the cognitive-centric model is concerned almost entirely with the *content* of education: thus a "Christian" education is focused

45. For a relevant historical overview, culminating in a focus on Heidegger, see Eva Brann, "Are Humans Ultimately Affective?" *Expositions: Interdisciplinary Studies in the Humanities* 1 (2007): 53–70.

FIGURE 2
Shifting the Center of Gravity of the Self: From Cognitive to Affective

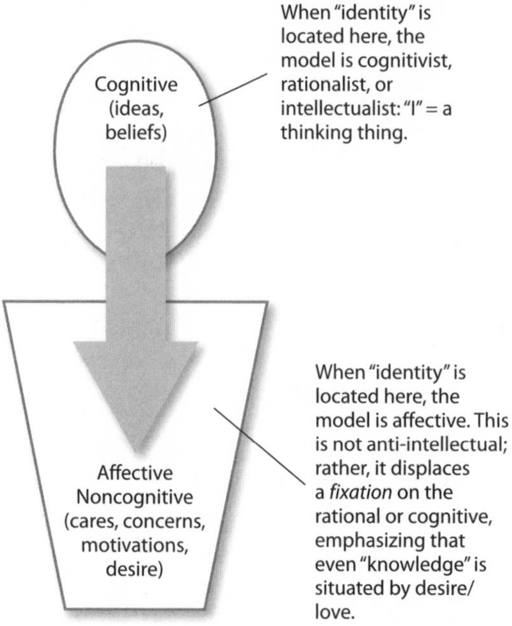

When "identity" is located here, the model is cognitivist, rationalist, or intellectualist: "I" = a thinking thing.

Cognitive (ideas, beliefs)

Affective Noncognitive (cares, concerns, motivations, desire)

When "identity" is located here, the model is affective. This is not anti-intellectual; rather, it displaces a *fixation* on the rational or cognitive, emphasizing that even "knowledge" is situated by desire/love.

on "distinctively Christian" ideas and beliefs that will be deposited into "minds in the making."

There are two correlates to this cognitive emphasis: First, this focus on a Christian worldview as a system of beliefs and doctrines marginalizes or ignores the centrality of distinctly Christian *practices* that constitute worship—arguably the single most important thing that Christians *do*. From most expositions of "the Christian worldview," you would never guess that Christians worship! From the pictures of Christians implied in worldview-talk, one would never guess that we become disciples by engaging in communal practices of baptism, communion, prayer, singing, and dancing. Second, this focus on beliefs is inattentive to the pedagogical significance of material practices. The cognitive-centric approach exhibits a fixation on the cognitive region, a kind of tunnel vision that is narrowly focused on the mind. Because of this, the body—and all the things associated with the body, like the imagination—doesn't really show up on the radar. And that has two significant implications: on the one hand, it means that such an approach is blind to the *pedagogical* effect that all sorts of cultural practices have. Inattentive to the formative effect that material rituals have, such a worldview-ish understanding of the person fails to recognize that cultural practices like shopping and athletics actually constitute formative pedagogies of desire. On the other hand, the cognitive-centric picture associated with worldview-talk fails to think about the role of practices in a distinctively Christian education—and more specifically, it fails to provide any account of or place for the centrality of Christian worship as integral to the task of Christian education.

As a way of working out this shifting of the center of gravity of human identity from the cognitive to the affective, from minds to embodied hearts, I want also to suggest that we consider a (temporary) moratorium on the notion of "worldview" and instead consider adopting Charles Taylor's notion of "the social imaginary."[46] Taylor is also convinced that understanding culture requires us to give up our fixation on ideas and theory and instead focus on the "understanding" that is embedded in practices. So just as we're trying to turn our attention from a fixation on ideas to the bodily formation of desire, Taylor's account of modernity shifts from a fixation on "theories" (what modern people "think" or "believe") to an attentive description of the specifically *modern* "social imaginary." He emphasizes that all societies and communities are animated by a social imaginary, but this does not mean that all are oriented by a theory. The social imaginary, he says, is "much broader and deeper than the intellectual schemes people may entertain when they *think* about social reality in a disengaged mode."[47] Congruent with Wilson's account of the importance of the adaptive unconscious, Taylor intuits that what we "think about" is just the tip of the iceberg and cannot fully or even adequately account for how and why we make our way in the world. There's something else and something more rumbling beneath the cognitive that drives much of our action and behavior. Taylor describes this as an *imaginary* in order to refer to "the way ordinary people 'imagine' their social surroundings," which is "not expressed in theoretical terms, but is carried in images, stories, and legends."

To call this an "imaginary" is already to shift the center of gravity from the cognitive region of ideas to the more affective region, which is "closer" to the body, as it were—since the imagination runs off the fuel of the body. So *imaginary* already hints at a more embodied sense of how we are oriented in the world. The imaginary is more a kind of noncognitive *understanding* than a cognitive *knowledge* or set of beliefs. Taylor invokes Martin Heidegger's distinction between "knowledge" (*Wissen*), which is objective and propositional, and "understanding" (*Verstehen*), which is an "inarticulate understanding of our whole situation" and constitutes

46. Charles Taylor, *Modern Social Imaginaries* (Durham, NC: Duke University Press, 2004), 23–30, now expanded in Taylor, *A Secular Age*, 171–76. For this concept, Taylor acknowledges his debt to Benedict Anderson, *Imagined Communities* (London: Verso, 1991).

47. Taylor, *Modern Social Imaginaries*, 23, emphasis added.

the "background" of our knowledge (*Wissen*).[48] This "understanding" is more on the order of know-how than propositional knowledge, more on the order of the *imagination* than intellect.[49] To describe this in terms of the imagination (an "imaginary") is meant to signal that our most basic way of intending and constituting the world is visceral and tactile—it runs off the fuel of "images" provided by the senses.

So when Taylor emphasizes the fundamental and necessary function of the "social *imaginary*" as a noncognitive director of our actions and our entire comportment to the world, I think it is important to hear in that an emphasis on the imagination as an affective faculty of sorts that constitutes the world for us on a level that is bodily. It is a way of intending the world meaningfully—giving it significance—but in a way that is not cognitive or propositional. In common parlance we might describe it as a kind of intuition that, as Taylor observes, eludes propositional articulation: "it can never be adequately expressed in the form of explicit doctrines."[50] Instead, as something functioning on the order of the imagination rather than the intellect, a social imaginary is "often not expressed in theoretical terms, but is carried in images, stories, and legends."[51] A social imaginary is not how we *think* about the world, but how we *imagine* the world before we ever think about it; hence the social imaginary is made up of the stuff that funds the imagination—stories, myths, pictures, narratives. Furthermore, such stories are always already communal and traditioned. There are no private stories: every narrative draws upon tellings that have been handed down (*traditio*). So the imaginary is social in two ways: on the one hand, it is a social phenomenon received from and shared with others; on the other hand, it is a vision *of* and *for* social life—a vision of what counts as human flourishing, what counts as meaningful relationships, what counts as "good" families, and so forth.

This shifting of our center of gravity from the cognitive to the affective—which is the whole point of describing this as an "imaginary"—finds its completion in the role of bodily practices in this picture. Taylor emphasizes a dynamic relationship between such understanding and practice: "If the understanding makes the practice possible, it is also true that it is the

48. Ibid., 25, drawing particularly on Hubert Dreyfus's reading of Heidegger in *Being-in-the-World* (Cambridge, MA: MIT Press, 1991). For the relevant discussion in Heidegger, see *Being and Time*, §31. Heidegger's articulation grows out of a critique of Husserl's "cognitivism"—a charge echoed by Dreyfus. For a defense of Husserl in this regard, see Christian Lotz, "Cognitivism and Practical Intentionality: A Critique of Dreyfus's Critique of Husserl," *International Philosophical Quarterly* (2007): 153–66. Taylor finds analogous notions of "understanding" in Wittgenstein and Polanyi.

49. By "imagination," I don't mean a Romantic sense of "invention." Unfortunately, a full treatment of "imagination" will have to wait until volume 2.

50. Taylor, *Modern Social Imaginaries*, 25.

51. Ibid., 23.

practice that largely carries the understanding."[52] Or, to put it otherwise, the understanding is "implicit in practice."[53] Such "understanding" is still distinct from, and irreducible to, "theoretical" or propositional knowledge. This is akin to Pierre Bourdieu's sense of the "logic of practice": there is a kind of rationality characterizing practices that cannot be adequately disclosed in any theoretical articulation of it. Echoing a Pascalian dictum ("The heart has reasons of which reason knows nothing"), Bourdieu emphasizes that "practice has a logic which is not that of the logician."[54] And I can—and most often *do*—function with an understanding without ever needing a "theory."

Here Taylor suggests a helpful analogy: The understanding implicit in practice is akin to knowing how to get around your neighborhood or town. This is a kind of know-how that is embedded in your adaptive unconscious. Often if we've grown up in an area, we've never looked at a map of the neighborhood. Rather, we have an understanding of our environment and surroundings that has been built up from our absorption in it: we've been biking and walking these streets for years. We could get home from the ball diamond without even thinking about it. If we're longtime residents and have never lived anywhere else, and a stranger stops us on the sidewalk and asks us how to get to Baldwin Street, we might actually be stumped because we've never really even paid attention to street signs. We know *how* to get from our house to the arena, our friend's house, and the corner store—but we "know" this in a way that doesn't translate well into giving directions to someone looking at a map. Map knowledge of the town is very different from the sort of know-how that been inscribed in us by years of walking home from school.

Taylor is emphasizing that a social imaginary is an "understanding" of the world that functions on the same level as our hometown know-how,

---

52. Ibid., 25.

53. Ibid., 26. Here we might quibble with Taylor a bit. While he wants to emphasize that the relationship between "imaginary" (understanding) and practice is "not one-sided" (25), there does seem to be some ambiguity in his account. At times he speaks as if the understanding "makes possible" common practices (23), as if practices "express" a preexistent understanding. However, at other times Taylor emphasizes that it is the practices that "carry" the understanding (25). While I think he is right to honor the dynamic, dialectical relation between the two, I think it particularly important to emphasize the latter. If there is a priority in this chicken-or-the-egg-like question, I would think the practices precede the understanding. As he later emphasizes, "Ideas [and so, *mutatis mutandis*, understanding] always come in history wrapped up in certain practices" (33). Compare George Lindbeck, *The Nature of Doctrine: Religion and Theology in a Postliberal Age* (Philadelphia: Westminster, 1984), 35.

54. Pierre Bourdieu, *The Logic of Practice*, trans. Richard Nice (Stanford, CA: Stanford University Press, 1990), 86. He goes on to emphasize that this "logic of practice" is irreducible to theoretical articulation; there are "certain properties of the logic of practice which by definition escape theoretical apprehensions" (ibid.).

whereas a theory or doctrine is a kind of "knowledge" that is more akin to a map. And for most of us, most of the time, we make our way in the world without recourse to maps (I'll resist the typical stubborn-husband joke at this point). And such know-how or understanding, Taylor emphasizes, cannot be "adequately expressed" in a map. There is a certain amount of slippage in that move. The two (understanding and knowledge) are not wholly incommensurate; what's understood in the practice can be somewhat articulated in theory or doctrine. However, there will always be something lost in translation. Furthermore, Taylor emphasizes the priority of practices. As he succinctly puts it, "Humans operated with a social imaginary well before they ever got into the business of theorizing about themselves."[55]

With the key elements in place, we can perhaps map Taylor's account of the "social imaginary" into our earlier picture of the shift from a cognitive to affective "center of gravity" for the human person (see figure 3).

The "social imaginary" is an affective, noncognitive understanding of the world. It is described as an *imaginary* (rather than a *theory*) because it is fueled by the stuff of the imagination rather than the intellect: it is made up of, and embedded in, stories, narratives, myths, and icons. These visions capture our hearts and imaginations by "lining" our imagination, as it were—providing us with frameworks of "meaning" by which we make sense of our world and our calling in it. An irreducible understanding of the world resides in our intuitive, precognitive grasp of these stories.

Now, what does this have to do with a Christian worldview? I suggest that instead of thinking about worldview as a distinctly Christian "knowledge," we should talk about a Christian "social imaginary" that constitutes a distinctly Christian understanding of the world that is implicit in the practices of Christian worship. Discipleship and formation are less about erecting an edifice of Christian knowledge than they are a matter of developing a Christian know-how that intuitively "understands" the world in the light of the fullness of the gospel. And insofar as an understanding is implicit in practice, the practices of Christian worship are crucial—the sine qua non—for developing a distinctly Christian understanding of the world. The practices of Christian worship are the analogue of biking around the neighborhood, absorbing an understanding of our environment that is precognitive and becomes inscribed in our adaptive unconscious.

If we map this onto Taylor's account, we can see some important implications: First, if humans operate with a social imaginary well before they get into the business of cognitive theorizing, then by analogy we could say that humans were religious well before they ever developed a doctrinal theology; and for most ordinary people, religious devotion is rarely

---

55. Taylor, *Modern Social Imaginaries*, 26.

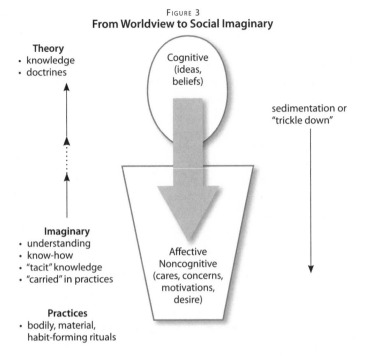

FIGURE 3
From Worldview to Social Imaginary

a matter of theory.[56] Rather, there is an understanding of the world that is carried in and implicit in the practices of religious worship and devotion. These rituals form the imagination of a people who thus construe their world as a particular kind of environment based on the formation implicit in such practices. In just this sense Christianity is a unique social imaginary that "inhabits" and emerges from the matrix of preaching and prayer. The rhythms and rituals of Christian worship are not the "expression of" a Christian worldview, but are themselves an "understanding" implicit in practice—an understanding that cannot be had *apart from* the practices. It's not that we start with beliefs and doctrine and then come up

56. Taylor's model can account for a dynamic that needs to be recognized here, namely, that "theory" sometimes "trickles down" and "infiltrates" the social imaginary (ibid., 24). In fact, he thinks this is exactly what happened in modernity: the "ideas" of Grotius and Locke gradually "infiltrate and transform" our social imaginary, producing what will become the unique understanding embedded in the *modern* social imaginary (28–29). (Heidegger has a similar account of how theory can become "sedimented" into our understanding; *Being and Time*, §62.) I suggest that something similar happens in the case of Christian worship: the "fruit" of theological reflection (e.g., the Nicene Creed) trickles down and infiltrates the Christian social imaginary such that this now becomes absorbed as a kind of noncognitive "understanding." I suggested something like this in *Introducing Radical Orthodoxy*, 178–79.

with worship practices that properly "express" these (cognitive) beliefs; rather, we begin with worship, and articulated beliefs bubble up from there. "Doctrines" are the cognitive, theoretical articulation of what we "understand" when we pray.

Second, the understanding implicit in practice cannot be simply identified with the sorts of ideas, beliefs, or doctrines that tend to be the currency of contemporary worldview-talk. The understanding—which is primary—can never be distilled into doctrines, ideas, or formulas without remainder. As Taylor emphasizes, there is a kind of irreducible genius that resides in the practices—in the same way that the "understanding" embedded in the paintings in the Sistine Chapel is not just a "substitute" for a treatise on Pauline theology, or vice versa.[57] While aspects of the social imaginary can be articulated and expressed—and even helpfully refined and reflected upon—in cognitive, propositional terms, this can never function as a substitute for participating in the practices that themselves "carry" an understanding that eludes articulation in cognitive categories. The distillation of the Christian worldview in terms of creation-fall-redemption-and-consummation can never adequately grasp what is *understood* when we participate in communion and eat the body of Christ, broken for the renewal of a broken world. And such an understanding is the condition of possibility for any later "knowledge."

To map this onto our earlier discussion, we might say that this is an understanding that *is* desire. It is an understanding that is a kind of love. So if, as Taylor and Heidegger emphasize, I understand before I know, we might also suggest that we love before we know. Our precognitive disposition—our fundamental mode of "intending" the world—is love or desire, and it is out of this fundamental "understanding" (*Verstehen*) that we can come to "know." This conclusion echoes an ancient wisdom in the Christian tradition, which might be formulated as an axiom: "desire forms knowledge."[58] What we do (practices) is intimately linked to what we desire (love), so what we do determines whether, how, and what we can know. This link—which we've culled from Taylor and Heidegger— was already discerned by the ancient Christian ascetic tradition, which

---

57. This analogy is suggested in Gordon Graham's discussion of the irreducibility of artistic "truth" in Gordon Graham, *Philosophy of the Arts*, 2nd ed. (London: Routledge, 2000), 46–51. Art's "understanding" should not be reduced to the sense of "assent to propositions," in which case art would be only one medium of many alternatives that can communicate propositional truth. Graham emphasizes that art cannot be "paraphrased" (51), nor can it be simply "exchanged" with other media for the same purpose. In the same way, theories and practices are not simply convertible; one can't drop the practice once one "gets" the theory.

58. Aristotle Papanikolaou, "Liberating Eros: Confession and Desire," *Journal of the Society of Christian Ethics* 26 (2006): 128.

emphasized the importance of shaping desire in order to know. Desire shapes how one sees and understands the world, and so the key question for the Christian in pursuit of knowledge is first to consider the shape and "aim" of one's desire, and to specifically seek to increase one's desire for God. How does that happen? According to Maximus the Confessor in *One Hundred Chapters of Love*, the key to directing and increasing one's desire for God is the acquisition of the virtues—which, you'll recall, we described above as noncognitive "dispositions" acquired through practices. So how does one acquire such virtues, such dispositions of desire? Through participation in concrete Christian practices like confession.[59]

I think we can begin to sense how this alternative anthropology of desire would shake up how we think about education, pedagogy, and the mission and task of a Christian school or university. Before unpacking those implications more specifically in the chapters that follow, I first want to briefly consider how this model of the human person should also change our understanding of cultural institutions, requiring a more nuanced theology of culture that is attentive to the dynamics of desire.

From Spheres to Aims: Liturgical Institutions

I have been suggesting that we picture human persons not as containers filled with ideas or beliefs, but rather as dynamic, desiring "arrows" aimed and pointed at something ultimate that in turn becomes a mirror of the sorts of people they (want to) become. We are fundamentally creatures of desire who crave particular visions of the kingdom—the good life—and our desire is shaped and directed by practices that point the heart, as it were.

To this point we have tended to focus on the person *as if* she were an individual. Thus figure 1 was to be a schematic picture of an individual person. However, the individual is always already embedded in a nexus of social relationships and institutions. And this is already embedded in the schematic picture: the self is always already shaped by practices that are themselves tethered to and embodied in concrete social institutions. There are no private practices; thus our hearts are constantly being formed by others, and most often through the cultural institutions that we create. Let's keep in mind that "culture" is not a thing that is "out there," but rather is an activity. Culture is, one might say, more of a verb than a noun; it is the fruit of human "making" or cultivation (*poiēsis*). So cultural institutions are those conglomerations of practices (and built-environment) that have unfolded and developed over time to address human needs, wants, and desires. These institutions don't fall from the sky ready-made; in other

59. See the lucid description of this in ibid., 128–31.

words, cultural institutions are not "created," they are sub-created (to use Tolkien's term in a different context).[60] They are engendered and unfolded by human creation, responding to invitations that are embedded in the earth, we might say. The family, for instance, is a cultural institution that has unfolded over time in response to all sorts of needs and wants, including bodily needs for provision and protection as well as higher-order cravings for intimacy and meaning-making.

Or consider the hospital or medicine: We can speak of "medicine" as an entity that names an entire constellation of practices, resources, and sites that arise in response to the need to foster health, curb disease, treat injury, and so forth. We move in and out of a plethora of institutions every single day; indeed, modernity is marked by an explosion of differentiation, from which many different kinds of institutions have emerged, such as the corporation, the state, the university, the market, the church, and so forth. At some fundamental level, these cultural institutions are products of human *poiēsis*, which is just to say that they are not "natural"—one doesn't bump into hospitals or universities as "naturally occurring" entities. Just as we know that smoke is a sign of fire, so cultural institutions are a sign of human making. However, there is also an important sense in which cultural institutions take on a life of their own; while they are ultimately human creations, once they're up and running, they cannot be reduced to the particular whims and interests of particular human beings. They take on a kind of systemic power that gives them an influence that is independent of individual agents. The result is that while cultural institutions are essentially human creations, there is also an important sense in which humans are the products of the formation we receive through cultural institutions.

As sub-creations, cultural institutions are also contingent—both in the sense that they could *not be* at all, but also in the sense that they could be *otherwise*. As human cultural products, they are pliable and malleable; they can be configured in different ways, depending on the ends to which they are oriented. Thus it is important to appreciate that just as persons are dynamic, intentional creatures oriented toward a *telos*, so too are institutions characterized by the same dynamic, "ek-static" orientation toward certain ends—in particular, toward certain visions of the kingdom and particular configurations of the good life. The practices that are part and parcel of cultural institutions aim to point our desire toward certain ends precisely because such orientations are inscribed into the institution itself. If figure 1 is a schematic diagram of the individual person, it is equally a diagram of the dynamics of cultural institutions. In other words, specific

60. See J. R. R. Tolkien, "On Fairy-Stories," in *Tree and Leaf* (San Francisco: Harper Collins, 2001), 70–71.

configurations of cultural practices and institutions function as liturgies, as pedagogies of (ultimate) desire.

Understanding cultural institutions as liturgical institutions, as dynamic structures of desire, primes us to have a more heightened and nuanced appreciation of what's at stake in those institutions. Just as we suggested with individual persons, such dynamic, intentional institutions cannot be understood in a snapshot. We will not adequately grasp what's at stake in given cultural institutions if we just look at what appears in the present or on the surface; we need to "read" these institutions and practices in order to discern the *telos* at which they're aimed. It is at the point of *teloi* that we'll discern the antithesis between a Christian vision of the kingdom and the visions of human flourishing that are implicit in so many current configurations of cultural institutions. Thus our cultural criticism should not be asking what ideas or beliefs are being bandied about in "culture"; rather, we should be discerning *to what ends* all sorts of cultural institutions are seeking to direct our *love*. In short, we will only adequately "read" our culture to the extent that we recognize operative there an array of liturgies that function as pedagogies of desire.

2

Love Takes Practice

LITURGY, FORMATION, AND COUNTER-FORMATION

Why Victoria's In on the Secret: Picturing Discipleship at *The Moulin Rouge*

The core argument of chapter 1 was that human beings are fundamentally *lovers*; that is, we are not primarily "thinking things" or "believing animals" but rather desiring agents with a *passional* orientation to the ultimate—to a vision of "the kingdom." This is a structural feature of being human: we can't *not* be lovers; we can't *not* be desiring *some* kingdom. The question is not *whether* we love but *what* we love. That structural orientation, operative for the most part at the level of the adaptive unconscious, can take different directions and be aimed at different ends or different visions of the good life. This model of the human person gives us new eyes to see the function of desire in our culture. For instance, it can help us to both recognize and understand the ubiquitous presence of sex in cultural phenomena from music to marketing. And I want to suggest that this is not all bad.

I'm guessing that I don't have to convince you that sex sells and that sex sells almost everything. It is so pervasive that we can perhaps become a bit blind to its ubiquity. We pretty much expect the association when someone is trying to convince us to buy cars or beer or body spray. But every once in a while the ubiquity of sex becomes just downright strange and thus jolts us into seeing again what is right in front of us. I remember, for instance, an advertising campaign for Uncle Ben's microwaveable rice that basically promised that the time saved from not having to boil water would translate into time spent in passionate sex with supermodels.

However, what's particularly interesting is the way in which marketing (and here one can include practically every aspect of the entertainment industry as ancillaries of the marketing industry) quite intentionally combines passion with transcendence, combines sex with religion. In a culture whose civic religion prizes consumption as the height of human flourishing, marketing taps into our erotic religious nature and seeks to shape us in such a way that this passion and desire is directed to strange gods, alternative worship, and another kingdom. And it does so by triggering and tapping into our erotic core—the heart. Thus in marketing one finds the promise of a kind of transcendence that is linked to a certain bastardization of the erotic. Certain modes of advertising appeal more directly to *eros*, to sexual desire and romantic love, and then in a move of substitution, channel our desire into a product—or at least associate the product with that desire and promise a kind of fulfillment. The standard versions of this tend to be more crass and are generally directed at men (think beer commercials, razor commercials, or more recently ads for AXE body spray). But this is also true for marketing directed toward women: you may recall a line of shampoo commercials promising that various states of ecstasy would attend mundane hygienic tasks like washing one's hair. But the ubiquity of Victoria's Secret is a particularly interesting case because it seems operative for both men and women: on the one hand, Victoria's Secret ads appear during football games broadcast on ESPN and TSN; on the other hand, the majority of shoppers at Victoria's Secret are women who want to be desirable. And all of this is communicated by very affective, visual means: tiny narratives packed into images that appeal to our faculties of desire and inscribe themselves into our imagination. The secret here is an industry that thrives on desire and knows how to get to it.

A common "churchy" response to this cultural situation runs along basically Platonic lines: to quell the raging passion of sexuality that courses its way through culture, our bodies and passions need to be disciplined by our "higher" parts—we need to get the brain to trump other organs and thus bring the passions into submission to the intellect. And the way to do this is to get *ideas* to trump *passions*. In other words, the church responds to the overwhelming cultural activation and formation of desire by trying to fill our head with ideas and beliefs.

I suggest that, on one level, Victoria's Secret is right just where the church has been wrong. More specifically, I think we should first recognize and admit that the marketing industry—which promises an erotically charged transcendence through media that connects to our heart and imagination—is operating with a better, more creational, more incarnational, more holistic anthropology than much of the (evangelical) church. In other words, I think we must admit that the marketing industry is able to capture, form, and direct our desires precisely because it has rightly discerned that we are embodied, desiring creatures whose being-in-the-world is governed by the imagination. Marketers have figured out the way to our heart because they "get it": they rightly understand that, at root, we are *erotic* creatures—creatures who are oriented primarily by love and passion and desire. In sum, I think Victoria is in on Augustine's secret. But meanwhile, the church has been duped by modernity and has bought into a kind of Cartesian model of the human person, wrongly assuming that the heady realm of ideas and beliefs is the core of our being. These are certainly part of being human, but I think they come second to embodied desire. And because of this, the church has been trying to counter the consumer formation of the heart by focusing on the head and missing the target: it's as if the church is pouring water on our head to put out a fire in our heart.

What if we approached this differently? What if we didn't see passion and desire *as such* as the problem, but rather sought to redirect it? What if we honored what the marketing industry has got right—that we are creatures primarily of love and desire—and then responded in kind with counter-measures that focus on our passions, not primarily on our thoughts or beliefs? What if the church began with an affirmation of our passional nature and then sought to redirect it?

The result would be what Inklings member Charles Williams called a "romantic theology." Developed in a number of (unfortunately) forgotten little books, Williams's argument is that the human experience of romantic love and sexual desire is itself a testimony to the desire for God. Williams would put it even more strongly: the person who experiences romantic love has experienced something of the God who is love. Treading a path opened by Dante's meditations on Beatrice, Williams suggests that romantic love "renews nature, if only for a moment; it flashes for a moment into the lover the life he was meant to possess."[1] Love, says Williams, is a testament to the in-breaking or emergence of the divine in human experience, and thus to be affirmed as an expression of our deepest erotic passion, the desire for God:

> Any occupation exercising itself with passion, with self-oblivion, with devotion, towards an end other than itself, is a gateway to divine things. If a lover contemplating in rapture the face of his lady, or a girl listening in joy to the call of the beloved, are worshippers in the hidden temples of our Lord, is not also the spectator who contemplates in rapture a batsman's stroke or the collector gazing with veneration at a unique example of [a stamp]?[2]

As we'll see later hinted in Walker Percy's *Love in the Ruins*, the erotic—even misdirected eros—is a sign of the kinds of animals we are: creatures who *desire* God. As Augustine famously put it, "You have made us for yourself, and our hearts are restless until they rest in you."[3] This is not a matter of intellect; Augustine doesn't focus on the fact that we don't "know" God. The problem here isn't ignorance or skepticism. At issue is a kind of in-the-bones angst and restlessness that finds its resolution in "rest"—when our precognitive desire settles, finally, on its proper end (the end for which it was made), rather than being constantly frustrated by objects of desire that don't return our love (idols). But this means that even desire wrongly "aimed" is still a testament to our nature as desiring animals. Operative behind Williams's "romantic theology" is a picture of the human person that appreciates affectivity and desire as the "heart" of the person.

An Augustinian anthropology of desire primes us to adopt just such a romantic theology. And this entails, I think, an interesting implication for how we'll think about

---

1. Charles Williams, *He Came Down from Heaven* (1938; repr., Grand Rapids: Eerdmans, 1984), 96.

2. Charles Williams, *Outlines of Romantic Theology*, ed. Alice M. Hadfield (Grand Rapids: Eerdmans, 1990), 70.

3. Augustine, *Confessions* 1.1.1.

learning and discipleship. I have in mind *The Moulin Rouge*—a film set in that den of iniquity, Montmartre, at the turn of the twentieth century, during the fervor of the Bohemian revolution. A starving artist named "Christian" has rejected the "respectable" and bourgeois lifestyle of his father (as a clerk or salesman) and instead sought to pursue a life devoted to literature and drama, all in the pursuit of beauty. He rejects the nine-to-five machinations of "normal" people, refuses to be reduced to a middle-class producer and consumer, and instead takes up residence with the colony of artists clustered in Montmartre—infamous home to burlesque shows and the red-light district, but also home to painters and artists like Renoir, Toulouse-Lautrec, and van Gogh—all taking place under the watchful eye of the Basilica Sacré-Coeur perched atop the hill. Thus Montmartre represents a certain mix of the sacred and the profane—both of which seem to be at odds with the bourgeois life of production and consumption that the young artist, Christian, has rejected. The proximity to Sacré-Coeur almost invites us to look for parallels and comparisons between the bohemian artists and the mendicant friars, the decadent painters and the celibate priests, both of whom reject a life of moneymaking for the sake of very different visions of the kingdom, of the good life. But if both the bohemian and the friar desire a kingdom that rejects the pursuit of comfort and wealth, could it be that there are some covert similarities between their visions of the kingdom? Does the Moulin Rouge already point up the hill toward the Basilica? What, at the end of the day, is Christian after?

Above all, Luhrmann's *Moulin Rouge* is a "spectacular" love story revolving around the play within the play—a production of another love story, "Spectacular, Spectacular."[4] It is desire that brings the young man to art, to commit himself to the voluntary poverty of a bohemian literary existence.[5] And it is in pursuit of this desire that another desire flames: his passion for Satine, a courtesan who reigns at the Moulin Rouge. Oddly, Satine herself represents the moneymaker, concerned primarily with acquisition, as attested in her hymn, "Diamonds Are a Girl's Best Friend." (Indeed, her profession represents the very commodification of love.) Thus she resists his advances; above all she rejects his bohemian ideal, his naive commitment to love (played out in the "Elephant Love Medley"). But love wins. Christian's evangelistic commitment to love captures the heart of Satine, and the effect is transformative: rejecting a lucrative offer from the duke, she too becomes a bohemian, and the desire for acquisition gives way to a passion for love and beauty. Love even has a kind of epistemological or perceptual effect, as indicated in their anthem, "Come What May": "Never knew I could feel like

4. Baz Luhrmann is the master of affective, adaptive unconscious. The film in its entirety is a spectacle. And its very spectacularity "works on you" in ways you can't quite articulate. One almost feels that one shouldn't be so moved, that perhaps this is some sort of "camp" production that's playing with us. And yet there is an affective, almost irresistible allure in the very medium itself.

5. For an interesting peek into the ideals of a bohemian life in a different context, see Virginia Nicholson, *Among the Bohemians: Experiments in Living, 1900–1930* (New York: William Morrow, 2002).

this, like I've never seen the sky before." The world is "seen" differently because of love.⁶
By the end of the film we learn that all of this has constituted a kind of *education*: "The
greatest thing you'll ever *learn* is just to love, and be loved in return."

On the one hand, this seems to be the very antithesis of the kingdom of God: a
realm of prostitutes and addicted artists given over to wanton pleasure-seeking. This
criticism is embodied in the figure of Christian's bourgeois father, who berates the
bohemian culture for its sinfulness, which seems to be most linked to its failure to be
"productive." But to "the children of the revolution" (try to hear Bono crooning the song
from the sound track), our highest calling is not to simply be producers. Instead, they
are committed to the bohemian ideals of "beauty, freedom, truth, and above all, *love.*"
And the spectacle of the film is ripe for analysis in terms of Williams's theology of romantic love—a love that is revelatory, that breaks open the world ("Never knew I could
feel like this, like I never saw the sky before . . ."). Christians will tend to say, "Ah, but
that's not love—that's *eros*, not *agapē*!" But a romantic theology refuses the distinction
because it recognizes that we are erotic creatures—that *agapē* is rightly ordered *eros*.
And so one could suggest that the kingdom looks more like Montmartre than Colorado
Springs! The kingdom might look more like the passionate world of the Moulin Rouge
than the staid, buttoned-down, talking-head world of the 700 Club. The end of learning
is love; the path of discipleship is romantic.⁷

6. Love also has its own economy (or an-economy). In watching a dress rehearsal of
"Spectacular, Spectacular," the duke (who's funding the play) rejects the ending: it doesn't
make any sense that the courtesan would choose the "penniless sitar player" over the monied
"security" of the maharaja. Why on earth would someone make such an absurd choice?
For love, is Christian's answer.

7. I think a philosophical anthropology centered around affectivity, love, or desire might
also be an occasion to somewhat reevaluate our criticisms of "mushy" worship choruses
that seem to confuse God with our boyfriend. While we might be rightly critical of the
self-centered grammar of such choruses (which, when parsed, often turn out to be more
about "me" than God, and "I" more than us), I don't think we should so quickly write
off their "romantic" or even "erotic" elements (the Song of Songs comes to mind in this
context). This, too, is testimony to why and how so many are deeply moved in worship by
such singing. While this can slide into an emotionalism and a certain kind of domestication of God's transcendence, there remains a kernel of "fittingness" about such worship.
While opening such doors is dangerous, I'm not sure that the primary goal of worship or
discipleship is safety. Catholic novelists such as Graham Greene (especially in *The Heart
of the Matter* [New York: Viking, 1948]), Walker Percy (in *Love in the Ruins* [New York:
Farrar, Straus & Giroux, 1971]), and Evelyn Waugh (in *Brideshead Revisited* [Boston:
Little, Brown, 1945]) recognize this thin fulcrum that tips from sexual desire to desire for
God—that on the cusp of this teetering, "dangerous" fulcrum, one is closest to God. The
quasi-rationalism that sneers at such erotic elements in worship and is concerned to keep
worship "safe" from such threats is the same rationalism that has consistently marginalized
the religious experience of women—and women mystics in particular. For a fascinating account along these lines, see Virginia Burrus, *The Sex Lives of Saints: An Erotics of Ancient
Hagiography* (Philadelphia: University of Pennsylvania Press, 2004).

Thick and *Thin* Practices: Ritual Forces of Cultural Formation

Our "desiring" model—our romantic theology—has emphasized that we are creatures who love first and foremost. The most basic way that we intend the world is on the affective order of love. This love constitutes our fundamental and governing orientation to the world. As such, our love is always ultimately aimed at a *telos*, a picture of the good life that pulls us toward it, thus shaping our actions and behavior. This orientation is something that comes before thinking; thus we've described it as precognitive. It is more at work at the level of the adaptive unconscious or the "social imaginary." Our love is aimed from the fulcrum of our desire—the habits that constitute our character, or core identity. And the way our love or desire gets aimed in specific directions is through practices that shape, mold, and direct our love.

So as we've suggested, habits (precognitive dispositions) are formed by practices: routines and rituals that inscribe particular ongoing habits into our character, such that they become second nature to us. According to research on the "new unconscious," such dispositions have a kind of "automaticity" about them: they are the default tendencies and inclinations that we follow without thinking.[8] They are not the same as mere biological instincts or "natural" responses to stimuli because they are learned; they are part of our "second" nature, not the first.[9] But how are such "automaticities" acquired? Research by Bargh and Chartrand shows that "the development of most acquired forms of automaticity (i.e., skill acquisition) depends on the frequent and consistent pairing of internal responses with external events." As this happens over time, "conscious choice drops out as it is not needed."[10] Some such acquisition of automatic dispositions and tendencies happens "intentionally"; that is, we choose to learn them by "frequent and consistent pairing"—namely, by practice. "We purposefully engage in the considerable practice (frequent and consistent performances) required to sublimate many of the components of

8. See John A. Bargh and Tanya L. Chartrand, "The Unbearable Automaticity of Being," *American Psychologist* 54 (1999): 462–79; and Neal J. Roese et al., "The Mechanics of Imagination: Automaticity and Control in Counterfactual Thinking," in *The New Unconscious*, ed. Ran R. Hassin (New York: Oxford University Press, 2006), 138–70.

9. Yet Bargh and Chartrand note that "some of the automatic guidance systems we've outlined are 'natural' and don't require experience to develop." However, "other forms of automatic self-regulation develop out of repeated and consistent experience" ("Unbearable Automaticity," 476). Our focus here is on the latter. But an interesting and relevant example of the former "natural" or "innate" automaticity is the "innate capacity for imitative behaviors and vicarious learning" possessed by humans and other primates (465). This involves an innate inclination to imitate the behavior of others. Once again, contemporary cognitive science seems to confirm the ancient wisdom of Aristotle.

10. Ibid., 468.

the skill."[11] Anyone who can remember first learning the piano, learning to type, or learning to drive can recall this process: at first doing the activity requires great mental ("conscious") energy and focus. Each movement requires intentional, conscious choice. But as one continues to engage in the practice over time, gradually more and more becomes "sublimated" or taken care of by the unconscious. Eventually, "one sees the teenager go from being an overwhelmed tangle of nerves at the first attempts to drive a car to soon being able to do so while conversing, tuning, and getting nervous instead over that evening's date."[12]

So many automatic dispositions become part of our adaptive unconscious because we consciously, intentionally choose to participate in practices and routines that will train the unconscious in this way. We choose to practice piano for an hour every day; we make a conscious choice to log our hours driving with Dad in the passenger seat. However, Bargh and Chartrand also note that automaticity can be acquired unintentionally. As they put it, "the process of automation itself is automatic." So there can be all sorts of "automating" going on that we do *not* choose and of which we are not conscious but that nevertheless happens because we are regularly immersed in environments that elicit commonly "paired" responses. In other words, all the ingredients for automation might be present without our consciously or intentionally *choosing* to be shaped in this way. In these cases, automation happens automatically. "These processes also become automated, but because we did not start out intending to make them that way, we are not aware that they have been and so, when that process operates automatically in that situation, we aren't aware of it."[13] (An example they consider is stereotypes.) Whether we intentionally choose to participate in a practice, or unintentionally just find ourselves immersed in it over time, the result is the same: the dispositions become inscribed into our unconscious so that we "automatically" respond the way we've been conditioned. Bargh and Chartrand note a rather chilling conclusion from this: "People should be able to put goals into gear through external means and thereby 'bypass the will' entirely."[14] Since research indicates that only about 5 percent of our daily activity is the product of conscious, intentional actions that we "choose," one can see that there's a lot at stake in the formation of our automatic unconscious. We'll return to this momentarily.

Both the philosophical tradition and recent cognitive psychology emphasize that our dispositions or automatic habits are acquired and shaped by

11. Ibid.

12. Ibid., 468–69.

13. Ibid., 469. Wilson discusses this as "implicit learning" (Timothy D. Wilson, *Strangers to Ourselves: Discovering the Adaptive Unconscious* [Cambridge, MA: Harvard University Press, 2002], 25–26).

14. Bargh and Chartrand, "Unbearable Automaticity," 469.

practices. These are rituals and routines that train our bodies, as it were, to react automatically in certain situations and environments. This happens because of what we've emphasized in chapter 1: the center of gravity of the self is located in the affective and unconscious. However, there is quite a range of things that would count as practices in this regard, precisely because there are different kinds of goals. There seems to be an important difference between the goal of learning to type automatically and the goal of being the sort of person who forgives "automatically." There's a difference between automatic habits that enable one to drive a car and automatic habits that make one dispositionally nonviolent. Brushing one's teeth may be an automated activity, but it seems significantly different from being compassionate automatically. So perhaps we might adopt a rough-and-ready, heuristic distinction between different "levels" or kinds of goals, habits, and practices.

- Some habits are very *thin*, or mundane, like brushing our teeth, or eating the same cereal for breakfast every day, or watching the eleven o'clock news every night, or exercising daily, and so on. Such things are not usually pursued for their own sake; rather, they are instrumental to some other end.[15] They also aren't the sort of things that tend to touch on our identity. It would be an odd thing, for instance, for me to think of myself first and foremost as a "tooth brusher." These practices and habits don't touch our *love* or fundamental *desire*.

- Other habits are what we could call *thick*, or meaning-full. These are habits that play a significant role in shaping our identity, who we are. Engaging in these habit-forming practices not only says something about us, but also keeps shaping us into that kind of person. So thick habits often both signal and shape our core values or our most significant desires. Here's where we would often locate religious habits and practices: going to Sunday worship, engaging in daily prayer, meeting with others for support and encouragement. But they might also include other kinds of habits and practices: for instance, if I regularly ride public transit, that might be a habit that not only says something significant about me, but also is a practice that could be regularly formative (or transformative) for me. So too would the regular habit of commuting by myself for three hours every day on the 405 freeway, all the while listening to inflammatory talk radio. So

15. This is just to say that such routines are not *really* "practices" in MacIntyre's sense, since the "goods" sought are external to the practice (see MacIntyre, *After Virtue*, 2nd ed. [Notre Dame, IN: University of Notre Dame Press, 1984], 187–88). However, such routines that lead to automation would be described as "practices" in Bargh and Chartrand's sense, so I'm using the term more loosely in this context.

not all thick habits are specifically religious, but all thick habits are meaningful and identity-significant.

Now, we should qualify this distinction a bit: at times, the line between thin and thick practices will be fuzzy and hard to draw. For instance, what might appear to be a thin habit—say, meeting with friends once every week for breakfast—might actually lean toward being a thick practice because it expresses something about our commitment to community and relationships. Or exercising every day could be a mundane, thin practice that actually serves a thicker matter of identity formation. And this could cut different ways: on the one hand, I might be doing this because I "want to look good naked" (as Lester Burnham put it in *American Beauty*), and I want that because being a hedonistic playboy is a central, meaningful aspect of *who I am*. Wanton pursuit of physical pleasure is my vision of the good life (while exercising Lester Burnham is listening to "The Seeker"), and so my thinner practice of daily exercise is actually taken up by my thicker desire to be that kind of person. On the other hand, I might engage in regular exercise because I want to stay healthy so that I can enjoy myself, see my children grow, spend many years of friendship with my wife, and so on. Here the thin practice of exercise serves the thick end of finding meaning in the sacrament of marriage and family.

This slippage perhaps helps us to recognize that—within the desiring framework we've constructed—no habit or practice is neutral. This is not to say that every habit is a thick one, but only that even our thinnest habits and practices ultimately get hooked up into desires that point at something ultimate. Certain kinds of habits and practices are aimed at certain ends (*teloi*), and other habits and practices are aimed at quite different ends— and at some important point, those different ends will be mutually exclusive; that is, it will come down to a matter of aiming at one or the other (cf. Matt. 6:24). All habits and practices are ultimately trying to make us into a certain kind of person. So one of the most important questions we need to ask is: Just what kind of person is this habit or practice trying to produce, and to what end is such a practice aimed?

With that in mind, there are two important things we need to recognize. First, what might seem to be thin practices are actually thick ones. In other words, recognizing that there are no neutral practices (even if there are mid-level practices that can be pointed to different ends) should push us to realize that perhaps some of the habits and practices that we are regularly immersed in are actually thick formative practices that over time embed in us desires for a particular version of the good life. In short, they are meaning-laden, identity-forming practices that subtly shape us precisely because they grab hold of our love—they are automating our desire and action without our conscious recognition. Our opening tour in the introduction was meant to shake us out of our familiarity with the mundane reality of the mall in order to see just this: what might appear to be the normal, everyday habit of going to the mall is actually a deeply formative ritual practice that subtly but powerfully shapes and aims our desire. Though we treat it as a thin practice, it is really a thick practice pointed at an end that is antithetical to being a disciple of Jesus.

Typical worldview-thinking is not primed to recognize something like this because it is too focused on the cognitive. If you think cultural critique is based on ideas or beliefs, and that cultural "threats" come in the form of messages and "values," then you'll have a cultural radar that is only equipped to pick up on ideas and beliefs. But the mall has never been guilty of being a think tank; one doesn't usually think of the Gap or Walmart

---

To Think About: A Practices Audit

So, the question is, Are there habits and practices that we acquire without knowing it? Are there ritual forces in our culture that we perhaps naively immerse ourselves in—and are thus formed by—that, when we consider them more closely, are pointed at some ultimate end? Are there mundane routines that we participate in that, if we are attentive, function as thick practices aimed at a particular vision of the good life?

To get at this requires quite a bit of patient reflection and analysis, both introspective and communal. Consider taking some time this week to engage in a bit of self-inventory—a "practices audit"—perhaps journaling about it. Then talk about these issues with friends. Use the following questions as prompts:

• What are some of the most significant habits and practices that really shape your actions and attitude—what you think and what you do?

• What does your time look like? What practices are you regularly immersed in each week? How much time is spent doing different sorts of activities?

• What do you think are the most important ritual forces in your life? And if you were honest with yourself, are these positive (forming you into the kind of person who embodies the kingdom of God) or negative (forming you into someone whose values and desires are antithetical to that kingdom, oriented toward another kingdom)?

• What do you think are some of the most potent practices in our culture? Or, if you have kids, what are the cultural forces that you *don't* want your children shaped by? What are the ritual forces that you *do* want to shape their desires? And why on both counts?

• If you step back and reflect on them, are there some habits and practices that you might have originally thought were neutral or thin, but upon further reflection, you see them as thicker and more significant?

• Is there any way in which you see worship as a thick habit? How so? How not?

• If Christian worship is a thick practice, what do you think are its most significant "competitors"?

as sites of the culture war because they don't traffic in ideas. As a result, the threat of these sites doesn't register on worldview radar; because such worldview approaches remain largely fixated on the cognitive, something like the mall drops off the radar (while an institution like the U.S. Supreme Court is unduly amplified). But all the while the ritual practices of the mall are grabbing hold of hearts and capturing imaginations, shaping our love and desire, and actually forming us in powerful, fundamental ways. If our cultural critique remains captivated by a cognitivist anthropology, then we'll fail to even see the role of practices. This constitutes a massive blind spot in much of the Christian cultural critique that takes place under the banner of worldview-thinking. But even if we might be primed to consider practices more centrally, if we mistakenly think that certain habits or practices are neutral, or even thin, when they are actually quite thick and loaded, then we will be unwittingly subjecting ourselves to a formation of our desire that is pointed away from the kingdom of God.

This raises the second concern: research on the "new unconscious" undertaken by cognitive psychologists like Bargh and Chartrand suggests that many kinds of automaticity—dispositions toward goals that become habituated in us to the point that they become automatic—are acquired unintentionally. While some of our habits (automaticities) are acquired by choosing to engage in certain practices (e.g., signing up for driver's ed or registering for piano lessons), many are acquired without our knowing it. And this might happen especially when we are unaware of it. If we are inattentive to the formative role of practices, or if we treat some practices as thin when they are thick, then we will be inattentive to all the ways that such practices unwittingly and unintentionally become automated. We will fail to recognize that they are forming in us habits and desires, oriented to particular ends, that function to draw us toward those ends at an affective, unconscious level such that we become certain kinds of people without even being aware of it.

Formation, *Mis*-formation, and *Counter*-formation: Liturgies Secular and Christian

I have suggested that our habits are formed by practices, and such practices can be either thin or thick. Thick practices are identity-forming, *telos*-laden, and get hold of our core desire—our ultimate love that defines us in some fundamental way. I want to ramp this up just one more notch and suggest that our thickest practices constitute and function as *liturgies*. But what would that mean? And why would we describe it this way?

We have suggested above that practices are sorts of rituals: they are material, embodied routines that we do over and over again; they are usually aimed at a specific end, or goal; and their repetition and practice has the effect of making them more and more automatic such that they become part of the very fiber of our character, wired into our second nature. Now lots of routines or rituals are very thin: you might always brush your teeth in exactly the same way, perhaps even religiously observe the ritual of eight brushstrokes for each sector of your mouth (Harold Crick in *Stranger Than Fiction* comes to mind). Or you might always put on your socks before your belt, such that your world might be off-kilter if one morning you looped your belt through your pants while still barefoot. Or you might always eat your vegetables, then your potatoes, and then finish with your meat. In any case, all of these might be quite scrupulous routines—the sort of thing we often describe (in a very loose sense) as *rituals*—as in, "My roommate has this whole *ritual* she goes through before getting into bed!" (*and it drives me crazy*, you're thinking). However, we would not be inclined to describe them as *liturgies*, largely because we associate *liturgy* specifically with religious rituals (and we might actually have a negative view of both liturgy and ritual in this respect).[16]

I want to shake up our habits of thought in this regard by suggesting that some so-called secular rituals actually constitute liturgies. Here I employ the term *liturgy* in a broad and generous sense (in order to see some kind of liturgy as integral to different religions), without diluting its meaning (such that any and all ritual would constitute liturgy). Thus we need a few distinctions in order to provide a map of the territory here. What is the relationship between practices, rituals, and liturgies? *Ritual* can be used in a very broad sense to refer to routines (as in the rituals of a batter before he steps into the batter's box); in this sense, not all rituals would be practices because not all rituals are directed toward an end. However, it would be hard to think of a practice that isn't already a ritual in some significant sense. So we might suggest that practices are a species of the genus ritual. What, then, of liturgies? Not all rituals would be liturgies; not even all practices would be liturgies (e.g., masonry could be understood as a practice but it doesn't seem to be a liturgy). Liturgies, then, are a certain species of practice.

More specifically, I want to distinguish liturgies as *rituals of ultimate concern*: rituals that are formative for identity, that inculcate particular visions of the good life, and do so in a way that means to trump other ritual formations. Admittedly, this might include rituals not associated with traditional religions (e.g., rituals of Nazi fascism or other rituals of totalizing nationalism); indeed, expanding our conception of what counts

16. If you have reservations about associating Christian worship with ritual and liturgy, turn to the excursus "The Shape of Christian Worship," 151–54.

FIGURE 4
Rituals, Practices, and Liturgies

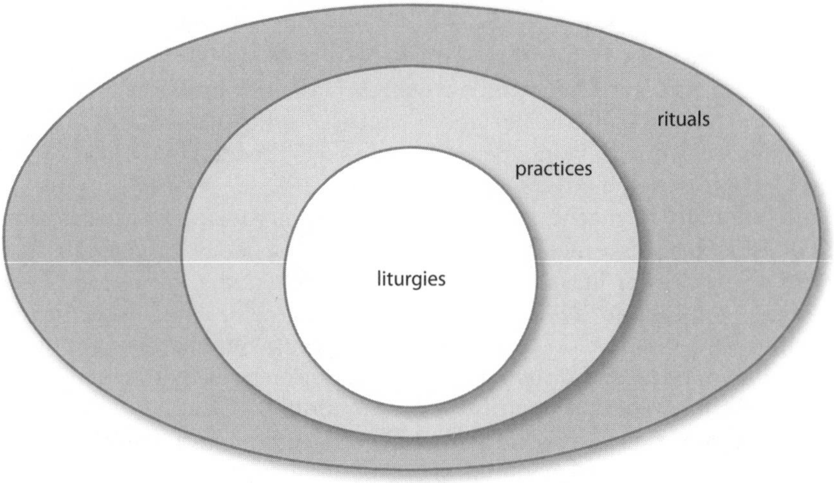

rituals

practices

liturgies

as "worship" is precisely the point.[17] Our thickest practices—which are not necessarily linked to institutional religion—have a *liturgical* function insofar as they are a certain species of ritual practice that aim to do nothing less than shape our identity by shaping our desire for what we envision as the kingdom—the ideal of human flourishing. Liturgies are the most loaded forms of ritual practice because they are after nothing less than our hearts. They want to determine what we love ultimately. By *ultimately* I mean what we love "above all," that to which we pledge allegiance, that to which we are devoted in a way that overrules other concerns and interests.[18] Our ultimate love is what defines us, what makes us the kind of people we are. In short, it is what we worship. Another way of putting this, in terms we've used before, is to say that liturgies are ritual practices that function as pedagogies of ultimate desire.

The reason to employ *liturgy* in this sense is to raise the stakes of what's happening in a range of cultural practices and rituals. Insofar as they aim to shape our desire and specify our ultimate concern, they function as nothing

17. See also Philip Kenneson, "Gathering: Worship, Imagination, and Formation," in *The Blackwell Companion to Christian Ethics*, ed. Stanley Hauerwas and Samuel Wells (Oxford: Blackwell, 2006), 53–67. Kenneson notes that since the basic feature of "worship" is "ascribing worth," then all sorts of human gatherings are "fundamentally formative" insofar as they train us to ascribe worth to certain ends (53–54).

18. This is *not* to suggest that we all love the same "ultimate"—which I take to be a roughly Tillichian claim. While I'm describing liturgies as "rituals of ultimate concern," this has no truck with Paul Tillich's project of locating an existential kernel that religions share in common. My account is pluralist about what people and communities worship *as* ultimate.

less than liturgies.[19] Above, we emphasized the importance of seeing what might appear to be thin practices (such as shopping at the mall, attending a football game, or taking part in "frosh week" at university) as thick practices that are identity-forming and *telos*-laden. We need then to take that recognition one step further and recognize these thick practices as liturgical in order to appreciate their religious nature. Such ritual forces of culture are not satisfied with being merely mundane; embedded in them is a sense of what ultimately matters (compare Phil. 1:10). "Secular"[20] liturgies are fundamentally formative, and implicit in them is a vision of the kingdom that needs to be discerned and evaluated. From the perspective of Christian faith, these secular liturgies will often constitute a *mis*-formation of our desires—aiming our heart away from the Creator to some aspect of the creation as if it were God. Secular liturgies capture our hearts by capturing our imaginations and drawing us into ritual practices that "teach" us to love something very different from the kingdom of God.

By the same token, Christian worship needs to be intentionally liturgical, formative, and pedagogical in order to *counter* such mis-formations and misdirections. While the practices of Christian worship are best understood as the restoration of an original, creational desire for God, practically speaking, Christian worship functions as a counter-formation to the mis-formation of secular liturgies into which we are "thrown" from an early age.[21] In chapter 3 we will exegete some dominant secular liturgies in order to discern the shape of the kingdom that is implicit in them; then in chapters 4 and 5 we will more fully explicate the social imaginary that is implicit in Christian worship and see how Christian liturgy functions as a *counter*-formation. This will then set us up to consider how a distinctly Christian education constitutes a counter-pedagogy.

19. In this respect, Lindbeck shrinks back from the implications of his own cultural-linguistic model of religion. Thus he recognizes "French Revolutionary *fraternité*" as a "quasi-religious phenomenon" (George Lindbeck, *The Nature of Doctrine: Religion and Theology in a Postliberal Age* [Philadelphia: Westminster, 1984], 40). But why only *quasi*-religious? In fact, it offers an "idiom for dealing with whatever is most important" (ibid.) and functions as a "ritual reiteration of certain definitions of what is ultimately good and true" (ibid., 41). I'm suggesting that we drop the "quasi" and recognize such formative "secular" rituals *as* properly "religious."

20. I use the term *secular* loosely since one of the implications of this analysis is that there is no secular. If humans are essentially liturgical animals, and cultural institutions are liturgical institutions, then there are no "secular" (a-religious or nonreligious) institutions. By describing them as "secular" liturgies, I'm heuristically conceding to some common habits of thought.

21. This is why, in the chapters that follow, I begin by first considering secular liturgies and then consider an exegesis of Christian worship. It is Christian worship that is normative and constitutes the creational norm of human love and desire. But we must begin from where we are, and for most of us, we find ourselves *first* immersed in disordered secular liturgies.

3

Lovers in a Dangerous Time

CULTURAL EXEGESIS OF "SECULAR" LITURGIES

"Reading" Culture through the Lens of Worship

Cultural Exegesis of Practices

I've been suggesting that a Christian analysis and critique of culture will be insufficient if it only looks at culture through the lens of the worldview paradigm. I'm inviting us to try on another pair of glasses for looking at culture, considering it through the lens of identity-forming practices, or what we're now calling liturgy. So the question we bring to culture is not primarily or only, What does this or that institution have to *say*? Or, What is the message being communicated in this film? Or, What ideas or values are contained in this or that policy? Rather, the questions we should be asking are quite different and will often be aimed at sectors of culture that have hitherto received little attention. We should be asking: What vision of human flourishing is implicit in this or that practice? What does the good life look like as embedded in cultural rituals? What sort of person will I become after being immersed in this or that cultural liturgy? This is a process that we can describe as cultural exegesis. The first question in cultural exegesis is discerning the shape of the kingdom toward which cultural practices and institutions are aimed. If we read *through* such cultural practices—if we read between the lines, so to speak, and discern their teleological aim—what do we see? What do these practices and institutions envision as the good life? What picture of human flourishing is implicit or "carried" in the practices? In this chapter we will focus on exegeting several "secular" liturgies in order to discern what's at stake in these practices and institutions, and to explicate the visions of the kingdom that are implicit within them.[1]

But then we also need to ask the same question regarding the practices of Christian worship (the focus of chapters 4 and 5): How do the practices of Christian worship inscribe a desire for the kingdom within us in a way that is more affective than grasping doctrines or beliefs? In what sense does worship precede a worldview? What picture of the kingdom is embedded in Christian liturgy? What vision of the good life is being "automated" in us when we participate in Christian worship? And how does this compare with the visions of human flourishing implicit in other cultural practices? Before we bring these questions to Christian worship, we'll first exegete cultural practices as secular liturgies.

Seeing through Babylon's Beauty: Cultural Critique as Apocalyptic

One of the reasons I'm describing cultural practices and institutions as secular liturgies is to raise the stakes: I want to give you a heightened awareness of the *religious* nature of many of the cultural institutions we inhabit that you might not otherwise think of as having anything to do with Christian discipleship. By *religious*, I mean that they are institutions that command our allegiance, that vie for our passion, and that aim to capture our heart with a particular vision of the good life. They don't want to just give us entertainment or an education; they want to make us into certain kinds of people. So one of the most important aspects of this theology of culture is first a moment of *recognition*: recognizing cultural practices and rituals *as* liturgies. We need to recognize that these practices are not neutral or benign, but rather intentionally loaded to form us into

1. In explicating what I'm calling *secular liturgies*, I cautiously and respectfully demur from Schmemann's account of the secular as "above all a *negation of worship*," and more specifically, "the negation of man as a worshipping being, as *homo adorans*." Alexander Schmemann, "Worship in a Secular Age," included as appendix 1 to *For the Life of the World: Sacraments and Orthodoxy*, 2nd ed. (Crestwood, NY: St. Vladimir's Seminary Press, 1973), 118. Schmemann later recognizes that "the secularist in a way is truly obsessed with worship" (124) and that "whatever the degree of his secularism or even atheism, man remains an essentially 'worshiping being,' forever nostalgic for rites and rituals no matter how empty and artificial is the ersatz offered to him" (125). However, he seems to reserve the descriptor *worship* for "genuine" (that is, Christian, for him) worship (125). I am making a distinction between worship as a formal, ineradicable structure of human being-in-the-world, and the particular *direction* that can take (which can be authentic or inauthentic). In my view, idolatry is still "worship."

To Think About: The "Doc Ock" Challenge

By describing these cultural institutions and practices as *liturgical*, my main purpose is to raise the stakes of concern regarding participation in them. Granted, given a long history of Christian retreat and isolation from culture into a dualistic fixation on "the spiritual," I don't mean to encourage a simple withdrawal. However, I do think it is important to heighten our sense of the risks of cultural engagement by recognizing cultural institutions as formative spaces of worship. We might describe this as the "Doc Ock Challenge." You may recall the infamous villain of Spiderman lore, particularly in the recent film version of *Spiderman 2*. Doctor Otto Octavius, a leading nuclear physicist and inventor, pursues high-level research in atomic physics. In order to push the envelope of that research, he develops a set of four mechanical arms that are resistant to radiation; in addition, they are highly precise, being controlled by a brain-computer interface that taps into Dr. Octavius's mind through inputs into his central nervous system. The apparatus straps onto his body, carefully inserting electrodes into his spine and neck, creating an interface with his brain that enables the arms to function as extensions of himself. He is, in a way, immersed in the technology. This enables him to pursue further research, all with the best of intentions.

But an experiment with the arms goes terribly wrong: a nuclear explosion fuses the arms to his body, cementing the electrodes into his central nervous system. In addition, the explosion causes the death of his wife, Rosie. Anger begins to overwhelm the doctor, who has now become a permanent, albeit artificial, octopus—"Doc Ock." His anger and rage are strangely harnessed by the arms, which seem to have a mind of their own. They speak to him, directing him to villainous actions, which are still justified by laudable ends. The doctor's intimate association with his own creation (the octopus-like apparatus) was assumed in order to effect transformation; but the sad result is that the apparatus has changed him.

- At what point does our attachment to cultural practices touch upon our central nervous system, so to speak?
- When does our engagement with culture become assimilation *to* culture?
- Is it possible that our laudable goal of transforming culture has unwittingly led, instead, to our transformation into its image, assuming its goals?

---

certain kinds of people—to unwittingly make us disciples of rival kings and patriotic citizens of rival kingdoms.

Seeing the world and our culture in this way requires a kind of wake-up call, a strategy for jolting us out of our humdrum familiarity and comfort with these institutions in order to see them for what they are. Interestingly, Scripture has a way of doing this: it's called *apocalyptic* literature.[2]

2. My thanks to Scott Daniels for the point that follows. See T. Scott Daniels, *Seven Deadly Spirits: The Message of Revelation's Letters for Today's Church* (Grand Rapids: Baker Academic, 2009). See also Wes Howard-Brook and Anthony Gwyther, *Unveiling Empire: Reading Revelation Then and Now* (Maryknoll, NY: Orbis Books, 2000).

Apocalyptic literature—the sort you find in the strange pages of Daniel and the book of Revelation—is a genre of Scripture that tries to get us to see (or see through) the empires that constitute our environment, in order to see them for what they really are. Unfortunately, we associate apocalyptic literature with end-times literature, as if its goal were a matter of prediction. But this is a misunderstanding of the biblical genre; the point of apocalyptic literature is not prediction but *unmasking*—unveiling the realities around us for what they really are. So apocalyptic literature is a genre that tries to get us to see the world on a slant and thus see through the spin. I imagine it as a bit like the vertical louvered blinds in my room: if the blinds are tilted to the left on a 45-degree angle, then from straight-on they'll appear to be closed and shutting out the light. But if I move slightly to the left and get parallel to the louvers, I'll find that I can see right through them to the outside world. Apocalyptic literature is like that: the empire (whether Babylon or Rome) has something to hide and so tilts the louvers just slightly to cover what it wants to hide. But apocalyptic is revealing precisely because it gives us this new perspective, just to the left, which lets us see through the blinders. Thus Richard Bauckham observes that the book of Revelation was meant to provide a set of "counter-images" to the official image purveyed by the Roman empire:

> Revelation's readers in the great cities of the province of Asia were constantly confronted with powerful images of the Roman vision of the world. Civic and religious architecture, iconography, statues, rituals and festivals, even the visual wonder of the cleverly engineered "miracles" (cf. Rev. 13:13–14) in the temples—all provided powerful visual impressions of Roman imperial power and of the splendour of pagan religion. In this context, Revelation provides a set of Christian prophetic counter-images which impress on its readers a different vision of the world: how it looks from the heaven to which John is caught up in chapter 4. The visual power of the book effects a kind of purging of the Christian imagination, refurbishing it with alternative visions of how the world is and will be.[3]

What we need, then, is a kind of contemporary apocalyptic—a language and a genre that sees through the spin and unveils for us the religious and idolatrous character of the contemporary institutions that constitute our own milieu.[4] My hope is that the shift of focus from ideas to practices, from

---

3. Richard Bauckham, *The Theology of the Book of Revelation* (Cambridge: Cambridge University Press, 1993), 17. In a way analogous to my notion of "secular" liturgies, Augustine saw such Roman civil ceremonies and rituals as "civil" theologies (*City of God* 6.7–8).

4. Bauckham emphasizes that the imagery of Revelation is not timeless, but is aimed at a very specific historical configuration of an idolatrous empire (*Theology of the Book*, 19–20). While we'll find resources and wisdom in Revelation's unveiling, we'll also have

beliefs to liturgy, will function as a methodological jolt that gets us into a position to see cultural practices and institutions in ways we've never seen them before. (I also hope it will help us to see the importance and centrality of Christian worship in ways that we perhaps haven't heretofore.) It's precisely because the liturgical nature of cultural practices is so *insidious* that we need to do the hard work of unveiling it as such.[5] In what follows, then, I will sketch a few case studies in cultural exegesis, taking up several common and influential cultural institutions (the mall, the stadium, and the university) in order to unveil the liturgical shape of their practices.

Consuming Transcendence: Worship at the Mall

Review and recall our opening "Martian anthropology" of the mall,[6] which took this familiar phenomenon that we find in every city, which we might visit every week, and suggested that it is actually a *religious* space because it is suffused with practices that constitute a kind of *worship*. Now you might say that the mall doesn't look very religious: there are no pews or pulpit, we don't go there to listen to a sermon, and we don't kneel and pray in the middle of the atrium. But just because it doesn't look like worship at church doesn't mean that it's not worship. Recall the working definition of worship or liturgy that we sketched in chapter 2: liturgies or worship practices are rituals of ultimate concern that are formative of our identity—they both *reflect* what matters to us and *shape* what matters to us. They also inculcate particular visions of the good life through affective, precognitive means, and do so in a way that trumps other ritual formations. In short, they are the rituals that grab hold of our *kardia* and want nothing less than our love. So they are "ultimate" in two senses: on one level, they determine what's most important, what really matters, what we think life is ultimately about; on

---

to do our own hard work of discerning the contemporary beasts that parade as angels of light.

5. If considering cultural practices and institutions as *liturgical* raises the stakes of cultural participation, we could ratchet up the stakes a bit further by looking at secular liturgies through the related lens of "powers and principalities," seeing them as expressions of fallen powers and perhaps even as demonic. Though Reformed confidence in the goodness of creation tends to be quite allergic to such language (and thus party to a certain disenchantment of the world), this fails to take seriously biblical language of "the powers." Cultural institutions and practices are "charged" not only with an implicit *telos*, but also by spirits or the Spirit. For a related discussion, see Marva J. Dawn, *Powers, Weakness, and the Tabernacling of God* (Grand Rapids: Eerdmans, 2001). Or listen to Uncle Tupelo's album *March 16–20, 1992* and notice the conjunction between "Coalminers" and "Satan, Your Kingdom Must Come Down."

6. I use the term *mall* as a bit of a shorthand for a web of practices and institutions associated with consumerism. I might have also spoken of "the market" or "Walmart." The mall is just a particularly representative site for the liturgies of consumerism.

another level, such practices are jealous: they want their particular vision of what really matters to supersede or trump all other competing practices. They don't mind if you brush your teeth and practice piano everyday, but they don't want you to engage in practices that would threaten their vision of the kingdom as the one that ultimately drives your desire, actions, and relationships. As ultimate they are also definitive.

If we bring this liturgical notion of "religious" to our analysis of the mall, if we shift to the left a bit and see through its everyday appearance (like those louvered blinds), we'll see the mall with new eyes. We'll begin to see that the rhythms, rituals, and spaces of the mall are loaded with meaning; and more specifically, they are loaded with a particular vision of the kingdom, a particular take on what constitutes the good life. What we need to undertake, then, is an exegesis of the sorts of practices associated with the mall (and consumerism more generally) in order to see that implicit in the practices of consumption is an "understanding" (in Taylor's sense) of what it means to be happy, fulfilled, and flourishing; in short, implicit in the mall's liturgies is an understanding of what it means to be *really* human.[7]

We also need to keep in mind just how this process works. Because we are embodied, affective, liturgical animals, our love and desire are shaped and directed by rituals and practices that work on our imaginary; this can often be a sort of automation that inscribes in us habits formed without our recognition because they are operative at the level of the adaptive unconscious—particularly if we fail to recognize the practices *as* formative rituals. Thus the rituals associated with secular liturgies constitute a pedagogy, a training of our hearts and loves; because education is a mode of formation, the formation that results from immersion in secular liturgies is its own education of desire. It is this fundamentally *educative* (i.e., formative) aspect of secular liturgies that concerns us here, precisely because so often the *telos* implicit in these pedagogies is antithetical to the biblical vision of the kingdom of God. And yet, subtly and covertly, by being immersed in these secular liturgies, we are being trained to be a people who desire the earthly city in all sorts of guises. These are not just neutral and benign "things we do"; they are formative liturgies, pedagogies of desire that function as veritable educations of our imagination. Thus, as we've emphasized, education is not confined to the classroom, nor is worship confined to the church. It is precisely because worship *is* a kind of education that secular liturgies function as pedagogies of desire. Our goal

---

7. I can offer only a selective sketch. For fuller considerations, see William Cavanaugh, *Being Consumed: Economics and Christian Desire* (Grand Rapids: Eerdmans, 2008); or Jon Pahl, *Shopping Malls and Other Sacred Spaces: Putting God in Place* (Grand Rapids: Brazos, 2003).

is to critically discern what these pedagogies are aimed at by determining the *telos*—the vision of the good life—that is embedded within them.

So, as a first case of a secular liturgy, what vision of the kingdom is implicit in the mall's liturgies? What story is embedded in its practices? What does it envision as the good life? What is the shape of the mall's worship? What kind of people does it want us to become? What does the mall want us to love?

First, let's keep in mind that the mall is a sort of intensification of a wider web of practices and rituals associated with consumer capitalism.[8] In that respect, one might say that marketing is the mall's evangelism; television commercials,[9] billboards, Internet pop-ups, and magazine advertisements are the mall's outreach. The rituals and practices of the mall and the market are tactile and visceral—they capture our imaginations through the senses of sight and sound, touch and taste, even smell.[10] The hip, happy people that populate television commercials are the moving icons of the consumer gospel, illustrations of what the good life looks like: carefree and independent, clean and sexy, perky and perfect. We see the embodiments of this ideal again in the icon-like mannequins in the windows of the mall. The mall, you might say, mimics that oft-repeated evangelical axiom that says, "We may be the only Bible that people ever read"; that is, the mall communicates its story not through tracts and

8. Lest my description of consumer capitalism as a liturgy should seem to be just the alarmism of a Christian socialist, note that a straight-laced economic policy wonk like Robert Nelson unapologetically makes similar claims about economics. See Robert H. Nelson, *Economics as Religion: From Samuelson to Chicago and Beyond* (University Park: Pennsylvania State University Press, 2001).

9. Keep in mind that what's happening *between* the commercials is very much part of this commercial outreach. Television was invented to create audiences for advertising, not the other way around. Whether it is sitcoms, evening dramas, sports, or news, all such programming is an extension of and support for the thirty-second spots that seem to "interrupt" what we're watching. For more on this, I still recommend Jean Kilbourne's series of documentaries on advertising, particularly the images of women in advertising: *Killing Us Softly* (1979); *Still Killing Us Softly* (1987); and *Killing Us Softly 3* (1999).

10. NPR's *Marketplace* program featured a fascinating conversation with the CEO of ScentAir, a leader in aroma marketing. The company's goal is to harness the sense of smell in order to lure shoppers into stores, keep them there long enough to buy something, and associate products with added, often nostalgic, values implied by scent ("smell being the sense most closely tied to memory"). See "Relax and breathe in the fresh . . . marketing" at http://marketplace.publicradio.org/display/web/2006/10/25/relax_and_breathe_in_the_fresh_nbspnbsp_marketing/. One can find an outline of "sense marketing" (including smell) in Bernd H. Schmitt, *Experiential Marketing: How to Get Customers to Sense, Feel, Think, Act, Relate* (New York: Free Press, 1999), 64–65. Interestingly, in the *Marketplace* segment, the interviewer speaks to a marketing professor who comments, "Be aware of your environment, if you don't want to be manipulated by it." In a way, that is a description of our project here: the goal is to become aware of the formative, liturgical nature of our environment in order to recognize it as such, and thus resist its formations.

didactic lectures but through visual embodiments of the happy life, 3-D icons that we come to revere as ideals worthy of imitation. And because these visual and visceral media operate on our imaginary more than our intellect—because they seep into our imagination—they are slowly and often surreptitiously absorbed into our *kardia*, into the very nerve center of how we orient ourselves to the world. In this sense, they function as very effective liturgies and pedagogies; they are making us into a certain kind of people without our realizing it.

What is the vision that seeps into us through the mall's liturgies? While this deserves much more careful attention than we can undertake here, we might note several features of the mall's version of the kingdom: (1) an implicit notion of brokenness akin to "sin"; (2) a strange configuration of sociality; (3) the hope of redemption in consumption; and (4) a vision of human flourishing ("quality of life") that is unsustainable. Let's briefly consider each of these.

1. *I'm broken, therefore I shop.* Given the smiling faces that peer at us from beer commercials and the wealthy people who populate the world of sitcoms, we are sometimes prone to suppose that the culture of consumerism is one of unbridled optimism looking at the world through rose-colored glasses. But this misses an important element of the mall's rituals—its own construal of the brokenness of the world, which issues not in confession but in consumption. One might say that this is the mall's equivalent of "sin" (though only superficially).[11] The point is this: implicit in those visual icons of success, happiness, pleasure, and fulfillment is a stabbing albeit unarticulated recognition that *that's not me.* I see these images on a billboard or moving in a sitcom, and while never articulated, an implicit recognition seeps into my adaptive unconscious (though the point is that I never really *articulate* this): "Huh," we (almost) say to ourselves. "Everything seems to work out for these people. They seem to enjoy the good life. Their life is not without its drama and struggles, but they seem to be enjoying family and friends who help them overcome adversity. And they sure have nice accessories to go with all that. Maybe at least part of the reason they're happy is because of what surrounds them. That sitcom dad has one of those mammoth chrome BBQs that could grill an entire side of beef in one go; who wouldn't be happier with something like that? That commercial kid has the latest mobile PDA that makes texting a cinch; who wouldn't be happier if it was that easy to stay in touch with your friends? That billboard mom has it all together: Her kids are smiling and seem

11. The radical difference between the two will become clear in chapter 5 when we try to unpack the Christian social imaginary that is implicit in Christian worship. There we'll see that Christian confession is what it is only in relation to assurance of pardon, whereas the mall points out our brokenness with no promise of forgiveness.

remarkably obedient; she's coifed and slim and seems so carefree—surely that new minivan with the DVD player and fourteen cupholders must have something to do with it." And so on.

Do you see how the images of happiness, fulfillment, and pleasure are actually insinuating something? "This isn't you," they tell us. "And you know it. So do we." What is covertly communicated to us is the disconnect and difference between their lives and our own, which often don't look or feel nearly as chipper and fulfilled as these images do. The insinuation is that there's something wrong with us, which only exacerbates what we often already feel about ourselves. Sometimes this is more direct, as in ads for pimple cream or diet pills—usually not much beating around the bush there, but rather direct, painful charges: "Do you find yourself alone at high school dances because of tumor-sized zits all over your face?" and so forth. But usually the liturgies of the mall and market inscribe in us a sense that something's wrong with us, that something's broken, by holding up for us the ideals of which we fall short.

On the one hand, those ideals draw on the power of authentic human desires for friendship, joy, love, and play. On the other hand, they also tend to implant and exaggerate less laudable ideals, focusing on particular conceptions of external beauty that are culturally relative and often impossible to achieve, being the products of digital manipulation; a supposedly ideal body type that can only be achieved in ways that are artificial and/or unhealthy; superficial fixations on image and the perceptions of others; and the celebration of a kind of irresponsibility masking itself as a "carefree" attitude but that is blind to questions of justice. In addition, such images are meant to impress upon us a deep sense of lack, thereby engendering a powerful sense of *need* that would otherwise be absent (as when a child begs a parent, "I *need* a PS3!").[12] So at the same time that these "perfect" images, these icons of happiness, are subliminally telling me what's wrong with myself, they are also valorizing ideals that run counter to *shalom*. As such, the liturgies of the market and mall convey a stealthy intuition about my own brokenness (and hence a veritable need for redemption), but in a way that plays off the power of shame and embarrassment.

2. *I shop with others.* It is something of a truism that consumerism is an expression of individualism—of both self-interest and self-absorption. But this perhaps misses a certain kind of relationality and sociality that attends the mall's liturgies. After all, it does seem that going to the mall is often a social phenomenon, something one does with others, even in

---

12. For an astute and practical analysis of the challenges that the liturgy of the market presents for children and their parents (though without using the language of "liturgy"), see Susan Linn, *Consuming Kids: The Hostile Takeover of Childhood* (New York: New Press, 2004).

order to be with others. However, just what vision of human relationships is implicit in the rituals of the market? While we might participate in the mall's liturgies in pairs or groups, what model of human intersubjectivity is implicit in the story it's selling us? It seems to me that, despite being a site of congregation and even a venue for a certain kind of "friendship," its practices inculcate an understanding of human intersubjectivity that fosters not community but competition; it inscribes in us habits of objectification rather than other-regarding love.

Because of its emphasis on ideals of image, and because we are immersed in such ideals almost everywhere, these slowly seep into our fundamental way of perceiving the world. As a result, we not only judge ourselves against that standard, but we also fall into the habit of evaluating others by the same standard. For example, if we could somehow analyze ourselves as a friend of a friend approaches "our circle" for the first time, we might catch ourselves looking him up and down, noting clothes that seem to be from Old Navy rather than Abercrombie & Fitch (and from last season at that!); he's got a big clunky cell phone that's about two years old; his tastes in music seem a bit dull and dated; and he's from a part of town we wouldn't walk through at night. Or while we're sitting at the Starbucks in the food court, we might find that our eyes are constantly darting to watch the other girls and women passing by. In just the blink of an eye, we find that we've sized them up from top to bottom; noticed their hair and sandals; wordlessly scorned their garish make-up and chubby ankles; or silently admired, even craved their D&G sunglasses or their naturally wavy hair.[13]

What's just happened in those habits of unstated judgment and evaluation? Two things, it seems to me: First, we've implicitly evaluated others vis-à-vis ourselves, and then triangulated this against the ideals we've all absorbed from the mall's evangelism. In doing so, we've also kept a running score in our head: either we've congratulated ourselves on having won this or that particular comparison, or we're demoralized to realize that, once again, we don't measure up. Subtly, then, we've construed our relationships largely in terms of *competition*—against one another and against the icons of the ideal that have been painted for us. And in the process, we have also objectified others: we have turned them into artifacts for observation and evaluation, things to be looked at, and by playing this game, we've also turned ourselves into similar sorts of objects, evaluating ourselves based on our success at being objects worth looking at. In both ways, the sociality of the mall, bustling with people, is merely a cover for

---

13. Jean Kilbourne's *Killing Us Softly* documentaries argue that advertising particularly heightens competition between women, and not only for the attention of men. A caricature of this intragender competition may be found in the 2004 film *Mean Girls*.

a construal of human intersubjectivity as fundamentally competitive and reductionistic. This is just to say that the mall's liturgies reflect a Hobbesian construal of human intersubjectivity as a war of all with all.

3. *I shop (and shop and shop), therefore I am.* If the icons of the ideal subtly impress upon us what's wrong and where we fail, then the market's liturgies are really an invitation to rectify the problem. Though its stories and images point out to us our blotches and blemishes, they are not pessimistic; to the contrary, they hold out a sort of redemption in the goods and services that the market provides. The mall holds out consumption *as* redemption in two senses: in one sense, the shopping itself is construed as a kind of therapy, a healing activity, a way of dealing with the sadness and frustrations of our broken world. The mall offers a sanctuary and a respite, where we can count on sales clerks greeting us with friendly smiles, where we can lose ourselves in the labyrinth of the racks and find new delights and surprises that—at least for a time—cover over the doldrums of our workaday existence. So the very activity of shopping is idealized as a means of quasi-redemption. In another sense, the *goal* of shopping is the acquisition of goods and the enjoyment of services that try to address the problem, that is, what's wrong with us—our pear-shaped figure, our pimply face, our drab and outdated wardrobe, our rusting old car, and so forth. To shop is to seek and to find: we come with a sense of need (given our failure to measure up to its iconic ideals), and the mall promises something to address that. The narratives of the mall's outreach, the veritable stained-glass presentations of the happy life, implant within us a desire to find *that* version of the kingdom, the good life, which requires acquisition of all the accoutrements in order to secure the ideal and combat our failures.

But here's the dirty little secret, which we get intimations of but are encouraged to quickly forget: when the shopping excursion is over and all the bags are brought into the house as the spoils of our adventure, we find that we've come back to the same old "real world" we left. The thrill of the shopping experience is over, and we now have to do our homework, cut the grass, and wash the dishes.[14] (When can we go again?!) And while the new product has a glitz and fascination about it for a little while, we know (but hate to admit) that the dazzle fades rather quickly. The new jacket we couldn't wait to wear to school somehow already seems a bit dingy in just a couple of months (or less); the latest and greatest mobile phone that seemed to have "everything" is already lacking something by the summer; the video game that we were craving sits unplayed after only a few weeks because we've already beaten every level. In short, what sparkled with the

14. Granted, I think many renditions of Christian worship—reflecting what we might call "refueling" models—are subject to the same disappointments and frustrations.

thrill of the new in the mall's slanted light quickly becomes flat and dull. It's not working anymore. This is why the mall's liturgy is not just a practice of acquisition; it is a practice of *consumption*. Its quasi-redemption lives off of two ephemeral elements: the thrill of the unsustainable "experience" or event and the sheen of the novel and new. Both of these are subject to a law of diminishing returns, and neither can last. They both slip away, requiring new experiences and new acquisitions.

The by-product of such persistent acquisition is a side we don't see or talk about much: the necessary *disposal* of the old and boring. So while the liturgy of the market invests products with an almost transcendent sheen and glow, enchanting them with a kind of magic and pseudo-grace, the strange fact is that the same liturgies encourage us to dispense with these products in a heartbeat. What the mall valorizes as sacred today will be profaned as "so five minutes ago" tomorrow.[15] Hence comes the irony that consumerism, which we often denounce as "materialism," is quite happy to reduce things to nothingness.[16] What makes such serial acquisition consumptive is just this treatment of things as disposable. On the one hand, this practice invests things with redemptive promise; on the other hand, they can never measure up to that and so must be discarded for new things that hold out the same (unsustainable) promise. By our immersion in this liturgy of consumption, we are being trained to both overvalue and undervalue things: we're being trained to invest them with a meaning and significance as objects of love and desire in which we place disproportionate hopes (Augustine would say we are hoping to *enjoy* them when we should only be *using* them) while at the same time treating them (as well as the labor and raw materials that go into them) as easily discarded.

15. This was diagnosed long ago by Marx and Engels, who, seeing the underside of the Industrial Revolution, already recognized that the revolutionary character of capitalism was a monster that would always demand new food, new sacrifices: "Constant revolutionizing of production, uninterrupted disturbance of all social conditions, everlasting uncertainty and agitation distinguish the bourgeois epoch from all earlier ones," they wrote. "All fixed, fast-frozen relations, with their train of ancient and venerable prejudices and opinions, are swept away, all new-formed ones become antiquated before they can ossify. All that is solid melts into air, all that is holy is profaned, and man is at last compelled to face with sober senses his real condition of life and his relations with his kind." Karl Marx and Friedrich Engels, *The Communist Manifesto* (Oxford: Oxford University Press, 1992), 6.
16. This is why folks like John Milbank and Graham Ward have suggested that most materialism amounts to a nihilism that reduces the world to nothingness, whereas it is only Christianity's creational (and participatory) ontology that truly values and invests the material. See John Milbank, Graham Ward, and Catherine Pickstock, "Introduction: Suspending the Material," in *Radical Orthodoxy: A New Theology* (London: Routledge, 1999), 1–5; and John Milbank, "Materialism and Transcendence," in *Theology and the Political*, ed. Creston Davis, John Milbank, and Slavoj Zizek (Durham, NC: Duke University Press, 2005), 393–426.

4. *Don't ask, don't tell.* The rituals of the mall and the liturgies of consumption that both sacralize and profane things have another element of ethereality about them: they live off of a kind of invisibility. Just as the mall is a haven and sanctuary, insulated from the noise of traffic and even the movement of the sun, so the liturgies of consumption induce in us a learned ignorance. In particular, they don't want us to ask, "Where does all this stuff come from?" Instead, they encourage us to accept a certain magic, the myth that the garments and equipment that circulate from the mall through our homes and into the landfill simply emerged in shops as if dropped by aliens. The processes of production and transport remain hidden and invisible, like the entrances and exits for the characters at Disney World.[17] This invisibility is not accidental; it is necessary in order for us not to see that this way of life is unsustainable and selfishly lives off of the backs of the majority of the world. What the liturgy of the mall trains us to desire as the good life and "the American way" requires such massive consumption of natural resources and cheap (exploitive) labor that there is no possible way for this way of life to be universalized. (Though the United States comprises only 5 percent of the world's population, we consume somewhere between 23 and 26 percent of the world's energy.) The liturgy of consumption births in us a desire for a way of life that is destructive of creation itself; moreover, it births in us a desire for a way of life that we can't feasibly extend to others, creating a system of privilege and exploitation. In short, the only way for this vision of this kingdom to be a reality is if we keep it to ourselves.[18] The mall's liturgy fosters habits and practices that are unjust, so it does everything it can to prevent us from asking such questions. Don't ask; don't tell; just consume.

17. This is not unlike Orwell's account of coal mining as the repressed injustice of an industrial society: "In a way it is even humiliating to watch coal-miners working. It raises in you a momentary doubt about your own status as an 'intellectual' and a superior person generally. For it is brought home to you, at least while you are watching, that it is only because miners sweat their guts out that superior persons can remain superior. You and I and the editor of the *Times Literary Supp.*, and the Nancy poets and the Archbishop of Canterbury and Comrade X, author of *Marxism for Infants*—all of us *really* owe the comparative decency of our lives to poor drudges underground, blackened to the eyes, with their throats full of coal dust, driving their shovels forward with arms and belly muscles of steel" (George Orwell, *The Road to Wigan Pier*, [London: Penguin, 2001], 30–31). Another intense example of such invisibility can also be found in our relation to food and our happy ignorance about its means of production. For an insightful discussion, see Matthew C. Halteman, *Compassionate Eating as Care of Creation* (Washington, DC: Humane Society of the United States, 2008), esp. 23–36.

18. For further discussion of these points, see Iain Wallace, "Space, Place, and the Gospel: Theological Exploration in the Anthropocene Era," in *After Modernity? Secularity, Globalization, and the Re-enchantment of the World*, ed. James K. A. Smith (Waco: Baylor University Press, 2008), 123–41.

Marketing (as) Evangelism: Picturing the Liturgy of Consumerism in "The Persuaders"

This reading of marketing and the mall as liturgies of pseudo-transcendence is not just an alarmist Christian diagnosis. Indeed, perhaps the best glimpse of the religious nature of consumer capitalism comes from the decidedly non-Christian studios of PBS. The *Frontline* documentary "The Persuaders" provides a wide range of interviews with ad executives and analysts, along with a selection of advertising artifacts in order to document the goals and strategies of "the persuasion industry."[19] What emerges is nothing short of the *theology* of marketing. Naomi Klein (author of *No Logo*) points out the pseudo-spiritual aims of the persuasion industry. Superbrands like Nike and Starbucks aim to forge "spiritual bonds" with consumers by channeling a sense that their product is the answer to the most basic and primal human needs, linking the sexual and the spiritual in an erotic, product-centered mysticism.[20]

Ad executive Douglas Atkin notes that a transformation has taken place in what's expected of the typical ad executive at a major corporation: rather than being responsible for design, packaging, and promotion, the brand manager is now asked "to create and maintain a whole meaning-system for people through which they get identity and an understanding of the world." Advertising is asked to induce devotion by investing products with transcendence. So Atkin asked himself, What makes people exhibit cult-like devotion? He thus undertook a study of cults precisely in order to figure out how brands could induce "loyalty beyond reason." When he heard people rhapsodize about sneakers or paper plates in terms that he described as "evangelical," he realized that people join brands for the same reasons they join cults and religions: to belong and to make meaning. They ceased being merely customers and now identified themselves as disciples, as "members of the tribe," whether that tribe be Saturn or VW owners, Starbucks drinkers, or Mac users. The advertisements for these products do not convey information about them; rather, they tell stories—they picture worlds of meaning and invite us to see ourselves within them (VW ads, aimed at twentysomethings, are particularly good examples of this). The goal of such marketing, this (very secular) documentary concludes, is "to fill the empty places where non-commercial institutions like schools and churches might have once done the job." They amount to "an invitation to a longed-for lifestyle."

Consider a Saturn car commercial, voiced-over by a slightly twangy, down-home voice (like those Motel 6 commercials), inviting Saturn owners to the factory in Tennessee for a gathering akin to an old-time revival or "camp meeting." Why? What brings them together? Why would owning the same kind of car be a reason to gather with people I've never met before? I don't see Ford Escort drivers doing the same. The dif-

19. The entire documentary can be viewed for free online at http://www.pbs.org/wgbh/pages/frontline/shows/persuaders/.

20. Compare her discussion of the "Nike myth machine" and her analysis of the Nike Store as a "temple" in Naomi Klein, *No Logo: Taking Aim at the Brand Bullies* (New York: Picador, 2000), 54, 56.

ference is that Saturn has invested the product with a sense of transcendence: Saturns aren't just cars; they are also nostalgic connections to an older, communal way of life. The result? Forty-five thousand people attended the festival.

Or consider the simple example of an advertisement for paper plates: It features brief glimpses of bright, cheery hostesses and hosts, surrounded by family, friends, and lots of good food, holding up paper plates on which various words are elegantly written. Against a charming soundtrack, a voice asks (with just that tinge of accusation we've noted): "What are you saying with your paper plates?" Because our hosts have chosen strong, durable, Chinet paper plates, theirs boldly proclaim, "Friends," "Tradition," "Confidence," "You're Special." The paper plates are charged with values, suffused with meaning. So what does that mean you're saying with your cheap, flimsy Dixie plates? Who would have guessed that disposable cutlery and dishware could say so much?

While we might think this is a kind of consumer Cartesianism ("I buy, therefore I am"), it might actually be closer to a consumer Augustinianism ("I love, therefore I buy"; or "I am what I love, and I love what I buy"). In either case, "The Persuaders" is a powerful portrayal of the quite intentionally liturgical nature of marketing.

Unfortunately, the Christian response to the liturgies of consumerism is often woefully inadequate, even a sort of parody of the mall. Rather than properly countering the liturgy of consumption, the church ends up mimicking it, merely substituting Christian commodities—"Jesufied" versions of worldly products, which are acquired, accumulated, and disposed of to make room for the new and the novel. This happens, I think, mainly because we fail to see the practices of consumption as *liturgies*. Typical Christian analysis of the situation, including the critique of materialism (where that still happens), tends to focus on *what* is being purchased, rather than calling into question the *gospel* of consumption— the sense that acquisition brings happiness and fulfillment. So instead, the evangelical community simply replays the gospel of consumption but with "Jesus" stuff (a quick visit to any local Christian bookstore—more likely now described as a "gift shop"—will confirm this point). We even end up reconfiguring "church" by this strange "other" gospel where God can be reduced to a commodity. In chapter 5 I'll suggest that the wisdom of historical liturgy offers a very different sort of response.

Sacrificial Violence: The "Military-Entertainment Complex"

If the mall is a ubiquitous and powerful secular liturgy in Western (and increasingly global) culture, we might consider the rituals of nationalism as another influential pedagogy of desire, particularly in the United States.[21] By this I mean certain constellations of rituals, ceremonies, and spaces that—like the mall's liturgies—invest certain practices with a charged sense of transcendence that calls for our allegiance and loyalty in a way meant to trump other ultimate loyalties. These nationalistic and patriotic rituals are intended to make us into certain kinds of people—good, loyal, productive citizens who, when called upon, are willing to make "the ultimate sacrifice" for the good of the nation (under whatever its particular banner might be, whether freedom or the *Volk*). As I've been emphasizing, this formation happens liturgically, not didactically; that is, such rituals grab hold of our desire and our love through our bodies—through material, visceral rhythms, images, and experiences that subtly inscribe in us a desire for other king-doms. And this isn't just true of the "fabulous" civic theologies of Rome (as Augustine called them), nor is it restricted to the overt nationalistic rituals of National Socialism or the stark May Day parades of Soviet com-munism. In some contexts, such liturgies are not necessarily (or primarily) state sponsored; instead, an overarching commitment to the nation or the people so suffuses a national ethos that liturgies and rituals that infuse this are orchestrated by all sorts of nongovernmental institutions.

In the United States, some of the most powerful rituals and icons of nationalism are channeled through sports and entertainment. Thus we get what Michael Hanby has coyly described as the "military-entertainment complex"—a powerful cultural machine that generates stories, images, and paeans to bravery, sacrifice, and devotion to the national cause, cho-reographed with bodily movements in contexts that are deeply affective.[22] These material, tactile rituals are formative precisely because they are material—because they get hold of our passions through the body, seep-ing into our imaginary. Such formation is less the fruit of civics class and more the fruit of repeated rituals—daily (the Pledge of Allegiance in the classroom), weekly (the national anthem at the high school football game),

21. I don't think that this is true *only* of the United States, but anecdotal experience of living in other countries suggests that the American context is somewhat unique among Western industrialist countries. I focus on it here only because most readers will find themselves in this context; readers outside of an American context can extrapolate from the analyses here.

22. Michael Hanby ("Democracy and Its Demons," in *Augustine and Politics*, ed. John Doody, Kevin L. Hughes, and Kim Paffenroth [Lanham, MD: Lexington Books, 2005], 129) sees these as a contemporary analogue to what Augustine described as the "fabulous" civic theology of the Roman theater (see Augustine, *City of God* 6.8). Hanby draws on Robert Dodaro's observation that Augustine "realized that Roman society was founded upon an extreme patriotism, a love for the *patria* above all else, which was promoted by means of Roman education, folklore, literature, civil religion and theatre" (Dodaro, "Pirates or Superpowers: Reading Augustine in a Hall of Mirrors," *New Blackfriars* 72 (1991): 9–19, as cited by Hanby, "Democracy," 135n20).

annually (the neighborhood Fourth of July parade)—that present powerful, moving portrayals of an ideal that seeps into our bones.[23] In short, this does not happen in the abstract; rather, such formation takes place in what might seem to be "normal," nonreligious events—like an NFL football game, a NASCAR race, or an evening at the movies. I want to just briefly consider a few examples of liturgies related to the military-entertainment complex: professional sports, "opening exercises," and the films of Jerry Bruckheimer.

1. *Please stand for the national anthem.* Consider the rituals that constitute the opening of a professional sporting event such as an NFL football game or a NASCAR race, even if only viewed on television. In a massive space thronging with people, eager for the beginning of the event, a crowd of a hundred thousand people can be brought into remarkable placidity by the exhortation, "Please stand for the national anthem." Like parishioners who know all the motions of the Mass by heart, these fans instinctively and automatically rise together. They remove their caps, and many place a hand over their heart as an artist or group sings a rendition of one of the world's most affecting national anthems, laden with military themes such that those singing it are transposed into battle, the identity of the nation being wrapped up in its revolutionary beginnings and legacy of military power. Perhaps even more importantly, this rehearses and renews the myth of national identity forged by blood sacrifice.

The sounds of the anthem are usually accompanied by big, dramatic sights of the flag:[24] a star-spangled banner the size of a football field is

23. Not all of these are oft-repeated rituals. But even "one-off" choreographed events situate themselves in a cumulative effect of nationalist rituals. This lifetime string of immersion in such rituals gives context and significance to less frequent events, and thus these "one-off" events can sometimes make powerful contributions to the cumulative effect of more frequently repeated rituals. For instance, during the funeral for former president Gerald R. Ford, the USAF staged a flyover of F-15 jets above downtown Grand Rapids in a missing-man formation, where a lone jet shoots heavenward in an ear-bursting blast of sound and speed. The effect of this was palpable because of its visual nature and the very weight of the sound; one could *feel* the jets flying by. Even one who wanted to resist what was implicit in this display couldn't help being moved by the ritual. The effect was amplified in a widely circulated video that reproduced the images with "Taps" playing as a sound track and a superimposed image of a waving American flag in the background (see the video at http://www.youtube.com/watch?v=IzgrZjJT-iA). For a fascinating discussion of the affectivity of war movies, including the matter of sound tracks, see Lawrence Weschler, "Valkyries over Iraq: The Trouble with War Movies," *Harper's* 311 (November 2005): 65–77.

24. Hanby expounds the centrality the flag in American civil religion, drawing on Carolyn Marvin and David W. Ingle, *Blood Sacrifice and the Nation: Totem Rituals and the American Flag* (Cambridge: Cambridge University Press, 1999). In particular he notes how the flag (and hence the nation) is invested with transcendence: "It is the flag's function to bind the nation together through blood sacrifice. As an object, it is to be treated with the utmost reverence: 'it must not touch the ground, it must hang in proper alignment, it must

unfurled across the field by a small army of young people whose movements make it undulate as if blowing in the winds of battle, proudly defiant, but almost dripping with blood in those red lines across it. And almost always, the concluding crescendo of the anthem—announcing that this is the "land of the free" and the "home of the brave"—is accompanied by a flyover from military aircraft, whether the searing slice of F-15 fighter jets across the sky or the pulsating presence of Apache helicopters chugging across the air space of the stadium. The presence of the aircraft has a double effect: it concretizes the militarism of the anthem and the flag while also making the scene something that is *felt*, as the sounds of the jets or choppers is a kind of noise one picks up in the chest more than the ears. A crowd larger than many American cities then erupts in cheers and applause as this ritual of national unity has united even fans of opposing teams.

I'm suggesting that this constitutes a liturgy because it is a material ritual of ultimate concern: through a multisensory display, the ritual both powerfully and subtly moves us, and in so doing implants within us a certain reverence and awe, a learned deference to an ideal that might some day call for our "sacrifice." This is true not only of professional sports; the rituals of national identity—and national*ism*—have been almost indelibly inscribed into the rituals of athletics from Little League to high school football.[25] "As is well known," Stanley Hauerwas once quipped, "Friday night high school football is the most significant liturgical event in Texas."[26] The imagination couples these spectacular displays at professional sporting events with the simplicity of the anthem and color guard at a high school football game, and together they build up a story of national unity forged by battle and sacrifice. Over time, these rituals have a cumulative, albeit covert, effect on our imaginary. And together, I'm arguing, these constitute liturgies of ultimate concern: the ideal of national unity and commitment to its ideals is willing to make room for *additional* loyalties, but it is not

---

not be lower than other flags, it must appear in the place of honor on the right, it must not be used as a receptacle or a covering.' This is because of the 'sacramental' quality the nation invests in it. 'For having flown in a particular lived battle or touched the casket of the remembered deceased,' a specific flag becomes a holy relic, communicating the 'real-presence' of those united in it" (Hanby, "Democracy," 130).

25. It might be interesting to consider how "extreme" sports are an exception to this rule. (Do they play the national anthem at the X Games? It would be tricky to have "Anarchy" scribbled all over your skateboard and then pause for the national anthem.) However, it seems to me that there is an individualism characteristic of extreme sports that is problematic in a different way.

26. Stanley Hauerwas, "The Liturgical Shape of the Christian Life: Teaching Christian Ethics as Worship," in *In Good Company: The Church as Polis* (Notre Dame, IN: University of Notre Dame Press, 1995), 153. I recall being particularly puzzled that the opening of a new stadium at a local Christian high school included a Marine color guard and the singing of the national anthem.

willing to entertain *trumping* loyalties. (Just try to remain seated at the next playing of the national anthem.) The fact that there seems to be little tension between Christianity and American nationalism is not a function of the generosity (let alone "Christianness") of the American ideal but rather a sign of a Christianity that has accommodated itself to these American ideals of battle, military sacrifice (which is very different from the Christian ideal of martyrdom),[27] individual (negative) freedom, and prosperity through property.

Implicit in the liturgies of American nationalism is a particular vision of human flourishing as material prosperity and ownership, as well as a particular take on intersubjectivity, beginning from a negative notion of liberty and thus fostering a generally libertarian view of human relationships that stresses noninterference. Related to this is a sense that competition and even violence is basically inscribed into the nature of the world, which thus valorizes competition and even violence, seeing war as the most intense opportunity to demonstrate these ideals. The vision of a kingdom implicit in this liturgy is antithetical to the vision of the kingdom implicit in Christian worship (which we'll explore in chapter 5). I think the liturgical take on American nationalism can help us to see why so few Christians experience a tension here; it can also help to diagnose the cause of the church's complacency and complicity: many Christians experience no tension between the gospel according to America and the gospel of Jesus Christ because, subtly and unwittingly, the liturgies of American nationalism have so significantly shaped our imagination that they have, in many ways, *trumped* other liturgies. Thus we now see and hear and read the gospel through the liturgical lenses of the "American gospel."[28]

2. *Opening exercises.* Not all national liturgies have the dazzle and power of the Super Bowl's opening spectacle. Most are much more mundane; but their repeated character perhaps lends them even more power. Consider the simple phenomenon of opening exercises in elementary school. Millions of young students begin each day with a ritual: the Pledge of Allegiance or the national anthem or perhaps both. Standing, in unison, as when a

---

27. See Craig Hovey, *To Share in the Body: A Theology of Martyrdom for Today's Church* (Grand Rapids: Brazos, 2008). Without romanticizing martyrdom, Hovey nonetheless suggests that the absence of martyrdom is not necessarily a sign of generous regimes but of a church not worthy of martyrdom because it poses no threat.

28. Compare Jon Meacham, *American Gospel: God, the Founding Fathers, and the Making of a Nation* (New York: Random House, 2006); and David Gelernter, *Americanism: The Fourth Great Western Religion* (New York: Doubleday, 2007). I have discussed "Americanism" further in James K. A. Smith, "The God of Americanism," in *The Devil Reads Derrida: And Other Essays on the University, the Church, Politics, and the Arts* (Grand Rapids: Eerdmans, 2009). Richard Gamble, in a review of Gelernter, rightly criticizes what he calls "demonic patriotism"; see Gamble, "The Allure of 'Demonic Patriotism,'" *Modern Age* 50 (2008): 80–83.

To Think About: Competing Allegiances

My friend Brent Laytham, who teaches at a Christian college in Chicago, recounts an interesting experience that highlighted some of the tensions I'm suggesting between the Pledge and the Creed. One day he was called to the college president's office to meet with an officer of the Department of Defense. One of his former students, Aaron, was becoming an Air Force pilot, and the DOD was conducting interviews to confirm his character. The officer's questions were a bit of a challenge for a Christian who has a sense of the transnational character of the church. "Did Aaron belong to any organization that puts him in contact with foreign nationals?" the officer asked. "Yes," Brent replied; "he's a member of the church." "I wasn't trying to be coy," Brent recounts. "In Christ we find ourselves placed in a body politic without territorial borders—the holy catholic church. . . . We have no foreign nationals in the church, or we are all foreigners; either way, we cannot imagine that some of us are 'us,' while others are 'them.' At least we shouldn't be able to imagine this."

The officer began to press him: "But did he associate with foreigners? How closely did he associate with them? Was it more than a normal amount?" Brent was perplexed at this line of questioning: "How could I answer such a question, given the church's calling to show the world that its version of 'normal' simply isn't? . . . I should have added, 'The church is a "sign, herald, and foretaste" of the coming kingdom; we refuse to allow national borders to be mapped onto the body of Christ.'" Finally the officer articulated a linchpin question: "Is he a loyal American?" While the answer in Aaron's case was undoubtedly yes, Brent heard echoes of Dorothy Day in his head:

> In the U.S. there is assumed to be a smooth fit between discipleship and killing. That assumption, held so easily and unreflectively, trespasses against our obedience to God alone. I wonder whether my questioner understands that for descendants of Jeremiah and followers of Jesus, obedience to God may require us to refuse the state's claim to our loyalty. Does the Department of Defense grant that my fundamental obligation is not loyalty to country but obedience to God? I doubt it. In such circumstances, where Caesar cannot distinguish between our proper subjection and our ultimate allegiance, it may be best to say bluntly, "A loyal American? Of course not. I'm a Christian!" (D. Brent Laytham, "Loyalty Oath: A Matter of Ultimate Allegiance," *Christian Century*, July 12, 2005)

---

congregation together confesses the Apostles' Creed, these students are united in a pledge of *allegiance*. For those familiar with the Creed, there is lilt and rhythm to the Pledge of Allegiance that has an analogous sacred feel about it:

> I pledge allegiance to the Flag of the United States of America,
> and to the Republic for which it stands:
> one Nation under God, indivisible,
> With Liberty and Justice for all.

While God is invoked, it is actually the flag and the republic to which one is pledging allegiance (that is, pledging devotion and loyalty). The republic claims to have an identity and unity about it, and even claims to have achieved the goal of *shalom*—to already be a nation "with" liberty and justice for all. (That last clause must have stuck in the throat of young black Americans in the Jim Crow South and, indeed, must still.) No hint of eschatological deferral; no sense of a "not yet" failure to measure up; but a confident claim of justice here and now, secured by the republic.

What are students doing when they recite this each day? Many will just be "going through the motions." However, given that we are liturgical animals who are deeply shaped by practices, I'm suggesting that a lot can happen when one just goes through the motions. The routine begins to inscribe habits of the imagination within us; the repeated saying of allegiance works itself into an *orienting* allegiance. What begins as a merely stated commitment begins to work itself into a functional commitment. Through the repeated ritual, a daily microliturgy, our very loyalties are aimed and shaped. And as I've tried to sketch above, I think there are good reasons to worry that the ideals of the republic are antithetical to some of the defining ideals of the people of God, called to imitate a suffering Savior, who was executed at the hands of military power. What's implicit in the Creed, if we tease it out, is in significant tension with what's implicit in the Pledge. And yet, it's tough for the weekly recital of the Creed to compete with daily utterance of the Pledge.[29]

3. *The gospel according to Jerry Bruckheimer.* One of the things that liturgies do is to visibly narrate a story about what really matters. In this respect, the story and ideals narrated and visualized in the star-spangled spectacles of nationalist liturgies are complemented and reinforced by those embedded in the entertainment industry—thus Hanby spoke of the "military-entertainment complex." Whether it's the compelling television of *24* or the masterful cinema of Steven Spielberg's *Saving Private Ryan*, the edgy drama of *Rescue Me* or predictable drama of *The Patriot*, the entertainment industry churns out remarkable amounts of material that solidify the myths of the national ideal, and they do so in a way that captures our imagination. Such media productions technically escape the charge of "propaganda" because they are not sponsored or directed by the state; indeed, what is intriguing is the

29. We might think more creatively about Christian day school education in this context vis-à-vis formation of allegiances. Unfortunately, though my children attend Christian schools, to my astonishment they have had teachers who also began the day with the Pledge of Allegiance. We'll think further about the shape of liturgies for Christian learning in chapter 6.

extent to which such nationalist productions bubble up from an *ethos* rather than government directions. Producers and directors willingly and eagerly engage in projects that tap into the nationalist ideal, finding a willing (and paying) audience for such ventures, which in turn further inscribes the ideals into the populace.

Perhaps one of the more prolific examples of this genre is found in the work of Jerry Bruckheimer, the producer of a wide range of films (and more recently television dramas) that draw upon and present the ideals of Americanism, in the obvious genre of war movies such as *Pearl Harbor* and *Black Hawk Down*, but also in near-related sports mythologies like *Remember the Titans* and *Glory Road*, or the new *National Treasure* franchise (which plays on the sacralization of American founding documents). In so much of his work, Bruckheimer (subtly or not so subtly) conveys the American ideals of individual freedom,[30] American power, and the valor of war. Though I can't offer a complete analysis here, I raise the case of Bruckheimer in order to suggest that, once again, a space (namely, the cinema) that we might have considered neutral or indifferent (or perhaps eagerly affirmed as "good" and "creational") is formative in a liturgical sense: here we have moving icons dancing across the screen, bathed in the affect of a calculated sound track, staging a story with implicit visions of the good life that, over time and because of their covert nature, seep into our imagination and shape not only how we see the world but also how we relate to it, how we orient ourselves within it, and what we ultimately are working toward.

Over time, the theater is a kind of classroom; it constitutes a pedagogy of desire. Insofar as the implicit mythologies and visions are antithetical to the visions of the gospel, we can find ourselves unwittingly becoming disciples of Americanism. This is not to say that we should avoid the cinema (though that might not always be a bad idea); rather, I think it is important to see that movies don't just "have" worldviews; rather, film is more like a liturgy. So it's not just a matter of being critical viewers who are looking for the message in the film; it's a matter of being awakened to their liturgical, formative nature. And in the case of nationalist entertainments, it requires further considering how the *telos* implicit in such media is antithetical to the shape of the hoped-for kingdom of God.

---

30. This becomes particularly ridiculous in Bruckheimer's rendition of the Arthurian legend (in *King Arthur*), in which he makes Arthur a zealous devotee of the heretic Pelagius (bit of a timing problem there), because both are so passionately committed to "freedom" (though "freedom" is here clearly understood in a post-Enlightenment fashion that would have been unfathomable not only to Arthur but probably even to Pelagius). Arthur's chivalry is much more in the orbit of Augustinian notions of "ordered" freedom than the proto-libertarianism of Pelagius.

Excursus: On Patriotism

Let me briefly anticipate a response to the analysis in this section. Some will be inclined to be dismissive, suggesting that the account is alarmist. Or, at the very least, they will assert that being "patriotic" is not a problem; it is something more like patrio*tism* that borders on idolatry. Consider, for instance, Richard Mouw's wise words about worship and nationalism. Recognizing that we de facto inhabit national and cultural contexts, he warns of "the constant danger of nationalistic pride": "When we come together for Christian worship, we are acknowledging our identity as members of 'a chosen race, a royal priesthood, a holy nation' (1 Peter 2:9). And we need to be reminded that other racial and priestly and national loyalties are constantly competing for our allegiance."[31] Thus he recognizes the limits of Christian enthusiasm for nationalist idolatry, including the habit of referring to soldiers' deaths as "the ultimate sacrifice." And he notes that "when nations and governments have exceeded their God-ordained boundaries by asking citizens for their ultimate loyalties, they have often borrowed religious language."[32] But Mouw is not ready to dismiss patriotism as such—only its distortions and excesses. He claims that there is "a legitimate place for patriotic sentiments in the Christian life" because to be a patriot is simply to "have affection for the 'fatherland.'"[33] His ensuing analogy with a child's love for her parents suggests that such patriotic affection is "natural."

But can there be a "natural" affection for an artificial reality? If there ever was something like a "natural" fatherland (I'm not convinced there was), the modern nation-state is a long way from such a reality. The makeup of most countries is variegated, often with rather artificial boundaries, and in any case they bring together citizens from around the globe who do not have any natural ties to "blood and soil." So in addition to being worried about the effects of patriotism as a de facto idolatry, I'm also skeptical about rationales that tried to make such nationalist affection "natural." Are those who lack such affections somehow unnatural? Moreover, there is a long legacy of Christians not identifying with any fatherland other than Christ. Thus Augustine emphasized that Christ is the true *patria* (*Con-*

31. Richard J. Mouw, "The Danger of Alien Loyalties," *Reformed Worship* 80 (2006): 20–22, at 21.

32. Ibid., 21. It seems to me this has intensified since 9/11 and the ensuing War on Terror. For instance, I recently witnessed a poster that included a translation of Psalm 20:7: "Some trust in chariots, and some in horses; but we will remember the name of the Lord our God" (KJV). Beside the verse was a painting of a shepherd Jesus, with a staff and cloth draped over his head and shoulders. But his headdress was the American flag! Or consider the "Support Our Troops" magnets emblazoned on cars across the country that include both the flag and the cross.

33. Ibid., 22.

fessions 7.21.27), and the early *Epistle to Diognetus* describes Christians as pilgrims and foreigners: "They live in their own countries, but only as nonresidents; they participate in everything as citizens, and endure everything as foreigners. Every foreign country is their fatherland, and every fatherland is foreign."[34]

So better than this notion of a sort of "natural" patriotism, I think, is Mouw's earlier, more persistently suspicious account of nationalism in *Political Evangelism*. There Mouw admonished Christians to look at the example of the Navajo nation: "The sense of tentativeness in the Navajo's commitment to the American nation, coupled with his genuine desire to participate in that nation, is instructive for the church."[35] When we see nationalist rituals as formative liturgies, such tentativeness should only be amplified.

Cathedrals of Learning: Liturgies of the University

Our public and private universities all generally pride themselves on being secular: spaces for the enlightened, dispassionate, objective pursuit of truth, unencumbered by the weight of tradition, especially religious tradition. The chief virtue of the university, on this telling, is that it is rational, not faithful. This story has rightly been called into question, focusing on the conditions of knowledge: everyone, it's pointed out, starts from some ultimate commitments that shape what they consider to be "rational." So in this sense, the scholar and the university can't help but be religious; or, in other words, there is no such thing as the secular.[36] However, here I want to make this point somewhat differently: the university remains a charged religious institution not (only) because of the epistemic conditions that undergird knowledge and research, but (also) because the university is a formative, liturgical institution, animated by rituals and liturgies that constitute a pedagogy of desire. The university is not just out to deposit information in our heads with a view to professional success (even if the university increasingly thinks of itself that way); rather, the university can't help but be a formative institution because of powerful (though

34. *Epistle to Diognetus* 6.5 in *The Apostolic Fathers: Greek Texts and English Translations*, ed. and trans. Michael W. Holmes, 3rd ed. (Grand Rapids: Baker Academic, 2007), 703.

35. Richard J. Mouw, *Political Evangelism* (Grand Rapids: Eerdmans, 1973), 48–49. Mouw continues: "The recognition of a distinct 'national identity' among members of the Body of Christ can keep before us our ties with Christians who live under different secular governments, with whom we have bonds that transcend and override our commitments to governments and groups outside the church" (49).

36. For further discussion, see James K. A. Smith, *Introducing Radical Orthodoxy: Mapping a Post-secular Theology* (Grand Rapids: Baker Academic, 2004), 143–83.

often unofficial) liturgies that shape our identity and self-understanding.[37] In short, the university is not only, and maybe not even primarily, about knowledge. It is, I suggest, after our imagination, our heart, our desire. It wants to make us into certain kinds of people who desire a certain *telos*, who are primed to pursue a particular vision of the good life.

This is why I've always thought it fitting that a deeply secular university like the University of Pittsburgh, which has no religious past, features one of the more stunning pieces of academic architecture in the United States: the Cathedral of Learning. Towering over the campus (and the city), the building is intentionally Gothic, invoking the architectural grammar of medieval churches and cathedrals. But here the aspiring, pointed architecture is no longer striving to point to the Creator, but rather seeks to serve a different, more immanent ideal: the truth of enlightened human reason, marshaled for the progress of the race. Thus the Cathedral of Learning represents the nature and limits of secularization at the university: while on the one hand it seeks to shut out reference to the divine, it nonetheless lives off the borrowed capital of religious aspiration. For instance, a copper plate engraved with these words was attached to the cornerstone of the Cathedral:

> Faith and peace are in their hearts. Good will has brought them together. Like the Magi of ancestral traditions and the shepherds of candid simplicity, they offer their gifts of what is precious, genuine and their own, to truth that shines forever and enlightens all people.

The Cathedral's inhabitants will be seekers, but unlike the magi who came seeking a king, these seekers are after the truth of immanence, a "human" reason. And what we get is not a creed, but a cathedral. This is an illustration of the claim I'm making here: what makes the university inherently religious is not just its teaching, and not even just its perspectives, but its practices. The Cathedral's architectural space is not just a concrete language with a message; it also invokes the materiality of religion, the spaces of worship. The Cathedral testifies to the material conditions for formation, for the pursuit of the university's *telos*, and is the incubator for the practices that will shape students into a certain kind of people.

---

37. Hauerwas echoes the same point, using the terms *education* and *moral formation* interchangeably: "A focus on the virtues means you cannot easily separate what you come to know from how you come to know. Any knowledge worth having cannot help but shape who we are and accordingly our understanding of the world. Thus I use the description, 'moral formation,' rather than education, because I think all education, whether acknowledged or not, is moral formation" (Stanley Hauerwas, "How Risky Is *The Risk of Education?*" in *The State of the University: Academic Knowledges and the Knowledge of God* [Oxford: Blackwell, 2007], 46).

114

Our cultural exegesis of the university will briefly consider it, not through the worldview-focus on perspectives, but through a liturgical focus on practices. With this focus, there are two sets of questions that we can bring to the university: (1) What *telos* does it "glorify"? What way of life or vision of the good life does it foster? What does the university want us to love? (2) What are the rituals and practices that constitute the secular liturgy of the university? The first set of questions concerns just what it is that the university loves; the second set concerns just how the university tries to make us the kind of people who love the same thing. The way to the first question is through the second: by reading the ritual practices that animate the university, we'll begin to discern what it is that the university worships, to what it ascribes worth.

To do this, we need once again to try to make the familiar strange. In other words, we need to try to find a way to shift gears, change our attitude, and step back from our familiar immersion in the rhythms and rituals of the university in order to see it as liturgical. So let's wriggle our imaginations into our Martian anthropologist suits once again and imaginatively set out on an expedition to the exotic locales of planet Earth, and the region of North America in particular. Our team of Martian researchers has been ably equipped with in-depth training in cultural anthropology and sociology, and in particular, a subdiscipline of both called "ritual studies." We've landed in North America with the goal of discerning the desires that animate the North American people by considering their ritual habits in various institutions. This time around, we'll descend upon a local university. So try to imagine, for a few moments, that you are part of this Martian anthropological team. You have embedded yourself in the university as a participant observer, but at the same time, the rhythms and rituals of this institution resemble nothing in your previous experience. What will you be struck by? Over time, what will you discern as the core practices that are most influential in forming the inhabitants of this place and the participants in these rituals? To an outside (Martian) observer, what aspects of our familiar experiences in the university would look liturgical?

Those who have inhabited universities know that the university has worlds within worlds. The university as inhabited by an undergraduate student is very different from the university as inhabited by the professor. What happens in the dorms looks little like what happens in the faculty lounge (one hopes!). Students are part of the university, whereas scholars are part of "the academy." Nevertheless, for both constituencies, the university is an identity-forming institution. Scholars who think about the university tend to identify its nerve center as the sites of teaching and research: the classrooms and lecture halls where knowledge is dispensed; the labs and libraries where knowledge is pursued. But for students, the university is much bigger than this: it is also the site of dorm rooms and dining halls, frat houses and football stadiums. In some ways, the classroom, lab, and library are only a slice of the student's experience of the university. And because scholars tend to focus on the "academic" spaces of the university, any discussion of the university as a place of liturgical formation will also tend to focus on those academic sites. But the university's formative, liturgical power extends well beyond the classroom and the lecture hall; indeed, it might be that the dorms, stadium, and frat houses are even more powerful liturgical sites within the university—shaping students into certain kinds of people, who develop certain loves, bent on certain ends. Thus in our analysis of the university's liturgies, it will be important to keep looking at it through a wide-angle lens. While these overlap and intertwine, in this context I will focus on the university as experienced by the student in its full array of practices: initiation, formation, commissioning.[38]

While university brochures and hopeful (perhaps naive) parents might still think about the university as a place of "higher *learning*" in which big ideas and marketable skills are implanted in eager receptacle-minds, students and those who otherwise "sell" the university know that the university is much more (and sometimes less) than that. The university is an experience, a rite of passage, a glandular adventure, both a postponement of and a rehearsal for the proverbial real world. A ritual analysis of the university might be inclined to consider the official rites of the learning community: the robed, ceremonial events of convocation and commencement or the more mundane routines of attending lectures, writing papers, and taking exams. While these are certainly important and remain central, my sense is that it is the unofficial liturgies of the university that might be more formative.

Consider, for instance, the consummate ritual of initiation: Freshers' Week (or "Frosh" Week, as it's known in Canada). This is an intensive experience of initial formation that functions as a veritable boot camp—a week of immersion in the life of the university that often has quite little to do with the task of learning or research. It is intensely communal and intergenerational, where older students initiate new students into the nooks and crannies of the university's life and not so subtly communicate what is valued, which often amounts to carefree social interaction lubricated

---

38. One could easily generate a similar analysis of the university's liturgies that form scholars. This would include a similar focus on the "novitiate" of graduate training as a quasi-monastic process of initiation, formation, and commissioning—all of which inculcate certain values and an "automated" commitment to certain *teloi*. Interestingly, Thomas Kuhn hints at just such an analysis when he describes graduate education as initiation into the paradigms of "normal science" in a given field through the inculcation of a scientific "tradition," which amounts to an absorption of academic orthodoxy by novices. See Thomas S. Kuhn, *The Structure of Scientific Revolutions*, 2nd ed. (Chicago: University of Chicago Press, 1970), esp. 23–51.

by alcohol, cult-like devotion to the football team, and the solidification of social networks that will be instrumental and instrumentalized for the sake of personal benefit and gain.[39] The Fresher Week novitiate is a retreat of sorts, an escape from the workaday world of the summer job as well as the anticipated drudgery of learning.[40] Indeed, this micro-novitiate sets up a construal of the university that tends to marginalize, or at least minimize and relativize, the task of learning. One of the gifts that seniors will give to the novices are tips and tricks for being able to maintain the lifestyle of Freshers' Week without letting the work of education ruin the party. This first week is multisensory, sometimes tingling senses the student didn't even know she had before. Some first-years arrive eager to dive into this way of life, having heard rumors of it from afar, from older siblings or Will Ferrell movies. Adopting this way of life will sometimes require a sort of conversion from the way of life they've pursued at home. Other wide-eyed freshmen will find themselves surprised by these rites of initiation. And though they might mount resistance, the liturgical force of these rituals, coupled with the social forces of stigmatization, will often make resistance futile.

Freshers' Week, we might say, amounts to a baptism by fire—an intensive immersion into the implicit and functional ideals of the university as construed by fellow students, though the university itself is also entirely complicit in this. Implicit in the practices of Freshers' Week is a vision of the good life that valorizes egoistic pursuit of personal pleasure, a passionate commitment to the tribe (expressed in "team spirit" at the football stadium or intensified in the "brotherhood" of fraternities), and an instrumental relation to learning that values it only insofar as it makes it possible to achieve the goods of prosperity, accumulation, status, and power. So despite widespread cynicism about the antics of Freshers' Week, its rituals turn out to be good preparation for the kind of people that the university ultimately wants to produce: productive, successful consumers who will be leaders in society. As such, the university is simply an outpost of the earthly city, an extension and training ground for the arenas of the market and the state we've considered above.[41]

39. That is, I'm not quite convinced that many of these social interactions would actually count as friendships.

40. It is perhaps clear that the university I have in mind is something like the state university, not necessarily a Christian college. However, that doesn't mean that the "Orientation Week" experience might not have similar problems even in the context of Christian higher education. Those orientations that function as mere extensions of summer camp sometimes subtly communicate a disjunction between "having fun at college" and pursuing the hard work of education.

41. This is particularly true as the university is increasingly co-opted by industry and government, serving sectors such as the defense industry or pharmaceutical companies—despite the stories that universities and academics tell themselves. For analysis, see Derek Bok, *Uni-*

After this intensive initiation that, through a full-bodied (!) experience, has primed students to inhabit the university in a certain way, the work of formation continues through other practices. Rush Week will be another intensification of Freshers' Week, but with an added layer of training for social networking. Implicit in the fraternity/sorority ideal is a particular take on intersubjectivity that tends to instrumentalize relationships as means to one's own (later) ends while at the same time providing an incubator for absorbing class distinctions and class sensibilities, which become their own hermeneutic framework for interpreting the world (recall Orwell's analysis of his haughty "public school" education in England, which amounted to learning that the working classes smell). Such instrumentalization of relationships will only be intensified in cross-gender practices of "hooking up."[42] The rhythms of football season and basketball season provide year-long opportunities to reinforce a tribal, competitive instinct, as well as a rhythm that makes education something one "fits in" to what otherwise *really* matters at college. Dorm life will be yet another incubator of habits and practices, providing opportunities to learn nocturnal habits of cliquishness, or other habits of avoidance and isolation.

Taken together, all of these facets of the university build up a generally frenetic and frantic pace, rhythms of expenditure and exhaustion, with little room for sabbath. This, too, turns out to be excellent formative preparation for the "real world" of corporate ladder climbing and white-collar overtime needed in order to secure the cottage, the boat, and the private education for the kids. In short, while the official story tells us that it's what we're learning in the classroom that will prepare us to be productive members of society, it is actually the rituals of the university outside the classroom that might constitute the most formative aspect of our education. Over time, these rituals—these veritable liturgies—mold, shape, and form us into certain kinds of people. And so the university experience ends with a commissioning; not quite a "Great" Commission, but something close. We are launched into career (and careerism) by the holistic formation we've received at college. The classroom and laboratory, lecture hall and library have played some role in this. But the *in*formation provided there has not been nearly as potent as the *form*ation we've received in the dorm and frat house, or the stadium and the dance club. We will look back on

---

versities in the Marketplace: The Commercialization of Higher Education (Princeton, NJ: Princeton University Press, 2004); and Jennifer Washburn, *University, Inc.: The Corporate Corruption of American Higher Education* (New York: Basic Books, 2005). My thanks to Peter Schuurman for pointing me to this literature.

42. See Tom Wolfe, "Hooking Up," in *Hooking Up* (New York: Picador, 2000), 3–15; and Kathleen Bogle, *Hooking Up: Sex, Dating and Relationships on Campus* (New York: New York University Press, 2008).

these years as "the best years of our lives"—a last hurrah for adolescence and a stern preparation for the rigors of "success."[43]

Picturing the University's Liturgies in Wolfe's *I Am Charlotte Simmons*

Tom Wolfe has long distinguished himself as a kind of Martian anthropologist keenly attentive to slices of contemporary American life. His novels, like *Bonfire of the Vanities* and *A Man in Full*, cloak keen sociological observation and description in stories that make us both wince and laugh. So what better ally could we have for our own anthropological exploration of the contemporary university in which we're trying to see it again for the first time? Wolfe's *I Am Charlotte Simmons* is a relentless description of life at "Dupont University," a Duke-like elite university, training ground for emerging aristocrats and the heirs of the nouveau riche at the turn of the twenty-first century. In particular, the novel tracks the first year of young Charlotte Simmons, valedictorian from tiny Sparta High School in the Blue Ridge Mountains, for whom Dupont represented Valhalla and Athens rolled into one. Spurred on by Momma and Miss Pennington, Charlotte had, in a rather un-Sparta-like way, actually aspired to leave home and reach for this pinnacle of higher education, which represented an enchanted oasis for nourishing the life of the mind.

What Charlotte didn't anticipate was the importance of the *body*. For the difference between the Dupont of her dreams and the Dupont of her experience was the difference between an ethereal space for minds and the gritty corridors occupied by bodies. While she came hoping for and expecting a life of the mind, what she encountered were bodies—bodies everywhere: massive, glistening bodies of athletes, who swaggered around campus like local deities; bodies grinding and writhing in the frat house and on the dance floor; bodies entwined and "rutting" on the floor of her dorm room; bodies with all their odors and excrement, smells and fluids:

> She felt a tug on her arm. It was Bettina, who had a bottle of beer in her hand. She motioned toward Mimi, who had a big glass of something. They headed toward the band, in the back. Charlotte followed as they made their way through a bewilderingly excited crowd. The odors—rotting malt, vomitus, cigarette smoke, bodies—became worse and worse. The sheer mass of bodies—it was so hot in here! Reminded her of the Saint Ray [frat] house that night . . . the heat, the smoky nocturnal gloom, the yowling drunks, the music that never stopped, the putrid air, the drunken cries of the male animal on all sides.[44]

43. In chapter 5, we'll return to ask whether "Christian education" really offers an alternative to the university's liturgies for "success" or whether it just offers the same *plus Jesus*. Just as the church can mistakenly remake itself as a "Jesufied" version of the mall, so too the Christian university often fashions itself as a "Jesufied" version of the university.

44. Tom Wolfe, *I Am Charlotte Simmons* (Toronto: HarperPerennial, 2004), 382. Subsequent references are in parentheses in the text.

One might say that Charlotte Simmons, who aspired to a life of the mind and dreamed of Dupont as the place to cultivate it, came to the university with a stunted philosophical anthropology: overestimating the power of the mind, she underestimated the influence of the body. And being unprepared in this regard, she was vulnerable to the material, bodily formations of the university's liturgies we've noted above.

Indeed, this is just what Wolfe narrates: the story of Charlotte's precipitous—albeit unintentional and even unwitting—fall from mind-cultivation to body-saturation. The novel is nothing less than a harrowing anthropological description of the micropractices that change how Charlotte imagines herself. This is why her name—and the title—are so central: "I am Charlotte Simmons" is a mantra, a refrain of *identity*, of knowing who she is and what she's about. She invokes her own name as a talisman, or even as an exorcist might invoke the name of Jesus: "This can't happen," she says to herself, "because *I* am Charlotte Simmons." But these self-reliant aspirations of the will are insufficient weapons against the formative practices of the university, its liturgies, its pedagogies of desire. She loses the ability to invoke her name as she loses herself in foreign practices. But what is disturbing is how quickly these foreign and strange practices become her own. By just the end of her first weekend at Dupont, having encountered the "pornography" of *Cosmopolitan* magazine while being "sexiled" from her dorm room, she already feels herself slipping away:

> If only she could call Miss Pennington . . . or Momma . . . Hello, Miss Pennington? Momma? You know Dupont, on the other side of the mountains? The Garden of Athena, Goddess of Wisdom, where great things are to be done? Well, Miss Pennington, Momma, I plumb forgot to ask: did anybody ever tell you about being sexiled? About being marooned in a public lounge in the middle of the night so that your roommate, so-called, can rut like a pig with some guy she just picked up? (157)

But she can say none of this. "So gutted, disemboweled, scoured out had she been, by loneliness, she had all but forgotten the Force: *I am Charlotte Simmons*" (157). This after just three days at the university.

While Charlotte underestimates the role of the body—and the covert machinations of bodily formation—Wolfe does not. If anything, he perhaps overestimates it by peppering the novel with references to evolutionary biology, which reduces these human students to animals, who "go on living from impulse to impulse" (140). These reductionistic, evolutionary musings are put into the mouth of Professor Starling, Dupont's resident neuroscientific guru. Starling's neuroscience course spends time on Darwin, not because he was a brain scientist, but because "Darwin did something more fundamental. He obliterated the distinction between man and the beasts of the field and the wilds. It has always been a truism that man is a rational being and animals live by 'instinct.' But what is instinct? It's what we know to be the genetic code an animal is born with" (306). Starling goes on to unpack humanity's animal, instinctual nature, moving "from impulse to impulse"—and Wolfe's (and Charlotte's) observations of the university student "in his natural habitat," so to speak, seem to confirm this animality. Later, recounting brain experiments in which a bull's behavior was altered by stimulating different sections of the brain tissue, Starling announces: "The more profound lesson was that not only emotions but also *purpose* and *intentions* are *physical* matters. They can be turned on and off physically" (425). Listening to Starling rhapsodize as only a neuroscientific guru can, "Charlotte was transported." In that moment, "Charlotte experienced a *kairos*, an ecstatic revelation of something too vast, too all-enveloping, too profound to be contained by mere words, and the rest of the world, a sordid world of flesh and animals grunting for the flesh, fell away" (427).[45]

One needn't embrace Wolfe's implicit reductionism to appreciate his insight into the role that material practices play in formation. Indeed, the novel well captures what we've been suggesting: that there are ways of construing the world and oneself, at the level of "the imaginary," that are not so much learned as absorbed. For instance, later in the story Wolfe notes that the evaluative word "skanky" had "slipped into Charlotte's vocabulary by social osmosis." Saint Ray's frat house amounts to a material training center, a pseudo-monastery for the priesthood of self-indulgence. Athletics on campus encouraged both tribalism and hedonism. "Tailgates were idiotic Saturday afternoon blackout parties for cretins whose idea of a fulfilling weekend was to drink until they passed out Saturday night and then tell war stories about it on Sunday and Monday" (356). And yet, this is just what you *do*; this is *what is done* at university. It's a question not so much of what you think but of what is done. All of Charlotte's preparation of the mind did nothing to prepare her for the embodied formation of her character, the meaty practices that would impose themselves on her identity through her body. And so she finds herself in the bar, once again immersed in all those bodies:

> As soon as they sat down, Mimi lit up a cigarette to show that . . . *she belonged*! Bettina began moving her torso languidly to the reggae beat to show that . . . *she belonged*! Cigarette in one hand, Mimi brought her bottle of beer near her lips, looked at Charlotte, and arched her eyebrows, pantomiming, "Don't you want something to drink?" which really meant, "Don't you want to *belong*?" Charlotte shook her head no, and leaned forward with her forearms braced on the edge of the table, and looked right past Mimi at all the young bodies clumped together. Why? Belong to—what? What was the point of this clump of humanity eagerly pressed against one another in a beaten-up place like the I.M. on a Friday night? She immediately answered her own question with another. What if I were in my room alone right now? She could *feel* it . . . sitting at her desk, staring out the window at the unlit library tower while loneliness *scoured* out all semblance of hope, ambition, or simple planning. Charlotte Simmons!— removed from all family, all friends, every family terrain, every worn and homely object. (383–84)

45. Wolfe is toying with us here: Charlotte's epiphany, which transports her beyond flesh and bodies, is occasioned by the revelations of neuroscience, which would reduce us to nothing *but* our bodies, tissues, and instincts.

Her resistance doesn't last for long. Without counter-measures—without the formative resources of a liturgy to counter the force of the university's liturgies[46]—Charlotte Simmons becomes just the sort of girl the university wants. A different "Charlotte Simmons" is reduced to a ghost—which also means that perhaps reductionism doesn't win out after all.

> She was Charlotte Simmons. Could she ever have that conversation with herself, the way Momma told her to? Mr. Starling put "soul" in quotes, which as much as said it was only a superstitious belief in the first place, an earlier, yet more primitive name for the ghost in the machine.
>
> So why do you keep waiting deep in the back of my head, Momma, during every conscious moment—waiting for me to have that conversation? Even if I were to pretend it were real, my "soul," the way you think it is, what could I possibly say? All right, I'll say, "I am Charlotte Simmons." That should satisfy the "soul," since it's not there in the first place. So why do I keep hearing the ghost asking the same tired questions over and over, "Yes, but what does that mean? Who *is* she?" You can't *define* a person who is unique, said Charlotte Simmons. It, the little ghost who wasn't there, said, "Well, then, why don't you mention some of the attributes that set her apart from every other girl at Dupont, some of the dreams, the ambitions? Wasn't it Charlotte Simmons who wanted a life of the mind? Or was what she wanted all along was to be considered special and to be admired for that in itself, no matter how she achieved it?" (737)

Charlotte came to the university focused on excelling at the "three R's," so to speak. Wolfe's keen, iconoclastic assessment of the university unwittingly highlights a fourth R that dominates higher education: ritual.

Apologetic Excursus: The Persisting Witness of Idolatry

My goal in providing these brief liturgical analyses of cultural institutions like the mall, the stadium, and the university has been to suggest that implicit in their liturgies are visions of the kingdom—visions of human flourishing—that are antithetical to the biblical vision of *shalom*. And because these are formative, liturgical institutions, they unwittingly but powerfully shape and mold our desires and love toward that end—which is why, in chapter 5, we need to see not only what vision of the kingdom

---

46. If there is a glitch in Wolfe's sketch of Charlotte Simmons, it is surely the absence of religious belief and participation, which, demographically, one would have expected to be a more significant part of her home formation and perhaps would have continued into her university habits.

is implicit in the practices of Christian worship but also the way in which Christian practices need to function as *counter*-formation.

Though my primary concern is to highlight the antitheses between these competing liturgies, it is important to note that even these pseudo, or false, liturgies are a testimony to the fact that humans are liturgical animals. In chapter 1 we emphasized that humans are essentially lovers and noted that the effect of the Fall is not that humans stop being lovers (i.e., it's not that the "love pump" is turned off), but rather that our love and desire is misdirected, aimed at ends other than the Creator and his kingdom. But even these misdirections are a testimony to the structure of human be-ing—a testimony to our nature as passional creatures and liturgical animals. This means that even the distorted and misdirected liturgies of the mall or the state are nonetheless signs of our liturgical nature. In other words, what we've been calling "secular liturgies" show that the so-called secular still testifies to our *religious* nature, not just because it involves beliefs or "spiritual" messages, but because even the secular is ultimately about love of something ultimate, with practices intended to form our love. Secular liturgies don't *create* our desire; they point it, aim it, direct it to certain ends.

So even in the midst of the trenchant critique I'm offering here, there remains a moment of affirmation, a point of what we might call "apologetic contact." While a Christian critique of culture through the lens of liturgy is meant to offer a more radical critique of cultural institutions (and to heighten the stakes of our participation in them), there is also an element of these secular liturgies that can be built upon in our witness and mission. By this I don't mean the strategies I've criticized above, whereby the church or Christian university refashions itself as a parody of these secular liturgies, remaking itself as a mall or outpost of University, Inc. Rather, Christian witness to culture can affirm that even these secular liturgies, with their misdirected desires, are a witness to the desire for God; the misdirections are a sign of a perduring structure that we can build upon.

This is just what John Calvin meant to affirm in his notion of the *sensus divinitatis*, an "awareness of divinity": "There is within the human mind, and indeed by natural instinct, an awareness of divinity."[47] (He later describes the same phenomenon, the same structure, as the "seed of religion.")[48] By this, Calvin does *not* mean to indicate that all human beings have a feeble, insufficient "knowledge" of God; he says that all human beings exhibit a "sense" of "divinity" (*sensus divinitatis*), not a

47. John Calvin, *Institutes of the Christian Religion*, ed. John T. McNeill, trans. Ford Lewis Battles (Philadelphia: Westminster, 1960), 1.3.1.
    48. Ibid., 1.4.1, 4.

"knowledge" of "God" (as if he spoke of a "natural" *scientia Dei*).[49] This is best understood not as a primarily intellectual disposition to form theistic beliefs but as a passional disposition to worship. Sin and the Fall may eradicate true knowledge of God because such requires a relationality that is lost by the Fall; but sin and the Fall cannot eradicate this seed of religion, this impulsion to worship. Thus for Calvin, even idolatry is a testament to humanity's essentially religious, liturgical nature:

> Indeed, even idolatry is ample proof of this conception. We know how man does not willingly humble himself so as to place other creatures over himself. Since, then, he prefers to worship wood and stone rather than to be thought of as having no God, clearly this is a most vivid impression of a divine being. So impossible is it to blot this from man's mind that natural disposition would be more easily altered, as altered indeed it is when man voluntarily sinks from his natural haughtiness to the very depths in order to honor God![50]

He later emphasizes that this "seed" of religion "can in no wise be uprooted," even though "this seed is so corrupted that by itself it produces only the worst fruits."[51] Calvin seems to suggest that, in a strange way, such idolatries give us something to work with, something to build on, a point of contact for articulating the gospel, for even idolatries are a sign of our nature as liturgical animals. In a similar way, then, I'm trying to extend Calvin's affirmation by suggesting that even the disordered direction of secular liturgies is testimony to the fact that we—even we "secular" moderns—are liturgical, desiring animals. I don't mean to say that secular liturgies give us implicit knowledge of God, but they are oblique signs that we *desire* God.

Such an oblique affirmation is at the heart of what we described as our "romantic theology" in chapter 2. For instance, in his *Outlines of Romantic Theology*, Charles Williams makes a similar claim: "He who, not in any sense for himself or to himself, is surrendered to an entire ardour cannot be said to be far from the Kingdom which will manifest Itself at Its chosen

---

49. Thus I disagree with Alvin Plantinga's reading of the *sensus divinitatis* (see, for instance, Plantinga, *Warranted Christian Belief* [Oxford: Oxford University Press, 2000], 170–75). Plantinga construes it as a "basic" knowledge of God, a natural disposition "to form *theistic* beliefs," whereas I think Calvin is asserting a natural instinct for *worship*, for investing things with transcendence (the sort of operation described in Romans 1). This is why, as we'll see, Calvin says that idolatry is a testament of this structural religious impulsion in human animals. For a related critique of Plantinga on this point, see John Beversluis, "Reforming the 'Reformed' Objection to Natural Theology," *Faith and Philosophy* 12 (1995): 189–206.

50. Calvin, *Institutes*, 1.3.1.

51. Ibid., 1.4.4.

time; the sooner if, as has been insisted throughout, this ardour is *directed* and controlled by the doctrines of the Christian Religion."[52] This is the intuition that animates some of our best literature, from Dante's *Vita nuova* to Graham Greene's *Heart of the Matter*.[53]

Consider, for example, the figure of Dr. Tom More in Walker Percy's *Love in the Ruins*. Despite the exemplary legacy of his namesake, Sir Thomas More, Tom More confesses to being "a Roman Catholic, albeit a bad one." "I believe in God and the whole business," he admits, "but I love women best, music and science next, whiskey next, God fourth, and my fellowman hardly at all."[54] His disordered loves lead to a disordered life, which he recognizes more than anyone and which is the primary cause of the fragmentation of his selfhood that he regularly experiences, echoing the scattering and distension of the disquieted Augustinian self. Thus he periodically finds himself committed to the psychiatric ward of which, at other times, he is an employee. His allergy to gin fizzes does not preclude his indulging them. Instead, suffering from the swelling as a result, he reflects: "My eyes are almost swelled shut, breath whistles in my throat, but my heart is full of love. Love of what?" he asks himself. "Women," is the reply. "Which women? All women. The first night I ever spent on the acute ward, a madman looked at me and said, not knowing me from Adam: 'You want to know your trouble? You don't love God, you love [women].'"[55] But at other times in the ward, a certain lucidity overcomes him and, like the madman, he diagnoses his own condition:

> Later, lust gave way to sorrow and I prayed, arms stretched out like a Mexican, tears streaming down my face. Dear God, I can see it now, why can't I see it other times, that it is you I love in the beauty of the world and in all

52. Charles Williams, *Outlines of Romantic Theology*, ed. Alice M. Hadfield (Grand Rapids: Eerdmans, 1990), 72. I would just tweak Williams's claim to say that such disordered ardor is first and best directed by Christian *practices*, then doctrines.

53. Greene's *Heart of the Matter* is a singular literary articulation of the axiom (often wrongly attributed to Chesterton) that a man knocking on the door of a brothel actually desires God. (Sadly, Greene's biography might be construed the same way.) The same is expressed in Sarah Miles's journals that are embedded in *The End of the Affair*, where she finally writes: "Did I ever love Maurice as much before I loved You? Or was it really You I loved all the time? Did I touch You when I touched him? Could I have touched You if I hadn't touched him first, touched him as I never touched Henry, anybody? And he loved me and touched me as he never did any other woman. But was it me he loved, or You? For he hated in me the things You hate. He was on Your side all the time without knowing it." Graham Greene, *The End of the Affair* (New York: Penguin, 2004), 99.

54. Walker Percy, *Love in the Ruins* (New York: Picador, 1971), 6. I think it's important to note that he *believes* in God, but it's his *love* (of women) that wins out most of the time. We'll consider the primacy of desire to belief in chapter 4.

55. Ibid., 46.

the lovely girls and dear good friends, and it is pilgrims we are, wayfarers on a journey, and not pigs, nor angels.[56]

At this moment he recognizes that even his disordered love—his lust, what Augustine would call *cupiditas*—is nonetheless a sorry shadow of *caritas*, of a desire and love for God, a "longing" he never shakes.[57]

One particularly powerful literary exploration of the theme is Evelyn Waugh's *Brideshead Revisited*.[58] The intense relationship of Charles Ryder and Sebastian Flyte, which is a portal for Ryder's rather dysfunctional relationship to the entire family, is disordered, misdirected, broken, at times torturous. And yet even in the early, infatuated phase of the relationship, Charles already has intimations of the importance of love: "that to know and love one other human being is the root of all wisdom."[59] In the end, after being abandoned by Sebastian (or after Sebastian's exile), after his troubled marriage and his conversion to faith, Charles would testify of Sebastian: "He was the forerunner."[60] "Perhaps . . . ," Charles muses,

perhaps all our loves are merely hints and symbols; a hill of many invisible crests; doors that open as in a dream to reveal only a further stretch of carpet and another door; perhaps you and I are types and this sadness which sometimes falls between us springs from disappointment in our search, each straining through and beyond the other, snatching a glimpse now and then of the shadow which turns the corner always a pace or two ahead of us.[61]

Echoing the Augustinian axiom that our hearts are restless, anxious, in the search for what they really desire, Charles Ryder sees in his earlier relationship with Sebastian a foretaste of his desire for God—and affirms that even that earlier, disordered love was a kind of prelude and

56. Ibid., 109. The "pigs" and "angels" refer to Dr. More's project throughout the story: to contest both "angelism" (which would construe human beings as essentially ethereal, disembodied minds) and "bestialism" (which would reduce us to merely biological machines; see ibid., 27 and passim). In this way, More's concerns anticipate themes we'll discuss in chapter 4.

57. "The first thing a man remembers is longing and the last thing he is conscious of before death is exactly the same longing. . . . At what age does a man get over this longing? The answer is, he doesn't" (ibid., 21).

58. Evelyn Waugh, *Brideshead Revisited: The Sacred and Profane Memories of Captain Charles Ryder* (Boston: Little, Brown, 1944). I also highly recommend the unabridged audio book narrated by Jeremy Irons (Chivers Audio Books, 2000). And the ITV television production *Brideshead Revisited* (1981), set in the sumptuous milieu of Castle Howard, also does a decent job of reproducing this theme, largely through a clever use of narrative voiceover.

59. Waugh, *Brideshead Revisited*, 45.

60. Ibid., 257, 303.

61. Ibid., 303.

propaedeutic to the love of God.[62] So, too, can even the secular liturgies of the mall and the disordered love of consumerism perhaps be such an occasion, a forerunner of sorts.

 Picturing Resistance in *1984*

I have been highlighting the liturgical nature of common cultural practices in order to help us recognize that these are not just "things we do"; they are habit-forming, identity-shaping, love-directing rituals that capture our imagination and hence our desire, directing it toward a *telos* that is often antithetical to the *telos* envisioned as the kingdom of God. Such material rituals are effective because of what we saw in chapter 1: that we are not (primarily) thinking things, or even (merely) believing things, but are embodied lovers whose love is aimed and primed by the practices and rituals that "train" our desires, as it were (chapter 2). Now, if Christian discipleship is understood as the formation of disciples who desire God and his kingdom, then that means we should have a heightened concern to *resist* the formation of secular liturgies.

However, at this point I think Christians often go wrong, for two reasons. First, sometimes Christians fail to articulate strategies of resistance because they fail to see a threat. Because they fail to see these cultural institutions and practices as formative—fail to see them as liturgies rather than just neutral, benign "things we do"—they also fail to recognize what's at stake in them. I hope this chapter has helped us to recognize these cultural practices for what they are and thus to appreciate the reality and nature of the threat.[63] But second, sometimes Christians fail to articulate adequate strategies of resistance because they misdiagnose the threat. And they misdiagnose the threat because of a flawed, stunted philosophical anthropology. This was Charlotte Simmons's problem: she thought fortitude of mind and will would be sufficient to counter the practices and rituals of Dupont University. Wolfe's narrative indicates the folly and failure of this cognitivist confidence; Charlotte falls fast and hard. Unfortunately, the church often adopts a similarly misguided strategy: while the mall, Victoria's Secret, and Jerry Bruckheimer are grabbing hold of our gut (*kardia*) by

---

62. Poor Sebastian, on the other hand, is doomed to the terrain of the unquiet heart, his desire perpetually sublimated and persistently frustrated, right up to his unsuccessful attempt to become a monk. Cf. Cordelia's evaluation of his "holiness" in ibid., 305–6, 308.

63. I'm a bit uncomfortable with the language of "threat" here but can't come up with an adequate alternative. I don't mean to communicate an alarmist fear of culture in the spirit of the "culture wars" (which, by the way, I think are often tilting at windmills rather than targeting the real, substantive threats to Christian discipleship—fixated on gay marriage but eagerly affirming capitalism). Ultimately, the stance I'm recommending is not anticultural, nor is it meant to counsel retreat, withdrawal, or isolation. Rather, the unveiling of secular liturgies should give us "eyes to see" so that we can engage (and, to some extent, participate in) these cultural spheres. What's important is that we not equate "majority" culture with culture *as such*.

means of our body and its senses—in stories and images, sights and sound, and commercial versions of "smells and bells"—the church's response is oddly rationalist. It plunks us down in a "worship" service, the culmination of which is a forty-five-minute didactic sermon, a sort of holy lecture, trying to *convince* us of the dangers by implanting doctrines and beliefs in our minds. While the mall paradoxically appreciates that we are liturgical, desiring animals, the (Protestant) church still tends to see us as Cartesian minds. While secular liturgies are after our hearts through our bodies, the church thinks it only has to get into our heads. While Victoria's Secret is fanning a flame in our *kardia*, the church is trucking water to our minds. While secular liturgies are enticing us with affective images of a good life, the church is trying to convince us otherwise by depositing ideas.

Such a rationalist response is inadequate and mistargeted because it continues to assume a flawed anthropology. One can see the futility of such a strategy, not only in Charlotte Simmons's transformation, but also in the haunting narrative of Orwell's *1984*.[64] In the privacy of his own home, Winston Smith is a resister. We meet him trying to carve out a hidden little alcove in the corner of his flat that somehow escapes the panoptical eye of Big Brother. He is writing in a journal, which he regularly hides ("To mark the paper was the decisive act" [94]). He sees through Big Brother's (re)construction of the world through the transformation of Oceania's available lexicon; he recognizes the revisionism of the so-called Ministry of Truth and the demonization of Emmanuel Goldstein; he endures the charades of the Two Minute Hate and other civic rituals because he possesses something internal and secret: within him are *memories* that tell him these things aren't so. "Was he, then, *alone* in the possession of a memory" (142)?

So despite the rather defeated tone of Winston's narrative, it is actually suffused with a certain careful confidence, a sense of immunity that leads him to some rash decisions and ill-advised routines, particularly his regular rendezvous with Julia. Together they extend Winston's habit of carving out hidden spaces that are supposedly immune to the gaze and control of Big Brother: first Winston's mind and memories, then his journal and alcove, and then together, a little love nest above Mr. Charrington's shop in the Proles sector of the city, where they engage in activities prohibited by the Party. While haunted in all these ventures, they all indicate in Winston a certain prideful sense of being able to secure interiority and privacy.

During a conversation in which Winston voices his persistent fears of detection, he admonishes Julia about what's important if they should ever be found out:

> "If I confess they'll shoot you, and if I refuse to confess, they'll shoot you just the same. . . . The one thing that matters is that we shouldn't betray one another, although even that can't make the slightest difference."
>
> "If you mean confessing," she said, "we shall do that, right enough. Everybody always confesses. You can't help it. They torture you."

64. George Orwell, *1984*, in *Animal Farm/1984* (New York: Harcourt, 2003). Subsequent references are in parentheses in the text.

"I don't mean confessing. Confession is not betrayal. What you say or do doesn't matter; only feelings matter. If they could make me stop loving you—that would be real betrayal."

She thought it over. "They can't do that," she said finally. "It's the one thing they can't do. They can make you say anything—*anything*—but they can't make you believe it. They can't get inside of you."

"No," he said a little more hopefully, "no; that's quite true. They can't get inside you." (243)

And so Julia, a fellow devotee, articulated the creed of Winston's "interiorism": his philosophical anthropology that carves out a mental inside that is immune and secure from whatever external and material practices Big Brother might subject him to, whether the Two Minute Hate or inevitable torture. Such (merely) material, bodily strategies could never reach his "inside"—the interior space of his memories, will, mind, and above all, love.

What he sensed was inevitable comes to pass: found out (or betrayed), he becomes a prisoner subjected to all sorts of strategies of brainwashing and transformation. And what the Party requires is not just obedience, not just belief, but love. When O'Brien finally comes to gather Winston, he asks him, "Tell me, Winston—and remember, no lies; you know that I am always able to detect a lie—tell me, what are your true feelings toward Big Brother?"

"I hate him" is Winston's response.

"You hate him. Good," O'Brien affirms. "Then the time has come for you to take the last step. You must love Big Brother. It is not enough to obey him; you must love him" (356).

Winston is then taken to the dreaded Room 101, and the worst of his dreaded nightmares come true: Rats. His torture would be a heinous, horrific device: "an oblong wire cage with a handle on top for carrying it by. Fixed to the front of it was something that looked like a fencing mask, with the concave side outwards. Although it was three or four meters away from him, he could see that the cage was divided lengthways into two compartments, and there was some kind of creature in each. They were rats" (357). In one of the most chilling passages of twentieth-century literature, the device filled with hungry rats is strapped to his face.

The outcome? A conversion. "'They can't get inside you,' she had said. But they could get inside you." The fire of Winston's interiorism has been extinguished, and with it the latent dualism that pictured the human body as containing a private, immune "inside" that was somehow unattached to and unaffected by the movements and experiences of the body. But now he realized the folly of his dualism; the very materiality of his torture was its own kind of education, nothing short of a pedagogy of desire. He now "gazed up at the enormous face" of Big Brother. "Forty years it had taken him to learn what kind of smile was hidden beneath the dark mustache. O cruel, needless misunderstanding! O stubborn, self-willed exile from the loving breast! Two gin-scented tears trickled down the sides of his nose. But it was all right, everything was all right, the struggle had finished. He had won the victory over himself. He loved Big Brother" (370).

Christians can be prone to something like Winston's interiorism and mistakenly assume that our loves are insulated and isolated, untouchable and unaffected by so-called external rituals and bodily routines. But Orwell's chilling narrative echoes a biblical picture of the integrity of the human person as an embodied creature, a material lover, whose loves are primed and shaped by concrete rituals—whose love is educated by liturgies. How much more important is it, then, to be intentional about the shape of Christian worship as a pedagogy of desire trained to make us love the Father and desire his kingdom? And how crucial must it be that what we call "Christian education" should be informed and infused by such liturgical practices? It is to these questions that we turn in part 2.

Desiring the Kingdom

THE PRACTICED SHAPE
OF THE CHRISTIAN LIFE

In part 1, we laid out a formal claim: that human beings are essentially and fundamentally creatures who are oriented and defined by what they love, by desire. We are fundamentally affective beings; thus being human takes practice, so to speak. We are shaped by material bodily practices that aim or point our love to ultimate visions of human flourishing—to particular configurations of what "the kingdom" should look like. We have described practices or rituals of ultimate concern as *liturgies*. And in chapter 3 we exegeted some "secular" liturgies in order to discern the shape of the kingdom implicit in and carried in the practices associated with them. Thus we tried to sketch a mode of cultural critique that focuses on cultural practices rather than fixating on ideas.

In part 2, we turn to our constructive task. In chapter 4 we'll explore the relationship between worship and a Christian worldview and consider a fundamental aspect of Christian worship, what we'll call *sacramentality*. The heart of the book is then chapter 5, which is an exegesis of the Christian social imaginary as embedded and carried in the practices of Christian worship. Here we finally unpack the particularities of the vision of the "kingdom *of God*" as it is implicit in Christian worship. In chapter 6 we then consider the implications of this model, and this understanding of the kingdom, for the project of Christian education.

4

From Worship to Worldview

CHRISTIAN WORSHIP AND THE FORMATION OF DESIRE

The Primacy of Worship to Worldview

In the previous chapters we have emphasized that human persons are not primarily thinking things, or even believing things, but rather imaginative, desiring animals who are defined fundamentally by love. We are embodied, affective creatures who are shaped and primed by material practices or liturgies that aim our hearts to certain ends, which in turn draw us to them in a way that transforms our actions by inscribing in us habits or dispositions to act in certain ways. In short, being human takes practice—and implicit in those practices is a social imaginary that orients, guides, and shapes our desire and action. A social imaginary, you'll recall, is an understanding of the world that is precognitive and prereflective: it functions on an order before both thinking and believing, and it is "carried," Taylor says, in images, stories, myths, and related practices. Thus we have suggested that it might be more helpful to talk about a Christian social imaginary than to focus on a Christian worldview, given that the latter seems tinged with a lingering cognitivism. By focusing on social imaginaries, the radar of cultural critique is calibrated to focus on exegeting practices, not just waiting for the blips of ideas to show up on the screen. Thus in chapter 3 we considered some secular liturgies in order to read between the lines, as it were, to discern the shape of the social imaginary (and, in particular, the vision of the kingdom of human flourishing) embedded in these practices.

Our project culminates in chapter 5, in which we'll provide a summary exegesis of the Christian social imaginary as it is embedded in the practices of Christian worship. Thus we'll bring to Christian worship the same questions we brought to secular liturgies in chapter 3: What is envisioned as the good life? What understanding of the world is carried in these practices? What vision of the kingdom is embedded in Christian worship? What picture of flourishing human community is envisioned by the practices of distinctly Christian liturgy? And how does this vision of the kingdom of God compare to the kingdoms aimed at in secular liturgies?

In other words, what does worship say about Christian faith? Too often we try to define the essence of Christianity by a summary of doctrines. We turn to texts and to theologians in order to discern the ideas and beliefs that are distinctive to Christianity. That's akin to thinking one can understand *Hamlet* just by reading the script; but it is only properly a play when it is performed, and there is a kind of understanding of *Hamlet* that comes from its performance that cannot be found just in the script.[1] So, what if we sought to discern not the essence of Christianity as a system of beliefs (or summarized in a worldview) but instead sought to discern the shape of Christian faith as a form of life? Instead of turning to texts, doctrines, and the theoretical articulations of theologians, we will consider what Christians *do*—or more specifically, what the church *as a people* does together in the "work of the people" (*leitourgos*). To discern the shape of a Christian worldview, we will read the practices of Christian worship in order to make out the shape of a distinctly Christian social imaginary.

Our move here stems from a conviction that follows from the philosophical anthropology sketched in part 1. In particular, because we've emphasized that humans are first and fundamentally affective creatures shaped by practices—creatures who love before they think, who imagine before they theorize—we need a corresponding account of the relationship between worship and worldview (or doctrine). This will require undoing some habits we've acquired in theology and philosophy, as well as in discussions of Christian education and the formation of Christian worldview. In particular, it requires that we reconsider the relationship between practice and belief.[2] In general, we have a tendency to think that doctrine and/

1. I was prompted to consider this analogy by Ben Faber, "Ethical Hermeneutics in the Theatre: Shakespeare's *Merchant of Venice*," in *Hermeneutics at Crossroads*, ed. Kevin Vanhoozer, James K. A. Smith, and Bruce Ellis Benson (Bloomington: Indiana University Press, 2006), 211–24.

2. I have addressed the following themes in a more technical way in James K. A. Smith, "Philosophy of Religion Takes Practice: Liturgy as Source and Method in Philosophy of Religion," in *Contemporary Practice and Method in the Philosophy of Religion: New Es-*

or belief comes first—either in a chronological or normative sense—and that this then finds expression or application in worship practices, as if we have a worldview in place and then devise practices that are consistent with that cognitive framework.[3] Such a top-down, ideas-first picture of the relation between practice and knowledge, worldview and worship, is often accompanied by a corresponding picture of the relationship between the Bible and worship. According to this model, we begin with the Bible as the source of our doctrines and beliefs and then "apply" it to come up with worship practices that are consistent with, and expressive of, what the Bible teaches.

But there are problems with this picture: First, it doesn't jibe with the historical record. The people of God called out (*ek-klēsia*) to be the church were worshiping long before they got all their doctrines in order or articulated the elements of a Christian worldview; and they were engaged in and developing worship practices long before what we now call our *Bible* emerged and was solidified, so to speak.[4] Thus we can see in the New Testament itself the remnants of early Christian hymns (Phil. 2:5–11) and doxologies (e.g., Rom. 16:25–27) that likely were taken up from worship practices in the early church. In addition, given the oral culture in which the Scriptures emerged, and the centrality of their public reading in gathered worship, the letters and documents that came to be the New Testament (in addition to the psalms prayed and sung by the early church) functioned primarily in a liturgical context of worship, not the private context of individual study.[5] And when the Scriptures are heard and read in the context of worship, they function differently. Rather than being approached as a "storehouse of facts" (Charles Hodge), the Scriptures are read and encountered as a site of divine action, as a means of grace, as a conduit of the Spirit's transformative power, as part of a pedagogy of desire. One could

---

says, ed. David Cheetham and Rolfe King (London: Continuum, 2008), 133–47; and idem, "How Religious Practices Matter: Peter Ochs' 'Alternative Nurturance' of Philosophy of Religion," *Modern Theology* 24 (2008): 469–78.

3. One can even find someone like Alexander Schmemann falling into the habit of talking this way, as when he says that "worship is . . . the *expression* thus not merely of 'piety,' but of an all-embracing 'world view'" (*For the Life of the World: Sacraments and Orthodoxy*, 2nd ed. [Crestwood, NY: St. Vladimir's, 1973], 123, emphasis added)—as if the worldview is in place before worship. But then later he will counsel that we need to recover "the genuine meaning and power of our *leitourgia*" so that it can become "the *source of* an all-embracing world view" (134).

4. For a helpful history on the Bible as, in some significant sense, a product *of* the church in the Spirit, see Craig D. Allert, *A High View of Scripture? The Authority of the Bible and the Formation of the New Testament Canon*, Evangelical Ressourcement (Grand Rapids: Baker Academic, 2007), esp. 67–130.

5. Much more deserves to be said about this, but for a relevant discussion, see Daniel J. Treier, *Introducing Theological Interpretation of Scripture: Recovering a Christian Practice* (Grand Rapids: Baker Academic, 2008), 42–45.

say that in the context of worship, Scripture constitutes a different kind of speech act, and thus is heard/received in a different mode.[6] The point here is that just as worship precedes the formation of the biblical canon ("the Bible"), so too does participation in Christian worship precede the formulation of doctrine and the articulation of worldview. Lived worship is the fount from which a worldview springs, rather than being the expression or application of some cognitive set of beliefs already in place.

Second, the common picture of doctrine or a worldview being "expressed" in worship—thus implying that worldview and/or doctrine *precedes* worship—doesn't jibe with the anthropology we've sketched above. This (I hope, biblical) anthropology suggests a different picture—not a top-down, ideas-first picture that prioritizes beliefs and doctrines ("worldview") but rather a bottom-up, practices-first model that prioritizes worship as a practice of desire. As I've been articulating this, I have had two special cases in my mind: children and mentally challenged adults. Both have limited capacities for grasping theological concepts or the sorts of theoretical formulations that characterize even worldview-talk. Their ability to process the sorts of abstractions that characterize even beliefs is limited, either temporarily (in the case of children) or chronically (in the case of the mentally handicapped). Does that mean that they cannot achieve fullness in Christ? Do the limits of their cognitive abilities impair the hope of their "growing up" *into* Christ (Eph. 4:15)? Does their inability to traffic in concepts preclude them from being educated? Not according to the anthropology I have sketched above; rather, because we are more fundamentally creatures of love and desire than knowledge and beliefs, our discipleship—our formation in Christ—is more fundamentally a matter of precognitive education of the heart. And Christian worship that is full-bodied reaches, touches, and transforms even those who cannot grasp theological abstractions.[7]

6. Or, as Daniel Treier elsewhere suggests, we might say that this is a difference between coming to the Scriptures for knowledge and coming to the Scriptures for wisdom—akin to a difference between theoretical and practical reason, *scientia* rather than *sapientia*. (One might say that *sapientia* is akin to Taylor's notion of precognitive "understanding" discussed in chapter 2.) Encountering the Scriptures first and foremost in the context of worship primes us for a *sapiential* engagement with the Word. For relevant discussion, see Daniel J. Treier, *Virtue and the Voice of God: Toward Theology as Wisdom* (Grand Rapids: Eerdmans, 2006).

7. This is yet another way in which churches need to think of making themselves "accessible" for the handicapped. While we have worried about elevators and barriers, too many Protestant churches continue to offer a (very modern) style of worship that is dominated by quite abstract, heady forms, centering on a sermon that communicates only on a cognitive level (often difficult even for those without college degrees)—rather than adopting historic forms of Christian liturgy that enact the whole person and thus reach those without such cognitive capacities with the story of the gospel. For a developed argument, see Amos Yong,

For instance, when our children were quite young, we would sometimes participate in Good Friday services that included a few hymns and an extensive sermon that would focus on the fine points of atonement theory. But sometimes we would have opportunity to participate in Tenebrae, a historic "service of shadows" that revolves around Christ's seven last words from the cross. In the service we have attended, the congregation enters a sanctuary lit only by seven clusters of candles. Through the service, Christ's last words from the cross are read—sometimes with a brief meditation, sometimes with a musical interpretation. After each word, one of the clusters of candles is extinguished (in this case by a person methodically doing so as part of a liturgical dance). The darkness of that dark day increasingly envelops the congregation, until after the final word when the last bit of light is extinguished. After a time of darkened silence, the *strepitus* sounds—a torrent of discordant noise generated by cymbals from a hidden location in the rear of the sanctuary, shuddering through the congregation like a cold wind of desolation. The congregation then departs in somber silence, in darkness, the realities of Good Friday having been enacted in a way that still lingers, almost oppressively. They will not gather again until Easter morn, when the darkened sanctuary will be ablaze with light and lilies in resurrection splendor. But for now they depart in heaviness to endure that dark Saturday between.

As you can perhaps imagine, the Tenebrae service has a much greater impact on my children than the long sermon on atonement. And as you also might expect, it tends to have much more impact on the adults too! Why is that? Because the heavy affectivity of the Tenebrae service—its ability to communicate Good Friday almost directly to our body, as it were—touches our gut, our embodied *kardia*. And *that* is something shared by all of us, including those who are either uninclined or unable to engage in theological abstractions. Historic Christian worship is fundamentally formative because it educates our hearts through our bodies (which in turn renews our mind), and does so in a way that is more universally accessible (and I would add, more universally effective) than many of the overly cognitive worship habits we have acquired in modernity. In this respect, Amos Yong rightly criticizes how Protestant worship has tended to configure Christian initiation and discipleship. "This is especially problematic in Protestantism," he notes,

> with its conviction that salvation is effectively mediated through "knowledge" (of theological or doctrinal content) and that the catechetical process

---

Theology and Down Syndrome: Reimagining Disability in Late Modernity (Waco: Baylor University Press, 2007), 203–15.

should be focused on cognitively imparting such knowledge to those seeking Christian initiation. However, we have now insisted that this Platonic and Cartesian anthropology is faulty precisely because of its subordination of the body. . . . Insofar as the Hebrew *yada* refers more to the knowledge of the heart than the head, Protestants can now learn from Catholic and Orthodox traditions, especially with regard to how human knowing of God is mediated through formation, imitation, affectivity, intuition, imagination, interiorization, and symbolic engagement.[8]

Because all human beings are more fundamentally affective than cognitive, such is true for all Christian worship. Emphasizing the primacy of worship practices to worldview formation both honors the fact that all humans are desiring animals while at the same time making sense of how Christian worship is developmentally significant for those who can participate in rituals but are unable to participate in theoretical reflection. In short, it helps us make sense of the moving testimony of someone like "Judy," a mentally challenged adult who eagerly confessed:

> I want to eat Jesus bread. . . . I can't wait until I can eat Jesus bread and drink Jesus juice. People who love Jesus are the ones who eat Jesus bread. . . . Jesus' skin and meat turned into bread and Jesus' blood and guts turned into juice—that's Jesus' bread and Jesus' juice, and I want to eat it and drink with all the other Christians at church 'cause I love him so.[9]

Responding to such a testimony with a didactic conversation aimed at theological correction would be a colossal adventure in missing the point. A better response would be to worship together at the table, eating Jesus bread and drinking Jesus juice together, opening ourselves up to the Spirit's transformative power.

So if we want to discern the shape of a Christian worldview, it is crucial that we recall the priority of liturgy to doctrine. Doctrines, beliefs, and a Christian worldview emerge *from* the nexus of Christian worship practices; worship is the *matrix* of Christian faith, not its "expression" or "illustration."[10] Just as Taylor emphasized that "humans operated with a social imaginary well before they ever got into the business of theorizing

8. Ibid., 208.

9. Cited in ibid., 193.

10. The argument I'm making here also has curricular import for seminary education: rather than being an addendum or foray in "applied" theology, liturgical training and "practical theology" should be at the center of the theological curriculum, displacing the privileged place of "systematic" theology. "Systematics" should be seen as an explication of the grammar of Christian worship. Something like this intuition is expressed in the structure and logic of *The Blackwell Companion to Christian Ethics*, ed. Stanley Hauerwas and Samuel Wells (Oxford: Blackwell, 2006).

about themselves,"[11] so too did Christians worship before they got around to abstract theologizing or formulating a Christian worldview. And developmentally, our orientation to the world is still more fundamentally shaped by embodied liturgical practices than doctrinal disquisitions (which is precisely why secular liturgies often trump our imaginations). The practices of the church as the gathered people of the coming King precede the formulas and codes that would later emerge from their theoretical reflection. Before Christians had systematic theologies and worldviews, they were singing hymns and psalms, saying prayers, celebrating the Eucharist, sharing their property, and becoming a people marked by a desire for God's coming kingdom—a desire that constituted them as a peculiar people in the present. So in the following chapter, rather than formulating the elements of a Christian worldview in abstraction, we will instead exegete the understanding or social imaginary that is implicit in the practices of Christian worship. What does Christian worship "say" about the sort of people the church is called to be? What vision of God and the world is implicit in Christian liturgy? What understanding of human intersubjectivity and political flourishing is embedded in Christian worship? What vision of the kingdom is being learned when we participate in these rituals?

The Sacramental Imagination: Resisting Naturalism and Supernaturalism

One of the first things that should strike us about Christian worship is how earthy, material, and mundane it is. To engage in worship requires a body—with lungs to sing, knees to kneel, legs to stand, arms to raise, eyes to weep, noses to smell, tongues to taste, ears to hear, hands to hold and raise. Christian worship is not the sort of thing that ethereal, disembodied spirits could engage in. Just as immaterial ghosts couldn't have eaten fish with the disciples on the shore of Galilee (Luke 24:36–43), neither could immaterial creatures worship so richly (angels could never have written the Psalms!). The rhythms and rituals of Christian worship invoke and feed off of our embodiment and traffic in the stuff of a material world: water, bread, and wine, each of which point us to their earthy emergence: the curvature of the riverbed, the shimmering fields that give forth grain, the grapes that hint of a unique *terroir*. It does not take much imagination for these in turn to evoke an entire environment: The gurgling water in the riverbed calls to mind the reeds and pussy willows along its edge, muskrats slinking quietly from the edge under

11. Charles Taylor, *Modern Social Imaginaries* (Durham, NC: Duke University Press, 2004), 26.

the water's surface, as the water wends its way to twist the crank of a gristmill or a hydroelectric turbine, both providing sustenance for a civilization of culture. The bread evokes images of Kansas wheat fields or of parched African expanses that have failed to yield grain for years.[12] The bread has not made it to this table without much labor, without hands (and machines) harvesting, sometimes toiling and despoiling in the process. The wine in the cup has its own rich history of grapes drooping on the ground, rescued from rot by caring hands of husbandry, perhaps also just escaping an early frost that threatened their ripe skins. So right here in Christian worship we have a sort of microcosm of creation—the "world in a wafer."[13]

And behind and under and in all of this is a core conviction, an implicit understanding that God inhabits all this earthy stuff, that we meet God in the material realities of water and wine, that God embraces our embodiment, embraces *us* in our embodiment. So before we articulate the conceptual affirmation of the goodness of creation (Gen. 1:31) that is integral to a Christian worldview, an understanding of this is enacted and performed in the church's worship. That God would meet us in the mundane and earthy is a *performance* of God's affirmation of creation and materiality as a good to be enjoyed and as a gift to be received, rather than a regrettable and lamentable condition from which we can hope to escape. The goodness of creation as a belief and even ontological claim makes sense for us because we first experience the blessing, sanctification, and riches of the material world in the joy and pleasure of Christian worship. There is a performative sanctioning of embodiment that is implicit in Christian worship, invoking the ultimate performative sanctioning of the body in the incarnation—which itself recalls the love of God that gave birth to the material creation[14]—its reaffirmation in the resurrection of Jesus, and looks forward to the resurrection of the body as an eschatological and eternal affirmation of the goodness of creation.

---

12. It is important to recall that God is present in *broken* bread, and God's affirmation of creation includes his inhabiting even its brokenness. This is powerfully portrayed in the stories of Flannery O'Connor and the novels of Graham Greene (*The Power and the Glory* especially comes to mind here). Compare also Anne Sexton's poem "The Earth," which hymns God's (incarnational) desire to inhabit a body: "God owns heaven / but he craves the earth, / the earth with its little sleepy caves" but *even* the world with "its murders lined up like broken chairs, / even its writers digging into their souls / with jackhammers." Anne Sexton, "The Earth," in *The Complete Poems of Anne Sexton* (New York: Houghton Mifflin, Mariner Books, 1999), 431.

13. I'm playing a bit with William Cavanaugh's phrase in *Theopolitical Imagination* (London: T&T Clark, 2002), 112.

14. Compare Jonathan Edwards, "The End for Which God Created the World," nicely situated in John Piper, *God's Passion for His Glory: Living the Vision of Jonathan Edwards* (Wheaton: Crossway, 1998), 117–252.

Any service of Christian worship that is given to a more dualistic or gnostic conception of the body (e.g., tending to see the body as a "prison" and the material world as an evil distraction) will actually be a performative contradiction, since any service of Christian worship will be inescapably material and embodied, even if it might not be considered liturgical or sacramental. Indeed, there is a sense in which human worship is inescapably sacramental insofar as it will always and only be an event of material meaning-making. Even the most didactic, minimalist "talking-head" kind of worship will require tongues and ears. Our essential embodiment will keep interrupting our Platonic desire to do away with the body, will keep insinuating itself into our dualistic discourses to remind us that the triune God of creation traffics in ashes and dust, blood and bodies, fish and bread. And he pronounces all of it "very good" (Gen. 1:31).

This liturgical affirmation of materiality is commonly described as a *sacramental* understanding of the world—that the physical, material stuff of creation and embodiment is the means by which God's grace meets us and gets hold of us. Now, you may find yourself a bit skittish about the word *sacramental* and what you associate with sacramentalism. If so, I would ask that you try to suspend judgment for just a few pages—just as I earlier asked you to withhold judgment about the use of the term *liturgy*. I hope that over the next few pages you'll see that a sacramental understanding of the world is simply a shorthand way of describing the psalmist's claim that "The earth is the LORD's and all that is in it, the world, and those who live in it" (Ps. 24:1), echoed in Paul's claim that *in* the Creator God "we live and move and have our being" (Acts 17:28). As Leonard Vander Zee notes, to speak of a sacramental understanding of the world is just to affirm that "God reveals himself through created things." Indeed, "that God can speak through the things he created" is a "biblical given."[15] "As God's creation," he continues, "the world may offer a sacramental window into transcendent reality."[16] And it is because the whole world is sacramental that God takes up nitty-gritty things like bread and water and wine to function as sacraments, special means of grace. "The only way in which particular sacraments can have meaning is if the universe is so created and structured that this can happen."[17] The sacraments, we might say, are particular intensifications of a general sacramental presence of God in and with his creation; they are particular

15. Leonard Vander Zee, *Christ, Baptism, and the Lord's Supper: Recovering the Sacraments for Evangelical Worship* (Downers Grove, IL: InterVarsity, 2004), 17.
    16. Ibid., 18.
    17. Ibid., 17.

To Think About: Sacramentality and Stuff in Percy's *Love in the Ruins*

In his fantastic yet prescient novel *Love in the Ruins*, Walker Percy often captures the scandal of this sacramental understanding of the world—a construal of the world that is scandalous to both gnostic supernaturalists who are longing to escape the evil of matter as well as naturalists who refuse to see anything beyond the visible. (Percy's character Dr. Tom More takes a swipe at the naturalistic establishment by noting that "there still persists in the medical profession the quaint superstition that only that which is visible is real" [*Love in the Ruins* (New York: Picador, 1971), 29].) Thus the novel's central character, Dr. Tom More, is regularly trying to cure people of either "angelism"—which makes them prone to disembodied, other-worldly abstraction— or "bestialism"—which tends to reduce people to biological (and primarily "reproductive") machines. Of particular interest here, however, is his critique of forms of Christian "spiritualism" that, in the name of holiness and spirituality, exhibit an allergy to things, to materiality, and thus are prone to fly off into disembodied abstraction. Thus when the "bad Catholic" Dr. More returns from Mass back to Doris in the interstate motel, he is "exhilarated." This prompts from Doris a question of exasperation and confusion: "My God, what is it you do in church?" she asks. "What she didn't understand," More tells us, "she being spiritual and seeing religion as a spirit, was that it took religion to save me from the spirit world, from orbiting the earth like Lucifer and the angels, that it took nothing less than touching the thread off the misty interstates and eating Christ himself to make me mortal man again and let me inhabit my own flesh and love her in the morning." (Ibid., 254). It is the earthiness and materiality of worship—the role of stuff that you can touch and taste—that keeps him from angelism. It is this "angelist" distrust of stuff and things—an implicit antisacramentalism—that he sees in Ellen, his Presbyterian liaison: "What bothers her is an ancient Presbyterian mistrust of *things*, things getting mixed up in religion. . . . What have these *things*, articles, to do with doing right? For she mistrusts the Old Church's traffic in things, sacraments, articles, bread, wine, salt, oil, water, ashes." (Ibid., 400). I'm suggesting that such a distrust of things is not inherently Presbyterian, and certainly not inherently Christian. It is a bad habit we have picked up at various times and places in the church's sojourn, but one that the Scriptures and the Spirit invite us to leave behind, seeing the very invitation to worship as a performative renunciation of such "angelism."

pieces of creation that God takes up as unique channels of grace, and to which he attaches a promise.[18]

This is incisively captured in Alexander Schmemann's articulation of *sacramental*: "The basic and primordial intuition which not only expresses itself in worship, but of which the entire worship is indeed the phenomenon—both effect and experience—is that the world, be it in its totality as cosmos, or in its life and becoming as time and history, is an *epiphany* of God."[19] Because

18. Thus Vander Zee notes that John Calvin could describe the Noahic rainbow as a "sacrament" (ibid., 22–23); cf. Calvin, *Institutes*, 4.14.18.
19. Schmemann, *For the Life of the World*, 120.

of the sort of animals we were created to be, "we *need* water and oil, bread and wine in order to be in communion with God and to know Him." And "it is this communion with God by means of 'matter' that reveals the true meaning of 'matter,' i.e., of the world itself."[20] Thus the term *sacramental* "means that for the world to be a means of worship and means of grace is not accidental, but the revelation of its meaning, the restoration of its essence, the fulfillment of its destiny."[21] Aspects of the material world like bread and water are not "made" to be sacramental by some kind of magical divine fiat that transforms their created nature; rather, when they are taken up as sacraments in the context of worship, their "natural sacramentality" is simply intensified and completed. So, too, worship is not some odd, extravagant, extra-human thing we do as an add-on to our earthly, physical, material nature; rather, "worship is the epiphany of the world."[22] Worship is the ordering and reordering of our material being to the end for which it was meant.

Implicit in the materiality of Christian worship is this sense that God meets us in materiality, and that the natural world is always more than just nature—it is charged with the presence and glory of God. Thus the very performance of Christian worship cuts against both dualistic gnosticism, which would construe matter and bodies as inherently evil, and reductionistic naturalism, which would construe the world as "merely" natural.[23] In short, the practice of Christian worship resists two sorts of reductionism: a dualistic, supernaturalistic gnosticism, on the one hand, and a materialistic, flattened naturalism, on the other. Both evacuate the world of God's presence, either by suggesting that a holy God would not traffic with the impurities of materiality, or by a "nothing-but" conception of the material as nothing *more* than material. The sacramental imagination runs counter to both of these reductionistic understandings of the world. The understanding of the world implicit in Christian worship walks the tightrope of a "theological materialism"[24] that both affirms the goodness of materiality but also that the material *is* only insofar as it participates in *more* than the material. Thus the sacramental imagination implicit in Christian worship eschews the dichotomies of both naturalism and supernaturalism. Instead, the whole world, as Hopkins lyricized, is charged with the grandeur of

---

20. Ibid., 121.

21. Ibid.

22. Ibid.

23. For further discussion of this point and the "participatory ontology" that is implied, see James K. A. Smith, *Introducing Radical Orthodoxy: Mapping a Post-secular Theology* (Grand Rapids: Baker Academic, 2004), 188–94.

24. See Graham Ward, "Theological Materialism," in *God and Reality*, ed. Colin Crowder (London: Mowbray, 1997), 144–59. Compare also John Milbank, *The Suspended Middle: Henri de Lubac and the Debate concerning the Supernatural* (Grand Rapids: Eerdmans, 2005), which walks the same tightrope.

God;[25] for the Christian social imaginary, the world is always more than it seems, without being less than it seems. It is characterized by a kind of enchantment.[26] That is an intuition and understanding that emerges from the very practices of Christian worship.

Picturing the Sacramental Imagination in Graham Greene and Anne Sexton

Worship forms us and aims us because its concrete, material practices catch hold of our imagination. This is why worship is more like art than science, more like literature than logic. Worship is fundamentally aesthetic, not didactic.[27] Hence there's a certain struggle, and even inability, to articulate these intuitions in the genre of this sort of book, whose mode is largely didactic and theoretical. This is why I have been regularly pointing to literature as a cognate portal into these questions, since there is more commensurability between the social imaginary of Christian worship and the imaginative worlds of litera-ture than there is with the staid, buttoned-down discourse of philosophy and theology. Thus one can often find the sacramental imagination better pictured in novels than dis-sertations. The very genre of the novel, though still textual, is more visceral and tactile: it functions on the same sort of register as the words and movements of Christian worship.[28] So we should expect to find a better testimony to the sacramental imagination in novels than philosophy books. Consider, for instance, the work of Graham Greene, particularly his masterpiece, *The End of the Affair*. In the midst of this complex psychological explora-tion of brokenness, love, desire, and hope, one finds powerful evocations of the enchant-ment of the world that is endemic to Christian worship. And as in the work of Waugh and others, the engine that drives human action is desire, love. All of this can be heard in the reflections of the narrator, Maurice Bendrix, on an episode of haunting:

25. Gerard Manley Hopkins, "God's Grandeur," line 1.

26. For further discussion of this, see James K. A. Smith, "Secularity, Globalization, and the Re-enchantment of the World," in *After Modernity? Secularity, Globalization, and the Re-enchantment of the World*, ed. James K. A. Smith (Waco: Baylor University Press, 2008), 3–13.

27. This is not to suggest that worship is merely aesthetic, nor am I suggesting that there is not a didactic moment to worship. Both worries betray a superficial understanding of "the aesthetic" (perhaps a Kierkegaardian notion of the irresponsible "aesthete"). For a richer notion of the aesthetic and a three-dimensional account of "artistic truth" that is relevant here, see Lambert Zuidervaart, *Artistic Truth: Aesthetics, Discourse, and Imagina-tive Disclosure* (Cambridge: Cambridge University Press, 2004).

28. My intuition—which needs to be followed up with a more rigorous consideration elsewhere—is that liturgical action, including liturgical speech acts, are a *kind* of doing and saying that are different from "doings" and "sayings" that take place in more didactic contexts. For instance, if I am in a theology classroom and read an article of the Nicene Creed for theological exposition, I am *doing* something different (and something different is "getting done") than when I recite the same article of the Creed with the congregation in the context of worship. Who, when reciting the Apostles' Creed in worship, doesn't find that it has a kind of poetic cadence to it?—which is precisely why it can so easily come to mind in other contexts too, sometimes haunting us by surprise.

I have never understood why people who can swallow the enormous improbabil-
ity of a personal God boggle at a personal Devil. I have known so intimately the
way that demon works in my imagination. No statement that Sarah ever made
was proof against his cunning doubts, though he would usually wait till she had
gone to utter them. He would prompt our quarrels long before they occurred:
he was not Sarah's enemy so much as the enemy of love, and isn't that what the
devil is supposed to be? I can imagine that if there existed a God who loved, the
devil would be driven to destroy even the weakest, the most faulty imitation of
that love. Wouldn't he be afraid that the habit of love might grow, and wouldn't
he trap us all into being traitors, into helping him extinguish love? If there is a God
who uses us and makes us his saints out of such material as we are, the devil too
may have his ambitions; he may dream of training even such a person as myself,
even poor Parkis, into being his saints, ready with borrowed fanaticism to destroy
love wherever we find it.[29]

Here we see all the messiness of love, sin, and redemption—and a first subtle reminder
that the saints are "material."

This theme continues to be expanded in the novel. In Sarah's journals, we catch
glimpses of her emerging Catholic faith, which begins with an intense repulsion, even
disgust. But in her aversion to it, she rightly grasps what's at stake in it. When, on a hot
and rainy day, she seeks shelter in a corner church, she looks around and realizes that "it
was a Roman church, full of plaster statues and bad art, realistic art." And what repulses
her is precisely all this emphasis on *bodies*, materiality, and tangible stuff:

I hated the statues, the crucifix, all the emphasis on the human body. I was trying
to escape from the human body and all it needed. I thought I could believe in
some kind of a God that bore no relation to ourselves, something vague, amor-
phous, cosmic, to which I had promised something and which had given me
something in return—stretching out of the vague into the concrete human life,
like a powerful vapour moving among the chairs and walls. One day I too would
become part of that vapour—I would escape myself forever. (87)

Sarah, who has done things with her body that she would like to forget, craves
escape from embodiment, is tempted by the "angelism" Dr. Tom More contests in *Love
in the Ruins*. But that is not Christianity, and the visceral environment of the church
reminds her of this. "And then I came into that dark church in Park Road and saw the
bodies standing around me on all the altars—hideous plaster statues with their com-
placent faces, and I remembered that *they* believed in the resurrection of the body,
the body I wanted destroyed forever" (87). But when her reflection turns to consider
the body of her lover, Maurice, with all its lines and scars, she finds a different desire
welling up within her. While she might want to be a vapor, she wants that scar to exist
through all eternity. A certain logic then catches up with her: "But could my vapour
love that scar? Then I began to want my body that I hated, but only because it could

29. Graham Greene, *The End of the Affair* (New York: Penguin, 2004), 47.

love that scar. We can love with our minds, but can we love only with our minds? Love extends itself all the time, so that we can even love with our senseless nails: we love even with our clothes, so that a sleeve can feel a sleeve" (88). So what both repels and attracts Sarah to Christianity at this point is the fact that it is a "materialistic" faith. She recalls her husband Henry's commentary on their visit to a Spanish church, whose statues of martyrs with all their blood and wounds drove Sarah from the church, sickened: "Of course it's a very materialistic faith," he said. "Materialism isn't only an attitude for the poor," he continued. "Some of the finest brains have been materialist, Pascal, Newman"[30]—an odd list of materialists since they were also rather ardent supernaturalists of a sort too. This washes back over Sarah on this hot, rainy day in the church on Park Road. "So today I looked at that material body on that material cross, and I wondered, how could the world have nailed a vapour there? . . . Am I a materialist after all, I wondered?"[31]

We have become so accustomed to a sort of Cartesian or Platonic diminution of the body, in the name of "Christianity," that we too might find ourselves scandalized by the embodiedness of Christian faith. And yet there is no Christian worship that is not material, that doesn't put bodies through motions and routines, that doesn't at some point evoke the body on the cross in (at the very least) the memory of the bread. Even if the content of our worship is bent on making us modern Platonic despisers of the body who long to become a vapor, the very gathering of a people at a certain time in a certain place to perform together certain acts—to (at the very least) sing with our tongues and lungs, read with our eyes, listen with our ears, pray with our voices, embrace one another in the foyer, nibble on crackers and sip grape juice—the very performance of Christian worship mitigates against such dualism. The Christian materialism that Sarah names is not just something confined to Catholicism; it is inextricably part of any sort of Christian worship, even in its "lowest" forms.[32] Participation in Christian worship is a performative opposition to "angelism," and it can't help but constitute a subtle training of our imagination to be disposed to bodies and materiality—to the stuff of God's good creation—in a mode of fundamental affirmation.

It's easy enough to find this sacramental imagination pictured in Catholic novelists like Graham Greene, Flannery O'Connor, and Evelyn Waugh; in the fantastic, enchanted worlds of J. R. R. Tolkien or C. S. Lewis; or in the Anglo-Catholic poetry of Herbert and Hopkins. But we can also find something similar in surprising places too. I have been most moved by the testimony to this sacramental affirmation in a rather surprising site: the poetry of Anne Sexton. In particular, consider her poem "Welcome Morning."

30. Ibid., 88–89.
31. Ibid., 89.
32. This is why Christian "materialism" (i.e., sacramentality) sometimes feels as if it teeters on the brink of paganism and superstition—because it sees the world as charged with the glory and grandeur of God. Thus later in the novel, a priest confides to Maurice, "I'm not against a bit of superstition. It gives people the idea that this world's not everything. . . . It could be the beginning of wisdom" (ibid., 146).

There is joy
in all:
in the hair I brush each morning,
in the Cannon towel, newly washed,
that I rub my body with each morning,
in the chapel of eggs I cook
each morning,
in the outcry from the kettle
that heats my coffee
each morning,
in the spoon and the chair
that cry "hello there, Anne"
each morning,
in the godhead of the table
that I set my silver, plate, cup upon
each morning.

All this is God,
right here in my pea-green house
each morning
and I mean,
though often forget,
to give thanks,
to faint down by the kitchen table
in a prayer of rejoicing
as the holy birds at the kitchen window
peck into their marriage of seeds.

So while I think of it,
let me paint a thank-you on my palm
for this God, this laughter of the morning,
lest it go unspoken.

The Joy that isn't shared, I've heard,
dies young.[33]

Such a sacramental imagination can make people nervous: it wavers on the edge, we worry, of confusing God with his creation.[34] But while the doctrine police get worried about blurring the Creator/creature distinction and thus position themselves at a distance from this enchanted space, they unwittingly evacuate the world of its charge and grandeur. In the name of avoiding the so-called paganism they find here, they end

33. In Sexton, *Complete Poems*, 455.
34. Leonard Vander Zee wards off this worry in *Christ, Baptism, and the Lord's Supper*, 22–23.

up with a flattened "nature" that is only a symbol or pointer rather than being creation that is charged with the Spirit's presence which makes it *more* than material. But that is the worry of those who lack imagination, who think truth only adheres in propositions and doctrines. At the end of the day, we shouldn't be surprised that it is poets who better intuit and express the elements of a Christian social imaginary and the sacramental imagination.

However, the sacramental imagination does come with some of its own challenges and temptations. I'll note just two. First, there is the curious possibility that the sacramentality learned in Christian worship, teaching us the goodness of creation and the sacramentality of the world, could end up marginalizing the church. The goodness of creation implicit in the sacramentality of worship could paradoxically lead to a kind of dissemination of the Spirit into the world in such a way that the church is left empty, leveled as just one more site of God's presence ("nothin' special"). If all the world is a sacrament, then who needs the church's liturgy? If the whole world is a sacrament, then what's so special about the Eucharist? (There is an analogue of this: If all of life is worship, including the life of the mind, then one might just as well spend time in the library as the chapel. Even if we might not *say* these things, sometimes our actions say quite enough.) In this respect, Aristotle Papanikolaou makes a helpful distinction in terms of *degrees*: "Although all of creation is sacramental, not all of creation is sacramental to the same degree."[35] I think we could extend this to understand the enduring and unique significance of the sacraments and the church's worship life as sites of a special presence of the Spirit that is both revelatory and formative in a unique way. While the whole world is a sacrament, we might say that *the* sacraments and the liturgy are unique "hot spots" where God's formative, illuminating presence is particularly "intense."[36] While the Spirit inhabits all of creation,

35. Aristotle Papanikolaou, "Liberating Eros: Confession and Desire," *Journal of the Society of Christian Ethics* 26 (2006): 126.
36. Before reading Papanikolaou, Amos Yong had already pressed me on a similar matter, asking how my account of Radical Orthodoxy's emphasis on a "participatory" ontology could be coupled with such a strong sense of antithesis and claims that the church is a unique *polis*. See Amos Yong, "Radically Orthodox, Reformed, and Pentecostal: Rethinking the Intersection of Post/Modernity and the Religions with James K. A. Smith," *Journal of Pentecostal Theology* 15 (2007): 233–50. In response, I suggested that we might think about this in terms of a continuum of participation that recognizes different *intensities* of participation (see James K. A. Smith, "The Spirit, the Religions, and the World as Sacrament: A Response to Amos Yong's Pneumatological Assist," *Journal of Pentecostal Theology* 15 [2007]: 251–61, esp. 256). A paradigmatic example of this would be regeneration: all human beings are created in the image of God, "participate" in God, and are sacramental

there is also a sense that the Spirit's presence is intensified in particular places, things, and actions.[37]

This intensity is suggested in the very words of institution of the Eucharist: "*This* is my body." Jesus didn't look around the room or out the window and abstractly announce, "Behold, the goodness of all creation. Look, remember, believe. These are the gifts of God for the people of God." Such a statement would be perfectly *true*; creation *is* just such a mediation of God's presence. But in addition to that truth, we also need to note that Jesus takes up particular things from creation and endues them with a sense of *special* presence, an especially intense presence. In this way Jesus seems to establish particular hot spots of sacramentality within a good creation, while also ordaining particularly packed practices. This selective intensity suggests that the affirmation that all the world is a sacrament is not meant to thereby level "the sacraments." In the same way, the affirmation that all of life is worship—that *all things* can be done to the glory of God—should not level the particular intensity of worship as the "work of the people" that especially praises God and forms us in unique, particularly intense ways.

If one temptation is to level the sacraments in the name of the sacramentality of the world, a second is the temptation to naturalize the liturgy as *just* an embodied practice like any other (another kind of leveling).[38] Sometimes our emphasis on liturgy as a formative, embodied practice that shapes us runs the risk of construing this as a wholly natural or immanent process—as if the formation of disciples in Christian worship operates in much the same way as the formation of Manny Ramirez as an excellent hitter through bodily rituals of batting practice. While worship is entirely embodied, it is not *only* material; and though worship is wholly natural, it is never *only* natural. Christian worship is nothing less than an invita-

---

images of God. But not all do so in the same way or to the same degree (which is why the *imago Dei* is a *task*, not a property; we'll discuss this further in chapter 5).

37. Vander Zee, following Michael Horton, makes the distinction between "sacramentality" and "sacraments" by emphasizing that the latter are also "ordinances"—particular things and actions taken up by Jesus and to which are attached promises (*Christ, Baptism, and the Lord's Supper*, 23). Or, as Horton puts it, "A sacrament not only reveals, it confers" (cited at ibid.). As a result, both restrict the sacraments to the Word, baptism, and the Lord's Supper. I refuse to take a strong line on this, since it seems to me, for instance, that my wife's love for me not only "reveals" God's love, but it also "confers" it and is a sacramental channel of God's grace—indeed, the most powerful expression of sanctifying grace in my life. Thus I find myself in fundamental sympathy with Schmemann's remarkable chapter on the orthodox sacrament of marriage (*For the Life of the World*, 81–94). However, though I'm not quite as worried about the mathematics regarding the number of sacraments, the notion of the church's sacraments as "hot spots" of the Spirit's gracious presence still gives these "ordinances" a privileged place in the life of discipleship.

38. My thanks to Doug Harink for pressing me on what follows.

tion to participate in the life of the triune God. In short, the centrality of embodiment should not be understood as a "naturalizing" of worship that would deny the dynamic presence of the Spirit; to the contrary, the Spirit meets, nourishes, transforms, and empowers us just *through* and *in* such material practices.

The church's worship is a uniquely intense site of the Spirit's transformative presence. We must never lose sight of the charged nature of these practices.[39] These are not just rituals that are unique because they are aimed at a different *telos*; they are also unique because they are practices that bring us face-to-face with the living God. If, in the context of this book, we have tended to focus on the formative power of Christian worship, we do well to remember that, in a sense, even this is a by-product of the fundamental aim of worship, which is praise and adoration of the triune God. The point of worship is not formation; rather, formation is an overflow effect of our encounter with the Redeemer in praise and prayer, adoration and communion. As Marva Dawn articulates, it is God who is both the subject and the object of our worship; the whole point of "liturgical lines and rituals" is to create "a powerful environment of God-centeredness."[40] Worship is not *for me*—it's not primarily meant to be an experience that "meets my felt needs," nor should we merely reduce it to a pedagogy of desire (which would be just a more sophisticated *pro me* construal of worship); rather, worship is about and for God. To say that God is both subject and object is to emphasize that the triune God is both the audience and the agent[41] of

39. Indeed, in chapter 3 I suggested that not even "secular" liturgies are wholly natural; they are animated by "the powers" that give them a different kind of "charge" that might even be demonic. This will return in our consideration of baptismal renunciations or "exorcisms" in chapter 5.

40. Marva J. Dawn, *Reaching Out without Dumbing Down: A Theology of Worship for the Turn-of-the-Century Culture* (Grand Rapids: Eerdmans, 1995), 79. In contrast to this, sometimes the grammar of our worship says something very different. For instance, consider the number of worship choruses that make "I" (the worshiper) the subject of the sentence rather than God. Thus, unwittingly, we actually end up singing about ourselves— *our* devotion, *our* worship, *our* surrender—rather than about God.

41. Nicholas Wolterstorff suggests that "the medieval Western liturgy" against which the Reformers reacted was beset by its own kind of "naturalization" insofar as it "was a liturgy in which, to an extraordinary degree, the action of God in the liturgy was lost from view. The actions were all human. The priest addressed God. The priest brought about Christ's bodily, but static, presence. . . . But God as agent is nowhere in view." Thus this sort of sacramentalism is "a sacramentalism of God's static presence" rather than one "of God's active doing." See Wolterstorff, "The Reformed Liturgy," in *Major Themes in the Reformed Tradition*, ed. Donald McKim (Grand Rapids: Eerdmans, 1992), 287, 288. Apropos of this, Peter Leithart criticizes the "zoom lens" approach to worship, which treats the sacraments as something to be *seen*, as symbols that merely "picture" something for us as spectators. In contrast, he reminds us that "the operative command in connection with the Supper is not 'Reflect on this' but 'Do this.'" See Peter J. Leithart, "The Way

worship: it is *to* and *for* God, and God is active *in* worship in the Word and sacraments. It is this emphasis on action, and particularly God's action in worship, that Wolterstorff distills as the "genius" of Reformed worship. "The liturgy as the Reformers understood and practiced it consists of God acting and us responding through the work of the Spirit." As such,

> the Reformers saw the liturgy as *God's action and our faithful reception of that action.* The governing idea of the Reformed liturgy is thus twofold: the conviction that to participate in the liturgy is to enter the sphere of God's acting, not just of God's presence, plus the conviction that we are to appropriate God's action in faith and gratitude through the work of the Spirit. . . . The liturgy is a meeting between God and God's people, a meeting in which both parties act, but in which God initiates and we respond.[42]

Emphasizing the material conditions of worship, and the formation that is effected by participation in such practices, is not meant to be a naturalization of worship but rather to honor the incarnational nature of God's dealing with humanity: that worship is a mediated encounter with the triune God, who condescends to meet us in the stuff of which we are made. And in and through that stuff, God is active.

Excursus: The Shape of Christian Worship

Now, you might find that your own experience of Christian worship doesn't exactly track with what I have described so far or what I'll articulate in the next chapter. For instance, you might find that I draw on particular forms or elements that are not common in your experience of Christian worship. Some of the language—terms like *Eucharist* or *benediction*—may not be familiar to you. Or worship at your church may not include specific elements of confession or recitation of the Apostles' Creed. "Worship" at your church might just refer to a time of music and singing that precedes the sermon. You might find that I draw on historical forms of worship that you've traditionally thought of as *liturgical* or "high church." You may even be a little suspicious about all this talk of ritual and liturgy and

---

Things Really Ought to Be: Eucharist, Eschatology, and Culture," *Westminster Theological Journal* 59 (1997): 176.

42. Wolterstorff, "Reformed Liturgy," 290–91, emphasis original. He goes on to emphasize that "the liturgy is the *continuation* of God's action in the world, and, in turn, God's action in the world is the *continuation* of God's action in the liturgy" (291). I worry that such a claim *can* (though need not) run in the direction of the leveling I've described above; on the other hand, as we've also discussed above, there is a sense in which the special presence and action of God in the sacraments is an intensification of a general presence and action of God in creation ("sacramentality").

sacraments. I can understand that; I think I know where you're coming from. But don't check out just yet. Let me try to assuage your concerns by noting a couple things in this regard.

First, it is not only high-church or liturgical contexts that are liturgical and formative. All Christian worship—whether Anglican or Anabaptist, Pentecostal or Presbyterian—is liturgical in the sense that it is governed by norms, draws on a tradition, includes bodily rituals or routines, and involves formative practices. For instance, though Pentecostal worship is often considered to be the antithesis of liturgy, it actually includes many of the same elements: charismatic worship is very embodied (hands raised in praise, kneeling at the altar in prayer, laying on hands in hope, etc.); it has a common, unwritten routine ("praise" music, followed by quieter "worship" music, followed by the sermon and then often "altar time"); and these practices of Pentecostal worship are deeply formative, shaping our imagination to relate to the world in a unique way. In this sense, even Pentecostal worship is liturgical; indeed, as we've emphasized above, Christian worship can't help but be embodied and material. So when I speak of worship as liturgical, I don't necessarily mean to favor a particular *style* of worship; rather, the emphasis is on the formative, embodied practices that constitute Christian worship—and many of these are shared across a diversity of styles, denominations, and theological traditions.[43] While it might not have a printed worship aid listing all the terms (e.g., Benediction, Prayers of the People, Eucharist, etc.), many of the elements of Christian worship I'll discuss below are nonetheless present. If you are used to worship contexts that don't use this lingo or these concepts, I still encourage you to pay careful attention to what happens in worship at your church to see whether most of these elements are nonetheless present. To that end, terms like *gathering, benediction, Eucharist,* and so on can function as a shorthand for us to recognize certain common elements of Christian worship.

Second, while I want to work with a generous understanding of worship and liturgy, this does not mean that all services of Christian worship would include the elements I'll describe below. Here I have to admit rather unapologetically that I think this is a problem: insofar as Christian worship doesn't include some of these elements, this represents a loss. In other words, I'm drawing on some of the historical riches of the church's worship in order to also invite us to rethink what our "services" look like. Here I try to explicate *catholic* (universal, historical)[44] elements of

43. For a lucid introduction to a generous understanding of Christian worship, see the prologue to *The Worship Sourcebook* (Grand Rapids: Calvin Institute of Christian Worship/Faith Alive Christian Resources/Baker Books, 2004), 15–28.

44. These have been described as the "constant norms for Christian worship that transcend cultures and keep us faithful to the gospel of Christ. Especially in an age that constantly focuses on worship style, it is crucial for all leaders to rehearse these transcultural, common

Christian worship that, over time, have been judged as essential aspects of the gathered body of Christ in its praise and worship of the triune God. The elements I describe below are by no means exhaustive (for instance, I don't speak about footwashing or pay close attention to aspects of church architecture), but I do hope that it is comprehensive in some way. These elements are deemed crucial parts of Christian worship precisely because they are essential showings (rather than tellings) of the gospel of Christ and because they are crucial aspects of training-by-doing, opportunities for practicing and rehearsing what it means to be the people of God, who desire the kingdom of God. To lose any element is to risk losing an element of the gospel of grace—and so to lose an opportunity for *counter*-formation vis-à-vis the secular liturgies we've described.

In this respect, I think it is important to own up to the fact that perhaps some of our worship habits are a missed opportunity; that we fail to draw on the formative riches of the tradition and thereby shut down channels for the Spirit's work. I think we need to be honest that Christians in North America (and elsewhere) have perhaps developed some bad habits in this regard. We may have construed worship as a primarily didactic, cognitive affair and thus organized it around a *message* that fails to reach our embodied hearts, and thus fails to touch our *desire*. Or we may have construed worship as a refueling event—a chance primarily to get what I "need" to make it through the week (perhaps with a top-up on Wednesday night), with the result that worship is more about *me* than about God, more about individual fulfillment than about the constitution of a people. Or we may have reduced gathered worship to evangelism and outreach, pushing us to drop some of the stranger elements of liturgy in order to be relevant and accessible. In all these cases, we'll notice that some key elements of the church's liturgical tradition drop out. Key historical practices are left behind. While we might be inclined to think of this as a way to update worship and make it contemporary, my concern is that in the process we lose key aspects of formation and discipleship. In particular, we lose precisely those worship practices that function as *counter*-formations to the liturgies of the mall, the stadium, and the frat

---

criteria for Christian worship and to actively seek to practice them faithfully" (*Worship Sourcebook*, 15). I would add that these criteria are "transcultural" *not* because they are acultural or ahistorical realities that dropped down from heaven, but precisely because they are part of the church *as* a distinct culture. They are contingent, historical, cultural formations—the fruit of human *poiēsis* like all other cultural phenomena—that the Spirit takes up and embraces. The incarnational God is not scandalized by such particularity; rather, the God who becomes flesh is the same God who embraces such historical, cultural contingency and takes it up into the life of the body. While some charges of Euro-centrism or liturgical colonialism have merit, affirming the logic of Incarnation requires affirming this scandal of the church's *cultural* particularity as a peculiar people.

house. We also lose a sense that worship is the "work of the people"—
that the "work of praise" is something we can only do *as a people* who
are an eschatological foretaste of the coming kingdom of God. In short,
we lose the sense in which Christian worship is also political: it marks us
out as and trains us to be a peculiar people who are citizens of another
city and subjects of a coming King.

The chapter that follows is meant to be a first exegesis of the Christian
social imaginary that is embedded in the practices of Christian worship.[45]
For those who find all these elements familiar, it is offered as an explication
of the irreducible understanding of the world that is implicit in Christian
worship and an invitation to consider how this can and should inform
the work of Christian scholarship, teaching, and the task of Christian
education (the focus of chapter 6). For those who might find some of these
elements strange or foreign, it is an invitation to discover the riches of the
church's ancient wisdom as embedded in worship of the global body of
Christ—and perhaps an invitation to consider how these elements of the
gospel's enactment can and should be incorporated into your own worship contexts.

45. Chapter 5 could easily be quite a long book; each of the elements I discuss ever so
briefly have generated shelves and shelves of books. I will not pretend to offer the definitive
exegesis of the Christian social imaginary that is "carried" in the practices of Christian
worship, but I hope this first attempt at such a project will provide some hints and clues as
to how others could further and deepen it—as well as a model for reflecting on worship
that one could undertake weekly as part of one's preparation for and participation in
worship. In short, the admittedly brief hints provided here are meant to be an invitation
to further reflection. I hope that this first take is sufficient to outline the core elements of
the Christian social imaginary's vision of human flourishing. I encourage readers to study
this in tandem with a worship resource such as *The Worship Sourcebook*.

5

Practicing (for) the Kingdom

AN EXEGESIS OF THE SOCIAL IMAGINARY
EMBEDDED IN CHRISTIAN WORSHIP

I invite you to put on your Martian anthropologist glasses again so that you can come to this exegesis of Christian worship with fresh eyes. Try to put out of play your assumptions and settled ideas about these matters, and let's, as it were, creak open the front door of the church—it could be the glass door of a storefront chapel, the curtain of an Asian hut, or the mammoth wooden door of a European cathedral—and make our way inside. What's happening? What are these Christians *doing*? And what does this say about who they are? What kind of a people is this? What vision of the kingdom is embedded in their practices? What's the shape of the social imaginary that's carried in the diverse practices of Christian worship? What do these people *love*? What sort of kingdom do they desire?

Liturgical Time: Rhythms and Cadences of Hope

Before we even make it to our seats, we may notice the environment of worship.[1] In particular, we may note the colors that adorn the space. Here

---

1. Space does not permit me to engage questions regarding the built environment within which worship happens (of course, worship also happens in the open air, more often than our North American assumptions might guess). For a recent discussion, see

we already bump into an instance in which our exercise runs up against a limit, missing what would be particularly notable if we had a series of time-lapse photographic shots (like the ones you've seen of clouds passing or the sun setting) of this same space over the course of a year. We would see the colors changing over time—from deep, royal purple to mournful black to a shimmering, triumphant white. At one point we might see the worship service extinguished in the darkness of shadows, the people departing in somber silence and later welcomed back to a space filled with light. Banners and flags and images in the space would move and change. In short, just the space of worship would tell a story that actually organizes time—an indication that here dwells a people with a unique sense of *temporality*, who inhabit a time that is out of joint with the regular, mundane ticking of commercial time or the standard shape of the academic year.

While this is visually represented in the color and adornment of worship space, it is even more integrally reflected in the shape of the practices—in the focus of prayer, in the spiritual disciplines that are observed, in unique rituals that happen annually rather than weekly (e.g., the lighting of the Advent candles or the imposition of ashes). This people relates to time in a way that is unique and peculiar, expressed in what is known as the liturgical year or the Christian year.[2] If we read the practices of Christian worship, we would conclude that Christians are a people whose year doesn't simply map onto the calendar of the dominant culture. Tensions and differences will be felt differently in different cultures. It might seem that in the West, the Christian liturgical calendar maps squarely onto the "secular" calendar (or the Hallmark quasi-liturgical year), whereas we might assume more dissonance between the Christian year and the Chinese calendar. But things are a little more complicated. While the Western calendar clearly shows the marks of Christendom and thus shows vestiges of the Christian year, these similarities can easily mask more significant differences.

For example, as the commercialization of Christmas has the "season" of consumption creeping from Thanksgiving all the way back to Halloween, the Christian observation of Advent marks a different orientation to time, particularly when it is recognized that Advent is a *penitential* season of denial and self-examination rather than of accumulation, consumption, and self-indulgence. Or while Easter makes it onto the Hallmark calendar and the mall's quasi-liturgical year, Lent certainly does not. And maybe there is something at stake in having our Day-Timers begin the week with

Mark Torgerson, *An Architecture of Immanence: Architecture for Worship and Ministry Today* (Grand Rapids: Eerdmans, 2007).

2. For an accessible, inviting introduction, see Robert E. Webber, *Ancient-Future Time: Forming Spirituality through the Christian Year* (Grand Rapids: Baker Books, 2004).

Sunday.[3] Thus the distinct marking of time that is integral to historic Christian worship establishes a sense that the church is a "peculiar people," and the liturgical calendar already constitutes a formative matrix that functions as *counter*-formation to the incessant 24/7-ness of our frenetic commercial culture.[4]

How so? What's so peculiar about Christian time? First, time here revolves around a person—Jesus of Nazareth, a first-century Jew who "suffered under Pontius Pilate, was crucified, died, and was buried. He descended into hell. And the third day he rose again from the dead. He ascended into heaven." The Apostles' Creed itself locates Jesus *in time*, in the historical reign of Pontius Pilate. The church is not a people gathered by abstract ideas or teachings or ideals; it is a people gathered to the historical person Jesus Christ. The church is a Messiah-people who worship a God who broke into and inhabited time, who suffered at the hands of historical regimes, and who rose "on the third day." They are gathered as a people to worship the Messiah, who does not float in some esoteric, ahistorical heaven, but who made a dent on the calendar—and will again.

Second, as a messianic people, the church is a people who inhabit the present with a certain lightness of being. If we are strangers and pilgrims in a foreign territory (1 Peter 2:11), then we are also pilgrims in a strange time—who will always relate to the present a bit like a time traveler (I can't shake pictures of Marty in *Back to the Future*). Resisting a presentism that can only imagine "living for the moment," the church is a people with a deeply ingrained orientation to the future, a habit we learn from Israel. During Advent each year, the Christian year teaches us to once again become Israel, recognizing our sin and need, thus waiting, longing, hoping, calling, praying for the coming of the Messiah, the advent of justice, and the in-breaking of *shalom*. We go through the ritual of desiring the kingdom—a kind of holy impatience—by reenacting Israel's longing for the coming of the King. The repetition of this year after year is a training in expectation (and it is replayed each week of the year in the celebration of the Eucharist, by which we "proclaim the Lord's death until he comes"). Thus Advent shakes us out of the presentist complacency that we can be lulled into. Instead, we are called and formed to be a people of *expectancy*—looking for the coming (again) of the Messiah. We are a futural people who will

3. On Sabbath-keeping as a potent Christian practice of counter-formation, see Marva Dawn, *Keeping the Sabbath Wholly: Ceasing, Resting, Embracing, Feasting* (Grand Rapids: Eerdmans, 1989); Norman Wirzba, *Living the Sabbath: Discovering the Rhythms of Rest and Delight* (Grand Rapids: Brazos, 2006).

4. For a succinct articulation of this, see Scott Waalkes, "Celebrating the Church Year as a Constructive Response to Globalization," in *After Modernity? Secularity, Globalization, and the Re-enchantment of the World*, ed. James K. A. Smith (Waco: Baylor University Press, 2008), chapter 11.

not seek to escape the present, but will always sit somewhat uneasy in the present, haunted by the brokenness of the "now."

The future we hope for—a future when justice rolls down like waters and righteousness like an ever-flowing stream—hangs over our present and gives us a vision of what to work for in the here and now as we continue to pray, "Your kingdom come." The temporality of Christian worship—macrocosmically expressed in the Christian year, microcosmically expressed in particular elements each Sunday—trains our imagination to be eschatological, looking forward *not* to the end of the world but to "the end of the world *as we know it.*"[5] In worship, we taste "the powers of the age to come" (Heb. 6:5), which births in us a longing for that kingdom to come, because this taste is also a bit of a teaser: it gives us enough of a sense of what's coming that we look around at our broken world and see all the ways that the kingdom has not yet arrived. "Come, Lord Jesus!" and "How long, O Lord?!" are both prayers of a futural people.

At the same time, the rhythms of Christian worship and the liturgical year stretch us backward. They are practices of remembering—another habit we learn from Israel. We remember with gratitude God's acts of redemption in the exodus (Ps. 78) and the cross. Lent and Easter invite us backward to remember the power unleashed in the cross and resurrection—a power that continues to break into the present (Phil. 3:10–11). The Christian year itself is an ancient inheritance reminding us that we are part of a people that is older than our present, that we are heirs of tradition. Thus we are constituted as a people who live between times, remembering and hoping at the same time. Each week this between-ness is performed in the Eucharist, which both invites us to "Do this in remembrance of me" and by doing so to "proclaim the Lord's death until he comes."

Charles Taylor thus notes a distinct difference between what he calls "secular time" and the "higher times" that is embedded in the Christian liturgical year. The liturgical year, he notes, draws on a kind of time consciousness for which "profane time existed in relation to (surrounded by, penetrated by; it is hard to find the right words here) higher times." There is a sense that the "here and now" is hooked up to *other* times—past, future, and "higher."[6] "Modern secularization," then, "can be seen from one angle as the rejection of higher times and the positing of time as purely profane." In particular, time becomes one-dimensional, issuing in what we've called *presentism* or what Taylor describes as the "modern notion of simultaneity," in which

---

5. Michael Horton, *A Better Way: Rediscovering the Drama of God-Centered Worship* (Grand Rapids: Baker Books, 2002), 127. Cf. R. E. M., "The End of the World as We Know It," on *Eponymous*.

6. Charles Taylor, *Modern Social Imaginaries* (Durham, NC: Duke University Press, 2004), 97–98.

events utterly unrelated in cause or meaning are held together simply by their co-occurrence at the same point in this single profane time line. Modern literature, as well as news media, seconded by social science, have accustomed us to think of society in terms of vertical time slices, holding together myriad happenings, related and unrelated. . . . This is a typically modern mode of social imagination, which our medieval forebears would have found difficult to understand, for where events in profane time are very differently related to a higher time, it seems unnatural just to group them side by side in the modern relation of simultaneity.[7]

We might describe this as the CNN-ization of time: a frenetic pursuit of "breaking news" that merely fixates on what has just happened before others have got the scoop. The thrilling drug of novelty is drunk deeply by such presentism; but it is a narcotic with diminishing returns. At stake here is a forgetting of "higher times" and the stretching of liturgical time. While such CNN-ized time is hungry for what will happen next, strangely it fails to be expectant about the future. It is an orientation to what's coming that lacks hope; instead, it simply records the onslaught of events.

There is a sense in which Christians are trained by the liturgy to be a people "untimely born," as Paul says of himself (1 Cor. 15:8). This is not because we are traditionalists who slavishly and nostalgically long for the old ways (Jer. 6:16). However, there is a deep sense in which the church is a people called to resist the presentism embedded in the tyranny of the contemporary. We are called to be a people of memory, who are shaped by a tradition that is millennia older than the last Billboard chart. And we are also called to be a people of expectation, praying for and looking forward to a coming kingdom that will break in upon our present as a thief in the night. We are a *stretched* people, citizens of a kingdom that is both older and newer than anything offered by "the contemporary." The practices of Christian worship over the liturgical year form in us something of an "old soul" that is perpetually pointed to a future, longing for a coming kingdom, and seeking to be such a stretched people in the present who are a foretaste of the coming kingdom.

Call to Worship: An Invitation to Be Human

Let's return to our worship setting. The milieu of the space—its color and adornment—has given us an indication of the unique temporality of this peculiar people. But the very next thing we should consider is something that easily slips from notice: the very fact that we're here—that on a Sunday morning, one of the few times that the city's streets are quiet and even

7. Ibid., 98.

the steady hum of consumption and production gets a bit quieter, here we find people streaming into a space to gather for worship of the triune God. Singles and families, seniors and toddlers, make the effort to gather together at an appointed time not of their choosing. We could be still snug in our beds at home, or enjoying the *New York Times Magazine* with a coffee on our front porch. But instead we are part of—let's be honest—a rather motley crew that has made its way here. Families have wrestled with children to make them presentable, and some probably argued in the car on the way here; students have perhaps only just felt the warmth of bed after a Saturday night of entertainment when they "have" to emerge, bleary-eyed, to "go to church"; senior citizens who find themselves secluded in nursing homes have been craving this day all week, when a deacon or friend drops by to pick them up to gather with the saints for worship.

Week after week, for millennia and around the globe, a peculiar people is gathered by a *call* to worship—a call that, in a sense, goes out before the service even begins, but that is then formally declared in the opening of the service in the "call to worship," often from the Psalms:

> Come, let us bow down in worship,
> let us kneel before the LORD our Maker;
> for he is our God
> and we are the people of his pasture,
> the flock under his care. (Ps. 95:6–7 NIV)

or

> Hallelujah!
> Praise! Praise God in the temple, in the highest heavens!
> Praise! Praise God's mighty deeds and noble majesty.
> All that is alive, praise!
> Praise the Lord.
> Hallelujah! (Ps. 150:1–2)[8]

The rather mundane fact that people show up is, however, an indicator of something fundamental: that a people has gathered in response to a call. "Whenever we gather for public worship," Horton declares, "it is because we have been summoned. That is what 'church' means: *ekklēsia*, 'called out.'"[9] It is not a voluntary society of those whose chief concern is to share, to build community, to enjoy fellowship, to have moral instruction

---

8. International Committee on English in the Liturgy, *The Psalter: A Faithful and Inclusive Rendering from the Hebrew into Contemporary English Poetry, Intended Primarily for Communal Song and Recitation* (Chicago: Liturgy Training Publications, 1995).

9. The New Testament term for the church is *ekklēsia*, from the verb *kaleō* (to call) and the preposition *ek-* (out). So the church is a called-out assembly.

for their children. Rather, it is a society of those who have been chosen, redeemed, called, justified, and are being sanctified until one day they will be glorified."[10] The very fact that we gather says something, implicitly trains our imagination in a way. "Gathering indicates that Christians are called from the world, from their homes, from their families, to be constituted into a community capable of praising God. . . . The church is constituted as a new people who have been gathered from the nations to remind the world that we are in fact one people. Gathering, therefore, is an eschatological act as it is the foretaste of the unity of the communion of the saints."[11]

There is a certain hint of scandal here, of a reality that cuts against the grain of our late-modern liberal sensibilities: for as we're making our way to worship, not everyone is coming. Our neighbor's home might still be quiet and darkened; folks down the street might already be mowing their lawn; we might walk softly through the dormitory hall because many of our peers won't emerge for hours; we may even be leaving family members in our own home who don't answer this call to worship, this summons to gather. Since we, on our own, don't have the inclination or ability to answer the call, our response in gathering is already a sign of God's redemption and regeneration at work. But the neighbors and strangers we pass on the way also remind us that God's peculiar people is also a *chosen* people (1 Peter 2:9), called out from among the nations, graced "without why," elected to be a renewed people *for* this still-sleeping world.

There is also another scandal that we experience in gathering: we will notice that others are gathering for worship in a different space just down the street; as we make our way to "our" church, other Christians are making their way to "their" church right in the same neighborhood. And we may also notice a tragic pattern that seems to emerge: those streaming into our church look like "us"—an "us" defined by a similar race or class or ethnicity—whereas those making their way into the neighboring church don't look like "us" (though they, too, all look like each other). Right here, just as we're responding to the call to gather for worship, we already experience the *eschatological* nature of what we're about to do, for our "gathering" does not look like that of which we'll sing, a congregation that can sing a new song to the Lamb upon the throne:

> You are worthy to take the scroll
> and to open its seals,
> for you were slaughtered and by your blood

10. Horton, *Better Way*, 24.

11. Stanley Hauerwas, "Liturgical Shape of the Christian Life: Teaching Christian Ethics as Worship," in *In Good Company: The Church as Polis* (Notre Dame, IN: University of Notre Dame Press, 1995), 157.

> you ransomed for God
> saints from every tribe and language and people and nation;
> you have made them to be a kingdom
> and priests serving our God,
> and they will reign on earth. (Rev. 5:9–10)

But *our* congregation doesn't look like this kingdom from every tribe and tongue and nation. And yet we'll sing of it, in confession and in hope. We know that this is the sort of people we are called to be, and because of this, our current not-yet gatherings will have to constantly confess their failures (that we are "a broken communion in a broken world"),[12] seek forgiveness, plead for mercy to undo these fractures, and yet "marvel that the Lord gathers the broken pieces to do his work."[13] Our gathering is an act of eschatological hope that amounts to a kind of defiance: while the faces and colors of our gathered congregation might constantly remind us that the kingdom remains to come, the Spirit also invites us to overcome, reminding us that, despite the failures internal to our gatherings, at the same time the worldwide chorus looks miraculously like this kingdom choir—prompting us to become a people that looks more and more like the "great multitude that no one could count, from every nation, from all tribes and peoples and languages, standing before the throne and before the Lamb," who together sing *one* song: "Salvation belongs to our God who is seated on the throne, and to the Lamb!" (Rev. 7:9–10).

We've hardly even done anything yet! We've merely showed up and heard the call to worship, but already we've glimpsed what is implicit in this action. Embedded in our gathering in response to this call is an implicit understanding of what is required for human flourishing. To be human is to be *called*. But called to what? Gathered for what? The congregation gathers in response to a call to *worship*, which is the fundamental vocation of being human. God is calling out and constituting a people who will look "peculiar"[14] in this broken world because they have been called to be renewed image bearers of God (Gen. 1:27–28)—to take up and reembrace our creational vocation, now empowered by the Spirit to do so. So this is not just a call to do something "religious," something to be merely added to our "normal" life. It is a call to be(come) *human*, to take up the

---

12. *Our World Belongs to God: A Contemporary Testimony* (Grand Rapids: Christian Reformed Church in North America, 2008), §43. Available online at http://www.crcna.org/pages/our_world_main.cfm.

13. Ibid.

14. The provocative notion of the church as a "peculiar people" is an echo of the KJV translation of Titus 2:14: "Who gave himself for us, that he might redeem us from all iniquity, and purify unto himself a peculiar people, zealous of good works." See also Rodney Clapp, *A Peculiar People: The Church as Culture in a Post-Christian Society* (Downers Grove, IL: InterVarsity, 1996).

vocation of being fully and authentically human, and to be a community and people who image God to the world. This call to worship is an echo of God's word that called humanity into being (Gen. 1:26–27); the call of God that brought creation into existence is echoed in God's call to worship that brings together a *new* creation (2 Cor. 5:17). And our calling as "new creatures" in Christ is a restatement of Adam and Eve's calling: to be God's image bearers to and for the world.

The "image of God" (*imago Dei*) is not some de facto property of *Homo sapiens* (whether will or reason or language or what have you); rather, the image of God is a *task*, a *mission*. As Richard Middleton comments, "The *imago Dei* designates the royal office or calling of human beings as God's representatives and agents in the world, granted authorized power to share in God's rule or administration of the earth's resources and creatures."[15] We are commissioned as God's image bearers, his vice-regents, charged with the task of "ruling"[16] and caring for creation, which includes the task of cultivating it, unfolding and unfurling its latent possibilities through human making—in short, through *culture*. "Imaging God thus involves representing and perhaps extending in some way God's rule on earth through ordinary communal practices of human sociocultural life."[17] Thus when, in the literary context of Genesis, God sets humanity in creation as his image bearer, it evokes images of a sort of priestly ambassador of the creation. "For just as no pagan temple in the ancient Near East could be complete without the installation of the cult image of the deity to whom the temple was dedicated, so creation in Genesis 1 is not complete (or 'very good') until God creates humanity on the sixth day as *imago Dei*, in order to represent and mediate the divine presence on earth."[18] But in this case it is creation that is the sanctuary, and humanity is commissioned "to liturgical service in the cosmic sanctuary."[19] To take up the task of being God's image bearer is both *cultural* work and *cultic* work; it is to be both prince/ss and priest.[20]

The very reason that we are gathered for worship under the cross is because of humanity's fundamental failure to carry out the task and mis-

---

15. J. Richard Middleton, *The Liberating Image: The* Imago Dei *in Genesis 1* (Grand Rapids: Brazos, 2005), 27. In what follows, I am entirely indebted to Middleton's brilliant analysis.

16. Middleton makes a careful case for the "royal" connotation of "image," in ibid., 50–55.

17. Ibid., 60.

18. Ibid., 87.

19. Ibid.

20. Middleton remarks that "the *imago Dei* also includes a priestly or cultic dimension"; so "the human vocation as *imago Dei* in God's world thus corresponds in important respects to Israel's vocation as a 'royal priesthood' among the nations (Exodus 19:6)" (ibid., 89–90).

sion of being the image of God. The *imago Dei* is not a thing or property that was lost (or retained); it was a calling and a vocation that Adam and Eve failed to carry out. Because of this failure to be God's vice-regents, God's cultural agents mediating his love and care for creation, a fundamental brokenness ruptures the world—and robs us of the ability to even measure up to the task. Thus God has to re-call and re-constitute a people for this task—a new call extended in Abraham, through Israel, called to be a peculiar nation among the nations, a people who would image what God's love for the world looks like. But they, too, failed in taking up this creational and human vocation. Thus the task of properly being God's image bearer is taken up and performed by the Son, who is "the image of the invisible God" (Col. 1:15). As the second Adam, Jesus shows us what it looks like to undertake that creational mission of being God's image bearer to and for the world.[21] Jesus takes up and completes the vocation of Israel, whose vocation was a recommissioning for the creational task of being God's image bearers.[22]

Thus Jesus is our exemplar of what it looks like to fulfill the cultural mandate. And he shows us what that looks like when the world is broken and violent: the shape of such image-bearing will be cruciform. Imaging God to this world we now inhabit—this world "between times," suspended between the "already" of Jesus's announcement of the kingdom and the "not yet" of its consummation—will require following Jesus's perfect image-bearing as the new Adam, an image-bearing that was not triumphant conquering *of* the world but submissive suffering *for* the world. This is central to Jesus's vocation of being the fullness of the image of God, thus accomplishing that creational task given to Adam—which remains our vocation as humans. As N. T. Wright provocatively puts it, "Jesus determined that it was his task and role, his vocation as Israel's representative, to lose the battle on Israel's behalf. This would be the means of Israel's becoming the light, not just of herself . . . but of the whole world."[23] If our vocation is to "follow Christ" as the way to take up our *human* vocation to be God's image bearers, then our image-bearing should look the same. "When we speak of 'following Christ,'" Wright cautions,

> it is the crucified Messiah we are talking about. His death was not simply the messy bit that enables our sins to be forgiven but that can then be forgotten.

---

21. Klaas Schilder rightly points out that as the second Adam, Christ is also the exemplar of what it looks like to carry out the cultural mandate. See Schilder, *Christ and Culture*, trans. G. van Rongen and W. Helder (Winnipeg, MB: Premier Printing, 1977), 47–48.

22. For an accessible and more detailed account of this story, for which I've provided only a thumbnail sketch, see N. T. Wright, *The Challenge of Jesus: Rediscovering Who Jesus Was and Is* (Downers Grove, IL: InterVarsity, 1999).

23. Ibid., 89.

The cross is the surest, truest, and deepest window on the very heart and character of the living and loving God. . . . And when therefore we speak . . . of shaping our world, we do not—we dare not—simply treat the cross as the thing that saves us "personally," but which can be left behind when we get on with the job. The task of shaping our world is best understood as the redemptive task of bringing the achievement of the cross to bear on the world, and in that task the methods, as well as the message, must be cross-shaped through and through.[24]

When we gather, we are responding to a call to worship; that call is an echo and renewal of the call of creation to be God's image bearers for the world, and we fulfill the *mission* of being God's image bearers by undertaking the work of culture making. In order for such cultural unfolding to be done well, it must find its animus and direction in a covenantal relationship with the Creator. This is why the call to worship is a call to a "covenant renewal ceremony."[25] Because of our sin—personally and collectively—our ability to undertake this vocation is lost; we lack the wisdom, discernment, and will to carry out the task. Thus God calls us to himself to find renewal, restoration, and reordering. We are called to an encounter with the life-giving God, who imparts transformative grace through the Spirit's empowerment, making it possible for us to entertain the vocation given to humanity at creation, but now with *more* than was given to Adam and Eve: with the perfect exemplar of Jesus, who shows us what it means to be human, and the empowerment of the indwelling Spirit, the fruit of the New Covenant (Rom. 8:1–11).

The congregation's response to the call to worship, after gathering, is the "invocation" of God's mercy and grace. We have a sense that we're in over our head; we've responded to a call—and even the response is by grace—to a vocation that we can't possibly fulfill on our own. In a strange and terrifying sense, the vocation of being human requires utter dependence on God; the task of being a creature requires being ordered to the Creator. Gathering as an answer to the call to worship is a displacement of any human self-confidence or presumption. Implicit in the very act of gathering is an understanding that human flourishing requires a dynamic

24. Ibid., 94–95. Michael Horton, from a Reformed perspective, echoes a similar point: "Jesus rules over a *kingdom of grace*, not yet a *kingdom of glory*. Just as he came in humiliation, suffering, and weakness, the kingdom advances not through the noisy or violent clashes of guns and tanks, nor through legislating the transformation of any earthly nation into God's chosen people" (*Better Way*, 129).

25. See ibid., 24; *The Worship Sourcebook* (Grand Rapids: Calvin Institute of Christian Worship/Faith Alive Christian Resources/Baker Books, 2004), 16; and John D. Witvliet, "Covenant Theology in Ecumenical Discussions of the Lord's Supper," in *Worship Seeking Understanding: Windows into Christian Practice* (Grand Rapids: Baker Academic, 2003), 67–89.

relationship with the Creator of humanity; in short, worship is at the heart of being human. The flourishing of creation—what the Scriptures describe as *shalom*—requires not only "right harmonious relationships" to other human beings and to nature, but also "right, harmonious relationships *to God* and delight in his service."[26] Thus as a called people, trying by the skin of our teeth to just measure up to being truly *human*, we invoke the grace of the covenant-making King:

> Lord, open to us the sea of your mercy,
> and water us with full streams
> from the riches of your grace
> and the springs of your kindness.
> Make us children of quietness and heirs of peace;
> kindle in us the fire of your love,
> and strengthen our weakness by your power
> as we become close to you and to each other. Amen.[27]

And God's delight is to answer.

God's Greeting and Mutual Greetings: Hospitality, Community, and Graced Dependence

I hope we have sensed just how charged the actions of Christian worship are, as already attested in our exegesis of the act of gathering in response to a call to worship. Please notice the emphasis on *action*: I'm not saying that this is what worship *means*, what it says or communicates if we step back and reflect on it as spectators. Instead, I'm suggesting that this is what *gets done* when we gather for worship; this is what's going on *in* the action, even if we don't stop to think about it. Of course, it's salutary to think about it, and reflection on what we do can deepen its significance.[28] But it is important also to keep in mind that worship is best understood on the order of action, not reflection; worship is something that we do. And even if we don't think about it in this reflective way—and even if some of us (children, the mentally handicapped) *can't* think about it in this way—the core claim of this book is that the practices of Christian worship *do* this work nonetheless because of the kind of creatures we are. The practices carry their own understanding that is implicit within them (*pace* Taylor), and that understanding can

---

26. Nicholas Wolterstorff, *Until Justice and Peace Embrace* (Grand Rapids: Eerdmans, 1983), 69–70.

27. From the Syrian Church, in *An Iona Prayer Book*, compiled by Peter W. Millar (Norwich, UK: Canterbury, 1998), 14. Used by permission.

28. Reflection is especially important for those who are responsible for *leading* worship, so that the rhythms and practices of worship are *intentional*.

be absorbed and imbibed in our imaginations without having to kick into a mode of cerebral reflection.[29] Reflection certainly deepens the doing; but the point is that there is always *more* happening: our imagination is being formed in ways that we are not (and perhaps cannot be) aware of. A way of construing the world becomes "automated," and this will affect our actions and behaviors outside the context of gathered worship in ways we don't always "think" about. In the action of gathering, there is a visceral training of our imagination that shapes how we subsequently think about our identity and our calling *as human*, in relation to God and in relation to others.

The same sort of education of desire happens in the next component of Christian worship, God's greeting to us. With hands raised, the minister extends God's welcome and blessing to the gathered congregation, who may receive the welcome and blessing with hands open in a spirit of mutual welcome and expectation. God's greeting is often extended in the language of Scripture:

> Grace to you and peace from him who is
> and who was and who is to come,
> and from the seven spirits who are before his throne,
> and from Jesus Christ, the faithful witness,
> the firstborn from the dead,
> and the ruler of the kings of the earth. (Rev. 1:4–5)

Or simply:

> The Lord be with you.
> *And also with you.* (based on Ruth 2:4)

29. I recognize that some might be uncomfortable with this claim, since it seems to suggest that there can be some sort of virtue in "going through the motions." On this point I'm afraid I have to confess that I do indeed think this is true. While it is not ideal, I do think that there can be a sort of implanting of the gospel that happens simply by virtue of participating in liturgical practices (this is in the ballpark of the principle of *ex opere operato*). For instance, one will often hear testimonies of those raised in the church, but who have strayed from the path of discipleship, nevertheless caught short by the cadences of the Apostles' Creed or the catechism while immersed in hedonistic pursuits of pleasure. The rhythms of the liturgy come back to haunt them, sometimes calling them back to a life of more intentional discipleship. Or one finds that their imagination—the very way they construe the world—is fundamentally shaped by Christian practices. This effect is documented in an illustrative way in Richard A. Blake, *Afterimage: The Indelible Catholic Imagination of Six American Filmmakers* (Chicago: Loyola, 2000). Blake uses the psychological term *afterimage*—"an image or sensation that remains or returns after the external stimulus has been removed"—to account for the persisting Catholic imagination that shapes the work of directors such as Martin Scorsese, John Ford, and Francis Ford Coppola. Even though they may reject the faith as such, their formation by Catholic liturgy and education nonetheless indelibly marks their imagination.

So having been called, we are welcomed.[30] The yearning for God that is implanted in us as creatures is not an instigation to strive after a deity who refuses to be caught; rather, the Creator in whom we find our "rest" is only all too eager to welcome us into communion. Like the father of the prodigal son who daily ventured to the end of the lane, looking for the wayward one to return, embracing him upon arrival, so God calls us and welcomes us at the very beginning of worship.

As part of that welcome, God extends a blessing to us, akin to the feast given for the prodigal son, but more importantly echoing the creational blessings of Genesis 1:28: After making humanity in his image, "God blessed them, and God said to them, 'Be fruitful and multiply, and fill the earth and subdue it; and have dominion over the fish of the sea and over the birds of the air and over every living thing that moves upon the earth.'" The blessing is both an affirmation and a conferral: at creation, God commissions humanity to be his image bearers by rightly ruling creation; in addition, the blessing confers God's power and sustenance.[31] Thus the creational blessing is a source of empowerment in both ways; it entrusts care for creation into the hands of humanity. The delegation of responsibility, as it were, is attended by gracious support. So, too, in the context of Christian worship: God's blessing is extended as both affirmation and empowerment to take up the calling to be human—to find one's identity and flourishing in relation to God in the context of creation. God summons us to worship not to scold us but to renew and restore us for our creational mandate, with which was promised flourishing and abundance. The blessing comes as a most welcome gift, even if a call is also implicit in it.

God's greeting indicates the dialogical nature of Christian worship, a give-and-take, back-and-forth interaction: God calls us; by his grace we respond by gathering, invoking his grace and mercy; and God in turn responds to our cry. This give-and-take indicates that we are dealing with a personal God who takes the initiative to engage in a relationship with humanity. It is an exchange of gifts that indicates God's gracious reciprocity. Implicit in this is also something fundamental about the nature of humanity: human flourishing is dependent upon our being oriented to and defined by this *relationship*. We are relational beings who are image bearers of a

30. For rich reflections on the theme of hospitality and worship, see Hans Boersma's meditations on evangelical hospitality, baptismal hospitality, eucharistic hospitality, and penitential hospitality in *Violence, Hospitality, and the Cross: Reappropriating the Atonement Tradition* (Grand Rapids: Baker Academic, 2004), 205–34.

31. The Hebrew term for "bless" in Gen. 1:28 means "to endue with power for success, prosperity, fecundity, longevity, etc.," transmitted from the greater to the lesser in order to "confer abundant and effective life upon something." See *Theological Wordbook of the Old Testament*, ed. R. Laird Harris (Chicago: Moody, 1980), 1:285.

relational God,[32] who graciously binds himself to us in a covenant from creation. And this relationship is not super-human; it does not go above and beyond what it means to be "merely" human. It is not a relationship that is a supplement to being a merely natural human being. Rather, because were are fundamentally *creatures*, being aimed at the Creator, so to speak, is a necessary condition for being fully or properly human. As Irenaeus put it, "The glory of God is a human being fully alive." Insofar as God calls us and welcomes us back into this relationship in Christian worship, what's going on in worship has relevance not just for my religious or spiritual life but also for my *human* life. God's greeting and welcome speaks to our fundamental dependence: that "in him we live and move and have our being" (Acts 17:28), and that this "him" is not a generic deity but the triune God, for it is in the Son that "all things hold together" (Col. 1:17). In short, God's welcome is a gracious way of reminding us of our utter dependence, cutting against the grain of myths of self-sufficiency that we've been immersed in all week long.

This dependence and lack of self-sufficiency is then often affirmed horizontally, as it were, by encouraging the congregation to greet one another, expressing welcome ("Good morning, welcome . . .") and extending blessing ("Christ be with you" or "The peace of Christ be with you").[33] Just as "we love because God first loved us" (1 John 4:19), so too we extend mutual greetings because God has welcomed us. As recipients of God's greeting, we become imitators of God by extending welcome to our neighbors and brothers and sisters. We are immediately reminded that worship is not a private affair; we have gathered as a people, as a congregation, and just as together we are dependent on our redeeming Creator, so too are we dependent on one another. All the parts of a body are dependent upon other parts and organs in order for the individual parts ("me") to function and flourish (1 Cor. 12:12–31). It is not only sin that makes us dependent upon others; our very finitude, as creatures, impels us to relationality because we need the gifts, talents, and resources of others. And such dependence is part of the very fiber of God's good creation. Worship is a space of welcome because we are, at root, relational creatures called into relationship with the Creator, in order to flourish as a people who bear his image to and for the world. In response to God's

---

32. God's relationality is not only extrinsic—a relation with humanity—it is also intrinsic, as seen in the trinitarian relations. For relevant discussion, see Miroslav Volf, "'The Trinity Is Our Social Program': The Doctrine of the Trinity and the Shape of Social Engagement," *Modern Theology* 41 (1998): 403–23.

33. In some worship traditions, a time of mutual greeting is known as "the passing of the peace" and is extended either after the assurance of pardon or during the celebration of the Lord's Supper.

gracious welcome, we practice hospitality in worship, which is practice for extending hospitality beyond it.[34]

Song: Hymning the Language of the Kingdom

At this point, and more than likely up to this point, Christian worship is usually animated by singing. But is this just adornment, something to jazz things up, shift gears, and give us a break from all the talking? Or is there something at stake in the people of God *singing*? While the church is often described as "a people of the book," isn't it the case that throughout its history it has also been a people of the *hymn*book? Could it be that there's something implicit here that is part of the fabric of the Christian social imaginary? We might suggest several features of singing that constitute elements of a Christian understanding of the world.

First, singing is a full-bodied action that activates the whole person—or at least more of the whole person than is affected by merely sitting and passively listening, or even reading and reciting texts. Singing requires us to call on parts of the body that might otherwise be rather dormant— stomach muscles and vocal chords, lungs and tongues. And since singing seems to tap into our joints and muscles, song often pulls us into dance or raising our hands in praise. Thus in song there is a performative affirmation of our embodiment, a marshaling of it for expression—whether beautiful songs of praise or mournful dirges of lament.[35] The delights of harmony also attest to an aesthetic expression of interdependence and intersubjectivity.[36] And the rigors and pleasures of musical creation attest to our vocation as subcreators.[37] In short, music and song seem to stand as packed microcosms of what it means to be human. How appropriate, then, for song to be such a primary means for reordering our desires in the context of Christian worship.

34. See Elizabeth Newman, *Untamed Hospitality: Welcoming God and Other Strangers* (Grand Rapids: Brazos, 2007), 41–69.

35. For a discussion of the role of the body in music, and even the body's own "music" and rhythms, see Don and Emily Saliers, *A Song to Sing, a Life to Live: Reflections on Music as Spiritual Practice* (San Francisco: Jossey-Bass, 2005), 19–37.

36. See David Ford's discussion of "a singing self" in *Self and Salvation: Being Transformed* (Cambridge: Cambridge University Press, 1999), 120–22, where he emphasizes that "the specific contribution of music to this building up of community in worship includes its encouragement of alertness to others, immediate responsiveness to changes in tone, tune and rhythm, and sharing in the confidence that can come from joint singing. Singing together embodies joint responsibility in which each singer waits on the others, is attentive with the intention of serving the common harmony" (122).

37. See Jeremy Begbie's discussion of music in the "ecology" of creation in *Resounding Truth: Christian Wisdom in the World of Music* (Grand Rapids: Baker Academic, 2007), 185–236.

Second, singing is a mode of expression that seems to reside in our imagination more than other forms of discourse. Partly because of cadence and rhyme, partly because of the rhythms of music, song seems to get implanted in us as a mode of bodily memory. Music gets "in" us in ways that other forms of discourse rarely do. A song gets absorbed into our imagination in a way that mere texts rarely do. Indeed, a song can come back to haunt us almost, catching us off guard or welling up within our memories because of situations or contexts that we find ourselves in, then perhaps spilling over into our mouths till we find ourselves humming a tune or quietly singing. The song can invoke a time and a place, even the smells and tastes of a moment.[38] The song seems to have a privileged channel to our imagination, to our *kardia*, because it involves our body in a unique way. Perhaps it is because of this that Paul admonishes Christians: "Let the word of Christ dwell in you richly; teach and admonish one another in all wisdom; and with gratitude in your hearts sing psalms, hymns, and spiritual songs to God" (Col. 3:16). In a similar way, in Ephesians 5:18–20 singing is related to the filling of the Holy Spirit.

Perhaps it is *by* hymns, songs, and choruses that the word of Christ "dwells in us richly" and we are filled with the Holy Spirit. Don Saliers suggests as much when, discussing the experiences of elderly saints in a local congregation, he comments, "Their music was 'by heart,' in the heart, and sung from the heart. Through the practice of singing, the dispositions and beliefs expressed in the words of the hymns—gratitude, trust, sadness, joy, hope—had become knit into their bodies as integral parts of the theology by which they lived." As he goes on to claim,

> This knitting of an embodied theology happens whenever Christian congregations sing, even though they do so in a great variety of ways from one culture to another. It has been happening since the earliest Christians extemporized variations of praise to God in the new images of Jesus' teaching and ministry, and above all in images of the mystery of his death and resurrection. The Trinitarian character of faith was sung long before it was put into the language of doctrinal theology. Indeed, the church's theology was embodied in its liturgical and singing practices before more formal theology developed.[39]

This knitting of song into our bodies is why memorization of Scripture through song is often so effective. Song soaks into the very core of our being,

---

38. This is captured in Trisha Yearwood's "The Song Remembers When," on *The Song Remembers When* © 1993, UMG Recordings, Inc.

39. Don Saliers, "Singing Our Lives," in *Practicing Our Faith: A Way of Life for a Searching People*, ed. Dorothy C. Bass (San Francisco: Jossey-Bass, 1997), 185–86.

which is why music is an important constitutive element of our identity.[40] Thus John Witvliet points to Psalms (the church's earliest hymnbook) as a sort of language training manual—an affective, embodied means of training our speech, which is so centrally constitutive of who we are and how we imagine ourselves. Following Thomas Long, Witvliet describes Christian worship as "God's language school," which "challenges us to practice forms of faithful speech to God that we are not likely to try on our own. Authentic worship, like toddler talk, expresses who we are and forms what we are becoming." The songs that constitute the Psalms have a crucial role to play in our learning the language of the kingdom: "The biblical Psalms are the foundational mentor and guide in this vocabulary and grammar for worship."[41] If being a participating member of a society is reflected by one's ability to speak the language, then one could say that song is one of the primary ways that we learn to speak the language of the kingdom.

Third, the church's music and songs constitute what Richard Mouw describes as a "compacted theology."[42] While I, following Saliers, want to equally emphasize the medium, so to speak—the materiality of song—it is also true that the content of Christian hymns and songs is a crucial incubator for Christian faith. Thus John Wesley famously described hymnody as "a 'body of practical divinity,' a sung theology."[43] Because of its nature as a "compacted" theology, coupled with the way that singing knits a vision into our bodies, song has a catechetical role to play in the formation of our understanding and the emergence of a Christian worldview.

Scripture envisions the identity and faith of the people of God as a song. For instance, when Israel finds itself in exile in Babylon, the psalmist expresses the challenge of being faithful amid idolatrous temptations in terms of singing:

> By the rivers of Babylon—
> there we sat down and there we wept
> when we remembered Zion.
> On the willows there
> we hung our harps.
> For there our captors

40. For further discussion of this point, see Saliers and Saliers, *Song to Sing*, 75–95.
41. John Witvliet, *The Biblical Psalms in Christian Worship* (Grand Rapids: Eerdmans, 2007), 12.
42. See Richard J. Mouw, introduction to *Wonderful Words of Life: Hymns in American Protestant History and Theology*, ed. Richard J. Mouw and Mark Noll (Grand Rapids: Eerdmans, 2004), xiii–xiv. Mouw also recognizes the point I've been pressing when he notes that a hymn "impresses the theological point on your consciousness as no scholarly treatise can do" (xiv).
43. Saliers, "Singing Our Lives," 193.

asked us for songs,
and our tormentors asked for mirth, saying,
"Sing us one of the songs of Zion!"

How could we sing the LORD's song
in a foreign land? (Ps. 137:1–4)[44]

Here singing is clearly tethered to identity: what we sing says something significant about who we are—and *whose* we are. Israel's challenge is not unlike our challenge: how do we live as the peculiar people of God in a foreign land, given that every land is "foreign" for the people of the city of God? Figuring out how to be faithful in exile is here tied up with learning how to sing in a strange land. And in such exilic singing, we already begin to hymn the "new song" that will resound in the coming kingdom (Rev. 5:9; 14:3) as a redeemed choir from every tribe and tongue and nation. Embedded in this sung hope we see something of the vision of the kingdom implicit in Christian worship: a world of delight and festivity, of joyful song, as well as a world of racial reconciliation where the choir is a reconciled community. The practice of singing together in Christian worship—singing *one* song, with different parts, in harmony[45]—is a small but significant performance of what we're looking forward to in the kingdom.

The Law: Order, Norms, and Freedom for the Good

In our exegesis of Christian worship, I have tried to emphasize that what is at stake in liturgy is not just the "religious" aspect of our lives; rather, the practices of Christian worship are nothing less than training to be *human*. This is the inverse of what I emphasized in chapter 3 regarding secular liturgies. In that case, because our tendency is to think that such cultural practices are not religious, I tried to make them strange by showing that they function as liturgies. In the case of Christian worship, because we are so prone to think of this as *just* a "religious" exercise or something we do in connection with our "personal salvation," we can miss the fact that Christian worship has much broader application and aspiration. This is why "naturalizing" Christian worship can sometimes help illumine its aspirations to train us to flourish in all aspects of life: social, political, economic, and so

44. Confirming the point above, this psalm has always stuck with me because of a rendition of it by a Canadian band, The Kry, that knit itself into my memory.

45. That is, the Christian vision of a reconciled, harmonious community is not one that eradicates difference in order to achieve uniformity. An affirmation of difference and plurality is built into the very fabric of God's good creation. For discussion, see James K. A. Smith, *The Fall of Interpretation: Philosophical Foundations for a Creational Hermeneutic* (Downers Grove, IL: InterVarsity, 2000), 56–60 and 183–84.

on. Implicit in Christian worship is a vision not just for spiritual flourishing but also for human flourishing; this is not just practice for eternal bliss; it is training for temporal, embodied human community.[46] When we say that Christian worship is eschatological, we are emphasizing that it anticipates the coming kingdom. But we must remember that the Christian hope is not a "spiritual" existence in a disembodied heaven but a renewed and resurrected existence in a new earth.[47] Christian discipleship is the shape of what it means to be a renewed human being and constitutes a restoration of the gift and call of being human that was given and announced in the Garden of Eden. Let's continue to unpack the understanding of human flourishing that is carried in the practices of Christian worship.

Now that we have gathered in response to God's call and been welcomed by God and one another, the dialogical principle of Christian worship continues in the reading of the law: in some traditions this will be a regular reading of the Ten Commandments; in many other traditions, the moment of law in worship will draw on a range of God's commands from across Scripture, including the Sermon on the Mount and other injunctions throughout the New Testament, such as the one Jesus called the greatest commandment: "You shall love the Lord your God with all your heart, and with all your soul, and with all your mind" and "You shall love your neighbor as yourself" (Matt. 22:37–39, echoing Deut. 6:5 and Lev. 19:18). Thus in some forms of Christian worship, this moment in the liturgy might not be named *law*; it might instead be articulated as that moment in the service where we hear "God's Will for Our Lives."

This moment of worship can also appear at different points in the service, depending on different traditions. In traditions that emphasize the announcement of the law as that which convicts us of our own sinfulness and need for confession, the reading of the law precedes and induces confession and assurance.[48] In other traditions, the law is seen as God's invitation to live a life of obedience out of gratitude; that is, God's law is not a stern restriction of our will but an invitation to find peace and rest in what Augustine would call the "right ordering" of our will. In this respect,

46. As we'll mention in chapter 6, this is why the social imaginary implicit in Christian worship is so crucial for the task of Christian scholarship. Insofar as every discipline and discourse—even so-called descriptive fields—assume certain *norms* of human flourishing, then Christian scholarship must find those norms for human flourishing in the thick particularity of Christian worship.

47. For accessible discussions of this point, see Paul Marshall, with Lela Gilbert, *Heaven Is Not My Home* (Nashville: Nelson, 1999); Nathan Bierma, *Bringing Heaven Down to Earth: Connecting This Life to the Next* (Phillipsburg, NJ: Presbyterian & Reformed, 2005); and most recently, N. T. Wright, *Surprised by Hope: Rethinking Heaven, the Resurrection, and the Mission of the Church* (San Francisco: HarperOne, 2008).

48. Michael Horton also notes that the reading of the law plays a role in covenant renewal: it constitutes "a reading of the terms of the treaty and its sanctions" (*Better Way*, 149).

the giving of commandments is an expression of love; the commandments are given as guardrails that encourage us to act in ways that are consistent with the "grain of the universe," so to speak. They are the means by which God invites and encourages us to find abundance and flourishing. The First Epistle of John captures this link between the commandments and love: "For the love of God is this, that we obey his commandments. And his commandments are not burdensome" (1 John 5:3). Whether before confession or after assurance, the announcement of God's law and will for our lives represents an invitation to engage in practices and actions that are conducive to the human good; they are protective, not restrictive.

Embedded in this practice is an understanding of freedom that runs counter to almost every other cultural institution of which we, in Western democracies, are a part. The announcement of the law and the articulation of God's will for our lives signals that our good is not something that we determine or choose for ourselves. The secular liturgies of late modern culture are bent on forming in us a notion of autonomy—a sense that we are a law unto ourselves and that we are only properly "free" when we can choose our own ends, determine our own *telos*. Since its early beginnings, Charles Taylor notes, modernity has been marked by a rejection of teleology, a rejection of the notion that there is a specified, normative end (*telos*) to which humanity *ought* to be directed in order to enjoy the good life. And this rejection was driven by a new notion of "libertarian" freedom, which identified freedom with freedom of choice. "Indeed, one of the reasons for the vigorous rejection of Aristotelian teleology was that it was seen, then as now, as potentially circumscribing our freedom to determine our own lives and build our own societies."[49] Such a conception of autonomous freedom as freedom of choice—freedom to construct our own ends and to invent our own visions of the good life—chafes against the very notion of a law outside of ourselves.[50] The announcement of "the law" is a scandal to those who are primarily formed by modern secular liturgies.

In contrast, right here in Christian worship we see a very different understanding of the good: humanity and all of creation flourish when they are rightly ordered to a *telos* that is not of their own choosing but rather is stipulated by God. Creation is created *for* something, *for* a particular

49. Taylor, *Modern Social Imaginaries*, 80. For a brilliant analysis of these issues, which is attuned to the theme of desire, see David Burrell, "Can We Be Free without a Creator?" in *God, Truth, and Witness: Engaging Stanley Hauerwas*, ed. L. Gregory Jones, Reinhard Hütter, and C. Rosallee Velloso Ewell (Grand Rapids: Brazos, 2005), 35–62. I also discuss these issues further in "The Gospel of Freedom, or Another Gospel? Augustinian Interrogations of the Bush Doctrine and *Empire*," in *Political Theology* 10.1 (2009).

50. The modern notion of autonomy indicates a sense that one gives oneself (*autos*) the law (*nomos*). Such a picture rejects "heteronomy," that is, the idea that the law comes from an other (*heteros*).

end envisioned by the Creator. "You have made us for yourself," Augustine confessed, which is precisely why "our hearts are restless until they find rest in you." The announcement of the law and the reading of God's will for our lives represents a significant challenge to the desire for autonomy that is impressed upon us by secular liturgies. The reading of the law is a displacement of our own wants and desires, reminding us that we find ourselves in a world not of our own making—which is why all our attempts to remake it as we want (as if we ourselves could be little creators) are not only doomed to failure; they are also doomed to exacerbate suffering. The announcement of the law reminds us that we inhabit not "nature," but *creation*, fashioned by a Creator, and that there is a certain grain to the universe—grooves and tracks and norms that are part of the fabric of the world.[51] And all of creation flourishes best when our communities and relationships run with the grain of those grooves. Indeed, the biblical vision of human flourishing implicit in worship means that we are only properly free when our desires are rightly ordered, when they are bounded and directed to the end that constitutes our good.[52] That is why the law, though it comes as a scandalous challenge to the modern desire for autonomy, is actually an invitation to be freed from a-teleological wandering.[53] It is an invitation to find the good life by welcoming the boundaries of law that guide us into the grooves that constitute the grain of the universe and are conducive to flourishing.

Confession and Assurance of Pardon: Brokenness, Grace, Hope

However, the announcement of the law and the articulation of God's will for our lives not only chastens our penchant for autonomy; it also reminds us of our inability to either pursue or measure up to this good. Now that we have been invited into a relationship with a holy God and been reminded of what he requires, a bright spotlight is shone upon not just our failures and trespasses but also our inability to do otherwise on our own. Rather than repressing this stark, haunting fact—of which we're not a little embarrassed

51. I'm alluding here to Stanley Hauerwas's adoption of John Howard Yoder's claim that "people who bear crosses" are "working with the grain of the universe." See Hauerwas, *With the Grain of the Universe: The Church's Witness and Natural Theology* (Grand Rapids: Brazos, 2001), 17.

52. Thus Augustine considered the situation of libertarian freedom—having no defined *telos* and thus being "free" to do whatever I want (so valorized in modernity)—as actually the situation of fallen, sinful freedom.

53. As Burrell puts it, "An action becomes more authentically one's own, and hence more integrally free, to the extent that one is freed from the hold of infatuations and thus able to follow those desires that contribute to fulfilling the orienting desire. So all is gift, and all is desire, while desires properly discerned lead to a freedom liberated from infatuations—*non est liber nisi liberatus*; no one is free until freed" ("Can We Be Free?" 49).

and ashamed[54]—and rather than papering over it or ignoring it, the practice of Christian worship calls us to own up to it in open confession, where we are honest with God about our transgressions and agree with God that they are violations of his law. We confess both our proclivity and actions that run against the grain of the universe, as, for instance, in a prayer of confession from the Anglican *Book of Common Prayer*, which would be recited by the congregation while kneeling in a position of humiliation:

> Most merciful God,
> we confess that we have sinned against you
> in thought, word, and deed,
> by what we have done,
> and by what we have left undone.
> We have not loved you with our whole heart;
> we have not loved our neighbors as ourselves.
> We are truly sorry and we humbly repent.
> For the sake of your Son Jesus Christ,
> have mercy on us and forgive us;
> that we may delight in your will,
> and walk in your ways,
> to the glory of your Name. Amen.

You'll notice this is not just a transgression of an abstract law; it is a sin "against you," against God. This is more like the breakdown of a marriage than the failure to hold up our end of a contract; our sin represents the violation of a trust. And at the root of wrong actions, the confession recognizes a failure to love—or rather, a failure to love well, to love rightly, to love the right things in the right order. Disordered action is a reflection and fruit of disordered desire, and our misdirected *desires* are as much a violation and transgression as sinful *actions*. Thus another prayer of confession honestly recognizes:

> There are many times we think we love you well, O God.
> But upon hearing your call to love you with all our heart,
> and all our mind, and all our strength,
> we confess that our love for you is a diluted love,
> made insipid and flat by lesser loyalties and a divided heart.[55]

54. But it should be noted that this confession is made as part of the people who have gathered in response to the covenant-keeping God, so we also come to confession with a kind of gifted confidence, an anticipation of assurance, having been promised that "if we confess our sins, he who is faithful and just will forgive us our sins and cleanse us from all unrighteousness" (1 John 1:9). This promise constitutes the context of our confession.

55. Adapted from Kenneth D. Koeman, "The Question That Focuses Us: 'Do You Love Me?'" *Reformed Worship* 8, no. 27 (1993): 41. http://www.reformedworship.org/magazine/article.cfm?article_id=1502&id=27.

What counts as a violation is filled in by all the particularities of the law that have preceded our confession. And as Christian worship over time rehearses the breadth of God's normative vision for human flourishing in its concrete aspects, we are regularly confronted by the various facets of our failure. We confess not only personal or private sins and transgressions; the moment of confession owns up to our complicity with all sorts of evil that disorders the world and corrupts creation. In short, we humans confess our failure to heed the call to *be human*, to be God's image bearers to and for the world. As a result, sin is not only personal and individual (a violation of a relationship); it also becomes inscribed into the cultural institutions of our human making (a refusal of our commission to be God's vice-regents). Culture-making—unfolding the latent possibilities that have been folded into creation—is a vocation given to us as image bearers of God. Just as the Fall means not that we stop desiring but rather that our desire becomes disordered, so too sin does not mean that we stop being culture makers; rather, it means that we do this poorly, sinfully, unjustly. As Schilder comments, "The cultural urge *per se* is, as we have seen, one of the 'natural' gifts, the 'gifts of creation.' . . . But the purposeful use of these gifts of creation, positive cultural activity in accordance with the commandment given by God with respect to purpose and eschatologically determined direction, is possible only in an obedience regained through the Spirit of Christ."[56] The "cultural urge" does not go away—it gets pointed in the wrong direction, toward the wrong ends; its teleology is sent off-kilter, and this skewing of creation is reflected in the cultural products that we produce. As a result, we create institutions and systems that are unjust, not only because of individual bad choices but also because the very structures and systems of these institutions are wrongly ordered, fostering systemic racism or patriarchy or exploitation of the poor. The practice of confession owns up to systemic sin as well, in concrete terms:

> Merciful God,
> in your gracious presence
> we confess our sin and the sin of this world.
> Although Christ is among us as our peace,
> we are a people divided against ourselves
> as we cling to the values of a broken world.
> The profit and pleasures we pursue
> lay waste the land and pollute the seas.
> The fears and jealousies that we harbor
> set neighbor against neighbor
> and nation against nation.
> We abuse your good gifts of imagination and freedom,

56. Schilder, *Christ and Culture*, 68–69.

> of intellect and reason,
> and turn them into bonds of oppression.
> Lord, have mercy upon us;
> heal and forgive us.
> Set us free to serve you in the world
> as agents of your reconciling love in Jesus Christ. Amen.[57]

Recognizing that it was human sin that effected a cosmic brokenness throughout creation (Rom. 8:20), this prayer owns up to the corruption of nature as yet another fallout of our sin. In this way our confession echoes the groaning of creation itself, which longs for redemption (Rom. 8:22), looking forward to the full reality of what Christ has already accomplished: reconciliation of all things to himself, "whether on earth or in heaven" (Col. 1:20).

As we noted earlier, the moment of confession in Christian worship, before it even commences, already anticipates what immediately follows: the announcement and assurance of God's pardon—the word of absolution and forgiveness that is accomplished in Christ. The dialogue continues: we have confessed our sins and God answers, "I forgive you!" If it seems a bit strange to crave confession, it certainly makes eminent sense to long for pardon. Here is the in-breaking of the good news!

> Hear the good news:
> Christ died for us while we were yet sinners;
> that proves God's love toward us.
> In the name of Jesus Christ, we are forgiven!
> *In the name of Jesus Christ, we are forgiven.*
> *Glory to God. Amen.*[58]

The following is from the *Book of Common Prayer*:

> The Almighty and merciful Lord grant you absolution and remission of all your sins, true repentance, amendment of life, and the grace and consolation of his Holy Spirit. *Amen.*

The good news speaks to our dependence, for our forgiveness comes as a gift, the overflowing of Christ's work on the cross. Our assurance does

---

57. *The Book of Common Worship* (Presbyterian Church in Canada, 1991), 28, alt. (used by permission). The *Worship Sourcebook* gathers a wide range of prayers of confession, including a number for specific systemic sins such as racism and exploitation, as well as prayers of lament that give us biblical language for expressing grief, frustration, and even anger at the brokenness of the world.

58. From "The Service of Healing I and II," in *The United Methodist Book of Worship* (Nashville: Abingdon, 1992), 615–26. © 1992 United Methodist Publishing House. Used by permission.

To Think About: Confession as Liberation

On the one hand, the moment of confession is not exactly something one would ever relish or enjoy. On the other hand, there is something about this moment of confession—this moment of imposed honesty, in the context of covenantal worship of a hospitable God, with a gathered people who *together* confess their sin—there is something about such an action that can also be incredibly liberating. Having been formed largely in churches that did not include confession as a regular part of worship, I now find that the liturgical act of confession, while it makes me uncomfortable, also gives honest voice to what I know about myself. It gives words to an impulse that I would rather repress. While on one level I would rather not be reminded of all my failures and sins and violations, on another level I never escape the knowledge of them, and the rite of confession makes room for honesty about that. We might say that there is a strange sense in which we *want* to confess, we *desire* to confess, and the rhythms of historic Christian liturgy recognize not only the need for confession but perhaps also this strange desire for confession.

Something like this strange desire is glimpsed at the very end of Graham Greene's novel *The Quiet American*. Set in Indochina in the middle of the last century, it recalls the colonialism of France and England and anticipates a different sort of colonialism that would come to grief in the American venture in Vietnam (a sort of quasi-colonial adventure not unlike more recent American ventures in Asia). A novel that explores the sins and hubris of both nations and individuals, of empires and souls, the story is a web of intrigue and selfishness, rife with instances of exploitation for personal and political gain—of things done and left undone, sins of commission and omission. At the nexus of both, the protagonist Fowler has violated every commandment on both tables of the law. It would seem that he has triumphed over

---

not stem from our own accomplishment, nor does God's forgiveness stem from simply dismissing the demands of justice or ignoring the brokenness of creation; rather, God himself takes on our sin and its effects in the Son, on the cross, who also triumphs over them in the resurrection. Our brokenness and violence are met by the grace of God, who suffered violence for our sake and in turn graces and empowers us to reorder our desires, to recalibrate our ultimate aims, and to take up once again our vocation as humans, to be his image bearers to and for the world.

Here again, in confession and assurance of pardon, we meet a moment where Christian worship runs counter to the formation of secular liturgies that either tend to nullify talk of guilt and responsibility or tend to point out failures without extending assurance of pardon. On the one hand, Oprah-fied secular liturgies tend to foster an illusory self-confidence ("Believe in yourself!") that refuses to recognize failure, guilt, or transgression, castigating such things as "negative energy" that compromises self-esteem. The we-can-do-it confidence of these liturgies of self-affirmation offers assurance without confession. On the other hand, many of the secular

his adversary Pyle (the "quiet American"), having emerged unscathed and even getting what he wants, namely, the woman they both loved, Phuong. And yet the narrative indicates that Fowler still wants something else:

> Opposite me in the bookcase *The Role of the West* stood out like a cabinet portrait—of a young man with a crew cut and a black dog at his heels. He could harm no one any more. I said to Phuong, "Do you miss him much?"
>
> "Who?"
>
> "Pyle." Strange how even now, even to her, it was impossible to use his first name.
>
> "Can I go please? My sister will be so excited."
>
> "You spoke his name once in your sleep."
>
> "I never remember my dreams."
>
> "There was so much you could have done together. He was young."
>
> "You are not old."
>
> "The skyscrapers. The Empire State Building."
>
> She said with a small hesitation, "I want to see the Cheddar Gorge."
>
> "It isn't the Grand Canyon." I pulled her down onto the bed. "I'm sorry, Phuong."
>
> "What are you sorry for? It is a wonderful telegram. My sister—"
>
> "Yes, go and tell your sister. Kiss me first." Her excited mouth skated over my face, and she was gone.
>
> I thought of the first day and Pyle sitting beside me at the Continental, with his eye on the soda fountain across the way. Everything had gone right with me since he had died, but how I wished there existed someone to whom I could say that I was sorry. (Graham Greene, *The Quiet American* [New York: Random House, 1992], 246–47)

liturgies of marketing play off of our deep knowledge of our faults and failures, but transform them into phenomena that yield shame but not guilt. In response, they promise not forgiveness or pardon, but opportunities to correct the problem via various goods and services. In this sense, they seem to require confession but make no promise of pardon or peace. In contrast to both, the rite of confession and assurance in Christian worship counters such secular liturgies by immersing us in a weekly practice that reminds us of a fundamental fracture that we find in ourselves and our world—and of the consequences of our choices. It forces us to be honest with God and ourselves about our complicity in injustice as well as to face up to the ways that we've failed to be good husbands or wives, daughters or sons, sisters or brothers, neighbors or ministers—and perhaps more importantly, how we as a people, the *ekklēsia*, have failed to be the foretaste of the kingdom to which we're called to be living witness. Yet the practice does not leave us in despair, but rather gives us hope, assuring us of forgiveness and reminding us that the curse is being rolled back. A reordering of creation has already broken into creation in the person of Jesus Christ, and we are gathering as a people in order to practice for the arrival of the kingdom in its fullness—and thus in order to be trained to be a kingdom-kind-of-people in the meantime, as witnesses to that kingdom, in and through our work as cultural agents.

Baptism: Initiation into a Royal Priesthood, Constitution of a New People

If we are attending a Christian worship service as Martian anthropologists, we might have occasion to observe what will seem to be an odd ritual, particularly vis-à-vis the other things we've observed in the surrounding culture. At this point in the service, a congregant may present herself at the front of the congregation; she may undergo what seems like an interrogation and then be submerged in water while completely clothed or have water poured over her head three times as what seems like a chant is muttered. Or it may be the case that a family comes forward with a baby, and after they are interrogated, the baby is dunked three times (perhaps even naked) into an ornate piece of equipment that looks like a giant birdbath, emerging from the experience screaming his lungs out while the parents and congregation seem to be overjoyed. What is going on here?

Most of us will recognize these admittedly odd practices as the sacrament of baptism. In many ways, like the sacrament of the Lord's Supper, baptism is a microcosm of the entirety of Christian worship and the story of God, in Christ, reconciling the world to himself. Thus it both recapitulates elements we have discussed and anticipates others that will still unfold in the service. But what "gets done" in baptism? How is baptism formative?[59] What does it picture and narrate? What sort of visceral training of desire could be going on here? I will highlight just three aspects: baptism's constitution of a new body politic, its reconfiguration of the family, and its ritualization of antithesis to "the world."

First, baptism is a rite of initiation into a people that at the same time effects the constitution *of* "a people."[60] While we might tend to focus on

59. I will not here offer a theology of baptism. However, we should at least note that as a sacrament, baptism is a means of grace, but it is significant and formative not just for the recipient. The entire congregation, we'll see, participates in every baptism. For a helpful and accessible theology of baptism, see Leonard Vander Zee, *Christ, Baptism, and the Lord's Supper: Recovering the Sacraments for Evangelical Worship* (Downers Grove, IL: InterVarsity, 2004), 71–120. For an outline of the elements of baptismal liturgies, see *Worship Sourcebook*, section 6.

60. Richard Hays emphasizes that for Paul, "the goal of God's redemptive action" is not the rescuing of individual souls but rather "to raise up a people to declare his praise" (Hays, *The Echoes of Scripture in the Letters of Paul* [New Haven: Yale University Press, 1989], 84, 183). Or as he summarizes elsewhere, "granting that Scripture tells the story of *God's* activ-

what baptism does to and for an individual (taking what Peter Leithart describes as a "zoom lens" approach to the sacraments),[61] baptism is situated in the context of gathered worship because it announces a social and political reality. When we zoom out and consider the reality that baptism signifies, we should be "awed . . . that God can throw down nations and plant new ones with a few drops of water."[62] While baptism illustrates new birth (dying and rising with Christ to become a "new" human; Rom. 6:3–4) and expresses one's new identity (one's confession that Jesus and not Caesar is Lord), it is not only an illustration or symbolic expression of personal redemption. Baptism is not just a picture; it also *does* something. As a sacrament, it *makes* what it promises: a new person and a new people. As such, it is a profoundly social reality. "Baptism," Leithart says, "announces the formation of a *polis* that offers priesthood to the plebs."[63] Historically, the plebeians were a class that was subservient to the patricians in ancient Rome; more generally, *plebs* refers to a despised and rejected class, a marginalized people. As Leithart argues, baptism signifies a radical reordering of the social world in Christ precisely because it signifies that the priesthood is open to all—which is just a way of saying that all, regardless of birth or class, are called and equipped to take up humanity's creational vocation of being prince(sse)s/priests for the world.[64]

In this respect, Leithart shows that the Christian practice of baptism was a sort of two-edged sword, cutting against the hierarchies of both Israel and Rome.[65] On the one hand, whereas in Israel the priesthood was

---

ity, we must say in the same breath that God's activity is directed toward the formation of a *people*" (Hays, *The Conversion of the Imagination: Paul as Interpreter of Israel's Scripture* [Grand Rapids: Eerdmans, 2005], 171). Consequently, Hays admonishes that if we want to adopt a Pauline hermeneutic—if we want to read the Scriptures as Paul did—then we need to adopt an "ecclesiocentric" (*Echoes*, 86, 183–84) or an "ecclesiotelic" hermeneutic that sees this social focus of God's creational and redemptive work as directed toward *re-creating a people* rather than saving individual people—"a people of his own" (Titus 2:14).

61. Peter J. Leithart, "The Way Things Really Ought to Be: Eucharist, Eschatology, and Culture," *Westminster Theological Journal* 59 (1997): 159–61.

62. Peter J. Leithart, *The Priesthood of the Plebs: A Theology of Baptism* (Eugene, OR: Wipf & Stock, 2003), xii.

63. Ibid., xxii. A *polis* was a city-state, a political entity; though as Leithart and others (like Augustine) emphasize, the Greek and Roman *polis* was suffused with religious liturgies that could not be distinguished from "the political."

64. On the priestly connotations of *imago Dei*, and the convergence of royal and priestly functions in humanity, see Middleton, *Liberating Image*, 87, 206–9.

65. As Leithart summarizes, "Baptism embodies a critique not only of antique Hebrew but also of antique Gentile order" (*Priesthood*, 186). This calls to mind N. T. Wright's emphasis that Jesus's announcement of the kingdom of God was a "double revolutionary" program that challenged both Israel's self-understanding and the pretensions of the Roman Empire (see Wright, *Challenge of Jesus*, 85).

restricted to the sons of Aaron (a kind of priestly aristocracy), in Christ the requirements and privileges of birth and lineage are abolished. Thus baptism functions as ordination did in Israel: just as through ordination Aaron "became a new man," so "baptism likewise forms new creatures."[66] Just as humanity was originally called to function as God's priestly image bearer, so now the vocation of priesthood (engaging in worship and mediating God's presence to the world) is open to all. And such image-bearing is a *social* reality: we are not deputized as little isolated images; rather, we bear the image in our collaborative cultural labors.

On the other hand, baptism into a people who are all priests also cuts against the hierarchies of privilege that characterized Greece and Rome. In both Greece and Rome, the *polis* (the political commonwealth) was also an inherently religious and liturgical community, but within it, priesthood and cultic service was organized according to the power and privilege of families and clans. Thus what we know as the traditional distinction and antagonism between "patricians" and "plebeians" was a religious divide, "a conflict over the distribution of priestly privilege within the ancient city."[67] But in the midst of this religio-political reality, Paul announces a very different religio-political reality, the church, which constitutes the people marked by baptism: "As many of you as were baptized into Christ have clothed yourselves with Christ. There is no longer Jew or Greek, there is no longer slave or free, there is no longer male and female; for all of you are one in Christ Jesus" (Gal. 3:27–28).

Baptism extends priesthood to the plebs—it is an investiture with Christ, the High Priest who clothes us as a priestly vestment. Recalling that Christ is the exemplary human, the one who finally fulfilled Adam's vocation to be God's image bearer, we see that central to that vocation is priesthood. And all of humanity is called to that vocation. "Baptism announces and creates a new *polis* where the 'one seed' of Jew and Greek share the Abrahamic blessing, where none are forced outside the city walls, where the marginal are welcomed to the *agora* and its joyful assembly."[68] Through baptism, God constitutes a peculiar people that makes up a new *polis*, a new religio-political reality (a "baptismal city")[69] that is marked by the obliteration of social class and aristocracies of blood. It is a motley crew: "Not many of you were wise by human standards, not many were powerful, not many were of noble birth" (1 Cor. 1:26). But that is the mark of the city of God, God's upside-down kingdom:

66. Leithart, *Priesthood*, 165.
67. Ibid., 205.
68. Ibid., 209.
69. Ibid., 210.

"God chose what is foolish in the world to shame the wise; God chose what is weak in the world to shame the strong; God chose what is low and despised in the world, things that are not, to reduce to nothing things that are" (1 Cor. 1:27–28). The citizens of the baptismal city are not just have-nots; they're also "are-nots"! And yet they are chosen and commissioned as God's image bearers, God's prince(sse)s and priests empowered to be witnesses of a coming kingdom and charged with the renewal of the world.

So baptism both makes and signifies a social reality, which is why it is situated in the context of gathered worship. We the congregation are there not just as spectators; rather, it is a sacrament in which all participate. On a minimal level, the ritual should call to mind our own baptism, thus rehearsing for us our own "pledge of allegiance," so to speak. (This is also why some churches have water at their entry, providing a tangible occasion for recalling *whose* we are. The stirring, touching, and perhaps self-anointing with water is a visceral reminder, as we enter for prayer or worship, that we are a marked people.) More substantively, the baptismal liturgy calls for us, the congregation, to also make a covenantal promise. For instance, when children[70] are presented for baptism, the minister turns to the congregation and asks something like this:

> Do you, the people of the Lord, promise to receive these children in love, pray for them, help instruct them in the faith, and encourage and sustain them in the fellowship of believers?[71]

The congregation then responds: "We do, God helping us." The covenant binds us together as a community, and if we are a new configuration of the *polis*, we are also a new configuration of the family, "the household of God" (Eph. 2:19). Here, too, there is a relativizing of "blood lines," which we also noted in the configuration of a priesthood of the plebs: our promises in baptism—as parents and as a congregation—signal that what counts most as family is not the closed, nuclear unit that is so often idolized as "the family."[72] Instead, the church constitutes our "first

70. I'll not provide an argument for baptizing children here; again, see Vander Zee, *Christ, Baptism, and the Lord's Supper*, 121–33.

71. CRC Service for Baptism (1981), in *The Psalter Hymnal* (Grand Rapids: CRC Publications, 1987), p. 955.

72. Thus Schmemann admonishes, "A marriage which does not constantly crucify its own selfishness and self-sufficiency, which does not 'die to itself' that it may point beyond itself, is not a Christian marriage. The real sin of marriage today is not adultery or lack of 'adjustment' or 'mental cruelty.' It is the idolization of the family itself, the refusal to understand marriage as directed toward the Kingdom of God" (*For the Life of the World: Sacraments and Orthodoxy*, 2nd ed. [Crestwood, NY: St. Vladimir's, 1973], 90).

family,"[73] which is both a challenge and a blessing. On the one hand, it challenges yet another sphere of rabid autonomy in late modernity: the privacy of the family. On the other hand, it comes as a welcome relief: we don't have to raise these kids on our own!

The "idolization" of the family noted by Schmemann results in an almost impossible pressure upon the family to function as a closed, self-sufficient, autonomous unit.[74] The rituals of political liberalism (whether "liberal" or "conservative") paint a picture of the family as the incubator of good citizens, dutiful producers, and eager consumers at the same time that it shuts up the family in a private "closed home" as part of the American ideal of independence.[75] The result, however, is an unbearable weight placed upon the family: "The predominant theology of the family" implicit in liberalism, McCarthy remarks, "isolates it with the formidable and lonely task of being a whole communion." But baptismal promises counter such a configuration: love and its obligations traverse the boundaries of "private residences" and "nuclear families" because they initiate us into a household that is bigger than what is under the roof of our house. The promises in baptism indicate a very different theology of the family, which recognizes that "families work well when we do not expect them to give us all we need." Instead, the social role of the family that is configured by baptism is to be a family "dependent upon a larger social body. . . . In theological terms, family is called to be part of the social adventure we call the church."[76]

Thus baptism becomes an almost subversive sacrament that revolutionizes many of the notions of social life that we have inherited, even those that claim to be "conservative" and "religious." For as McCarthy elsewhere notes, "Baptism establishes a communion that qualifies our relationships of birth."[77] Just as baptism relativizes the bloodlines of the priesthood, so it situates and positions even the bloodlines of the home and family. Our baptismal promises attest to the fact that "the church is our first family." And "if the church is our first family, then our second homes should be defined by it, and our doors ought to be open to the stranger, the sick, and the poor."[78] Baptism opens the home, liberating it from the burden of

73. David Matzko McCarthy, *The Good Life: Genuine Christianity for the Middle Class* (Grand Rapids: Brazos, 2004), 52.

74. As Schmemann laments, "It is not the lack of respect for the family, it is the idolization of the family that breaks the modern family so easily, making divorce its almost natural shadow. It is the identification of marriage with happiness and the refusal to accept the cross in it" (*For the Life of the World*, 90).

75. See the astute analysis of David Matzko McCarthy, *Sex and Love in the Home*, new ed. (London: SCM, 2004), 93–97.

76. Ibid., 111.

77. McCarthy, *Good Life*, 52.

78. Ibid.

impossible self-sufficiency, while also opening it to the "disruptive friend-ships" that are the mark of the kingdom of God.[79]

Finally, baptism is a moment when Christian worship articulates an antithesis with respect to the world. In constituting a people, God consti-tutes a *peculiar* people—a called-out people who are marked as strange because they are a community that desires the kingdom of God, and thus they reflect the cruciform shape exemplified by Christ. Since the early church, baptismal rites have included a series of "renunciations" or even "exorcisms" that renounce Satan and the world. Consider this liturgy from the Episcopal *Book of Common Prayer*:

> Do you renounce Satan and all the spiritual forces of wickedness that rebel against God?
> *I renounce them.*
> Do you renounce the evil powers of this world which corrupt and destroy the creatures of God?
> *I renounce them.*
> Do you renounce all sinful desires that draw you from the love of God?
> *I renounce them.*
> Do you turn to Jesus Christ and accept him as your Savior?
> *I do.*
> Do you put your whole trust in his grace and love?
> *I do.*
> Do you promise to follow and obey him as your Lord?
> *I do.*

If we have been emphasizing that Christian worship is training for being human, hearkening back to a fundamental continuity with creation, we must also recognize that Christian worship is a *counter*-formation. The renunciations that accompany baptism are to be ongoing renunciations that characterize life as a new creature. Though such renunciations are ritualized at the time of baptism, they are meant to be not a singular event but a way of life.

But don't these renunciations seem to contradict what we've been affirm-ing up to this point? Don't such renunciations of "the world" fly in the face of the sacramental imagination we noted earlier, which constitutes a fundamental affirmation of the goodness of creation? Don't these baptis-mal renunciations sound a little gnostic and otherworldly? To this point we've been emphasizing that we are called to be God's image bearers to and for the world, and that worship is material and embodied because that

---

79. On disruptive friendships, see ibid., 35–37.

is the stuff of God's good creation; so what are we now to make of these renunciations that seem to (literally) demonize the world?

A coherent answer to these questions requires that we think more carefully about "the world" and, particularly, about how the term *world* functions in Scripture. Consider, for instance, the following range of passages:

- "He [Christ] was in the world, and the world came into being through him; yet the world did not know him." (John 1:10)
- "For God so loved the world that he gave his only Son." (John 3:16)
- "The God who made the world and everything in it, he who is Lord of heaven and earth . . ." (Acts 17:24)
- "Do not be conformed to this world, but be transformed by the renewing of your minds." (Rom. 12:2)
- "Do not love the world or the things in the world. The love of the Father is not in those who love the world." (1 John 2:15)
- "The whole world lies under the power of the evil one." (1 John 5:19)

Just these few selections from the New Testament indicate that the word *world* runs a wide gamut of meanings. On one end of the spectrum, we see that God is the creator of the world and that God *loves* the world. On the other end of the spectrum, we are warned *not* to love the world and that it lies under the sway of the evil one. Can we reconcile what seem to be contradictory claims? And could this perhaps help us make sense of the renunciations of the world that are part of the baptismal liturgy?

Clearly the meaning of *world* in Scripture is not univocal; it can refer to various phenomena and realities. I suggest that the most helpful distinction to make when encountering reference to "the world" is to recall an earlier distinction we made between "structure" and "direction." With that distinction in hand, we can suggest that, on the one hand, the Scriptures affirm that the world as *structure* (as a given reality) is created by God and, as such, is fundamentally good.[80] On the other hand, *world* is sometimes a sort of name given to human society that has taken the world (as structure) in the wrong *direction*. In that case, *the world* names fallen, broken systems, idolatrous configurations, the Garden of Eden remade as Babylon.[81] In other words, in passages like

80. This does not refer only to "nature" but also includes the entirety of nature and culture per se.

81. We can see the same sort of distinction in the New Testament term *flesh*, which almost always has a negative connotation (e.g., Rom. 8:1–17; Gal. 3:3). But does this mean

---

To Think About: Contemporary, Concrete Renunciations

Our baptismal renunciations do not happen in a vacuum. While the baptismal formulas might seem rather generic, on the other hand they are quite concrete ("Satan and all the spiritual forces of wickedness that rebel against God"). But they could be even more concrete, and perhaps more contemporary. How would you articulate more concrete baptismal renunciations? If you were to name names, what "evil powers of this world" corrupt and destroy God's creation? What cultural practices and institutions are bent on forming in you "sinful desires that draw you from the love of God"? Think about the particular configurations of cultural institutions and practices that need to be (daily!) renounced in order to truly foster human flourishing; then write your own version of the baptismal renunciations. Consider using them as aids for meditation before receiving communion.

Romans 12:2 and 1 John 2:15, *world* is the name for *dis*ordered creation, often with a specific emphasis on the misdirected cultural formations of human society, but also including the "principalities and powers" (Eph. 6:12 KJV). It is in this sense that the world is to be spurned and renounced. Thus the baptismal formulas are rejecting not temporal material existence per se, nor cultural life as such, but rather the perversions and distortions of both that characterize fallen humanity—and that are so characteristic of the secular liturgies we have described in chapter 3.

The baptismal renunciations are clear echoes of biblical language that asserts a radical, even ontological, change that takes place when one becomes a member of the body of Christ, a citizen in this new configuration of the *polis*. "For once you were in the darkness," Paul says, "but now in the Lord you are light. Live as children of the light" (Eph. 5:8). This transformation and demarcation is a radical turning akin to resurrection, again calling to mind the image of resurrection pictured in baptism (cf. Rom. 6:12–13). As Paul elsewhere exhorts, "Put to death, therefore, whatever in you is earthly. . . . These are the ways you once followed, when you were living that life. . . . Do not lie to one another, seeing that you have stripped off the old self with its practices and have clothed yourselves with the new self" (Col. 3:5, 7, 9–10). Our baptism signals that we are new creatures, with new desires, a new passion for a very different kingdom; thus we renounce (and keep renouncing) our former desires.

---

that the New Testament condemns muscles and ligaments as somehow inherently evil? Wouldn't that contradict the announcement that such human bodies were "very good" (Gen. 1:31)? No; like the meaning of *world* as the *mis*direction of creation, so *flesh* actually names the *mis*direction of the will and embodiment.

Unfortunately, in the Reformed tradition, because we are rightly concerned not to accede to the modern gnosticism that would denigrate the goodness of creation, we can also be prone to blur Scripture's marked distinction between the world and the new creation (of which the church is a part). We even get a little embarrassed about the New Testament's stark claims about the people of God. In short, in the name of defending the goodness of creation, we paper over the distinction between structure and direction; thus our affirmation of creation slides into an affirmation of the world, which then slides toward an affirmation of "the world" even in its distorted, misdirected configurations. In the name of the goodness of creation, we bend over backward to affirm common grace and are embarrassed by the language of antithesis, which feels dualistic and otherworldly.[82] In short, we forget the renunciations that attend our baptism.[83]

The Creed: Situating Belief

The baptismal candidate, usually together with the congregation, affirms "the faith" by reciting the Apostles' Creed, which was originally developed as a baptismal confession. Indeed, many congregations recite the Apostles' Creed or the Nicene Creed every Sunday. An early Christian document that summarizes "the apostles' teaching" (Acts 2:42), the Creed functioned as a "rule of faith" (*regula fidei*) even before the formation of the canon of Scripture.[84] But what role does it have in the formation of a Christian social imaginary? What does reciting the creed *do*? I briefly highlight just three elements.

First, the Apostles' Creed functions like the church's pledge of allegiance.[85] Recited weekly, in unison, the Creed is a declaration—the positive affirmation that is the correlate of the renunciations we made in baptism.

82. In volume 3 of this project, which will focus on political theology in the Augustinian and Reformed traditions, I will attend to these issues in more detail. Here, suffice it to say that I think Kuyperians who are fixated on common grace mistakenly hear talk of "antithesis" as a kind of pietism. I think this is a mistake: *pietism*, as I would define it, is characterized by being not only anti-direction but also anti-structure; that is, it is marked by a rejection of culture as such. In contrast, what I would describe as an "antithetical" stance is anti-direction, but not anti-structure. And my concern is that the notion of common grace, particularly as it has been marshaled of late, slides toward being not only pro-structure vis-à-vis creation but also pro-direction vis-à-vis the world, largely because it fails to make the distinction (and seems to lack the imaginative nuance to do so).

83. Or, more likely, we omit such renunciations from the baptismal formula.

84. I will not even attempt to unpack the content of the Creed, which has generated shelves of books across the generations. For an exemplary commentary, see Justo Gonzalez, *The Apostles' Creed for Today* (Louisville: Westminster John Knox, 2007).

85. Indeed, it should *replace* the American Pledge of Allegiance, which seems to be recited in some Christian schools.

In it we confess our allegiance to a "foreign" king, the triune God. In that sense, if worship is like a renewal-of-vows ceremony, each week is also a citizenship-renewal ceremony. When we pledge that Jesus is Lord—not Caesar, not the emperor, not the president or prime minister, not the chairman of the Federal Reserve—we are engaged in a political act (recalling that our baptism constitutes us as a new *polis* and that the Creed was a baptismal document).[86] This is the pledge of those whose "citizenship is in heaven" (Phil. 3:20)—which is not citizenship in some otherworldly, ethereal kingdom but rather citizenship in an earthly kingdom that is *coming*.

Second, the shared recitation of the Creed constitutes us as a *historical* people. We are heirs to a tradition, indebted to those who have handed on the faith across the generations. Like many of the practices of Christian worship, the Creed comes to us from an ancient world, and yet it is on our lips as a contemporary confession. It is not our language, and yet it is, for the church's worship invites us to embrace the scandalous particularity of a language and culture that emerged "under Pontius Pilate," so to speak. In contrast to secular liturgies that are fixated on the novel and the new (including the liturgies of the university), which are trying their best to get us to forget what happened five minutes ago, Christian worship constitutes us as a people of memory. It cuts against the grain of myths of progress and chronological snobbery that assume "we" (late moderns) must know more and thus must know better. The communal recitation of the Creed conditions us to recognize the role of tradition in our construal of the world.[87] It forms in us salutary habits of deference and dependence (anathema in liberal democracy) in what we think and believe, recognizing and celebrating our debts and dependencies.

Third, the recitation of the Creed is the "I believe" moment in Christian worship. By emphasizing that the practices of Christian worship are formative at a fundamentally precognitive, affective level, I am not suggesting that in Christian worship we kiss our brains good-bye. Though the embodied and ritual nature of Christian worship takes hold of our imaginations in a way that eludes didactic formulation, this does not mean that Christian worship has nothing to teach us. By emphasizing that worship is material and visceral, on the order of the imagination, I don't mean to suggest that it is somehow incommensurate with assertions or propositions. By emphasizing the priority of the affective, I'm not rejecting the cognitive. Rather, the point is to *situate* the cognitive, propositional aspects of Christian faith:

86. See N. T. Wright, "Paul's Gospel and Caesar's Empire," in *Paul and Politics: Ekklesia, Israel, Imperium, Interpretation*, ed. Richard A. Horsley (Harrisburg, PA: Trinity, 2000), 161–62.

87. For related discussion of the Creed, see Nicholas Adams, "Confessing the Faith: Reasoning in Tradition," in *The Blackwell Companion to Christian Ethics*, ed. Stanley Hauerwas and Samuel Wells (Oxford: Blackwell, 2006), 209–21.

they emerge in and from practices.[88] The Creed is a moment in worship that gives us much to think about in the sense of conscious, intentional reflection; it teaches us something, formulated in assertions and propositions, and makes ontological claims about God, the world, and ourselves. Indeed, what is articulated in the Creed has been behind much of what we've been doing in worship. But its situation within worship—and in relation to baptism—also situates its function and end. What we believe is not a matter of intellectualizing salvation but rather a matter of knowing what to love, knowing to whom we pledge allegiance, and knowing what is at stake for us as people of the "baptismal city." In reciting it each week, we rehearse the skeletal structure of the story in which we find our identity. Its cadences become part of who we are, and they function as rival cadences, sometimes doing battle in our imagination with the cadences of other pledges that would ask for our allegiance and loyalty.

Prayer: Learning the Language of the Kingdom

After confession and absolution, after we have been ordained as priests in this new *polis* that is the baptismal city (which is just to say that we've been re-created to be the humans we're called to be), the way is opened for us to approach God in concerted prayer. "Since, then, we have a great high priest who has passed through the heavens, Jesus, the Son of God. . . . Let us therefore approach the throne of grace with boldness, so that we may receive mercy and find grace to help in time of need" (Heb. 4:14, 16). We should perhaps try to appreciate how strange this might look to Martian anthropologists, for here is a group of what appear to be otherwise (relatively) normal people engaged in a conversation with someone who seems to be absent. And this isn't like listening to just half of a conversation on a cell phone, where we can, from experience, postulate that there is another human being holding up the other end of the conversation. Rather, the

88. This requires more nuance and analysis than we can pursue here. In particular, it would require that we come up with a way to articulate different modes of intending "content." For instance, when I confess the Creed in the context of gathered worship, that will be a different kind of (speech?) act than when I read it for analysis at the front of a theology class (and it would be different in yet another way if I read it for analysis at the front of a history class, particularly if this was a history class at a Jewish university, say). (This puts us back in the terrain of George Lindbeck, *The Nature of Doctrine: Religion and Theology in a Postliberal Age* [Philadelphia: Westminster, 1984], 65–69.) It seems to me that, phenomenologically speaking, there are different modes of intentionality that are at stake in these different recitations of the same "content." My concern is to contest construals of both Christian faith and Christian worship that overprioritize the cognitive, and thus my claims (fuzzy as they may be) should be understood against that horizon. My thanks to Matt and Lisa Walhout for conversations on this point.

practice of prayer will, to particularly cynical Martians, seem more like the scruffy, bearded guy on the subway platform who is carrying on an animated conversation with himself.

Perhaps this is the first thing we should note about the practice of prayer with respect to the Christian social imaginary: it is a practice that makes us a people who refuse to settle for appearances. Or, to put it otherwise, it makes us a people who always see that there's more going on than meets the eye. One might even say it's another indication that for Christians who pray, the world must be characterized by a kind of enchantment. On the one hand, while the Martian anthropologist does not see God as present in our worship, the community in worship sees things very differently. God is present and engaged with us in worship—in his Word, in the sacraments, in the presence of the Spirit within us. On the other hand, the practice of prayer banks on God's exceeding our worship space, transcending the confines of place and time, and as the Creator of the universe, being interested and concerned about concrete realities that face us here in our finitude. Praying enacts an entire cosmology because implicit in the very act of prayer is an entire ontology and construal of the God-world relationship. This doesn't mean that we need to pursue a doctorate in metaphysics in order to pray; on the contrary, the point is that by *doing* it, by praying, we are engaged in a sort of performative ontology that could be teased out in reflection and analysis.

Christian worship usually includes at least two modes of prayer, often combined: intercessory prayer or "the prayers of the people" (sometimes called the "pastoral prayer") and, just before the proclamation of the Word, prayer for illumination. What do these say about the kind of people we are called to be? What vision of the kingdom is implicit in these? And what do these habits train us to do?

In intercessory prayer, we are reminded of at least two things: First, that we are called, even chosen, as a people not for our own sake but for the sake of the world. Just as Adam and Eve were created to be God's image bearers in and to the world, and just as Israel was chosen in order to be a light unto the nations, so the church is called to be the people of God to and for the world. It is because we are God's ambassadors and image bearers, charged with caring for creation, that we bring to him the concerns of creation, praying for each other, for the church, and for the world at large. As a royal priesthood, we are called to pray for the world; we are gathered in prayer like a monastic community that devotes itself to the world precisely by being devoted to prayer and worship. As individuals engaged in intercessory prayer, we are called outside of ourselves and our own interests to concern for the other (cf. Phil. 2:4–11). So, too, as a congregation, while we pray for one another, we also pray for those outside our community of faith: for our neighborhoods; for municipal and

194   Desiring the Kingdom

government leaders; for the poor and those in prison; for those suffering persecution, exploitation, or the effects of natural disasters; even for our enemies. Second, sometimes echoing confession, in intercessory prayer we are given words to articulate the vision of justice that is at the heart of the biblical vision of *shalom*. Often we do this in a backward sort of way: we pray for precisely the things that are continued evidence of the curse, of the way things are *not* supposed to be, and that thus make us hunger after the kingdom. We pray for healing from illness and disease, for protection from abuse, for the end of environmental exploitation, for the eradication of racism, for an end to war. This is why the intercessory prayer is so often accompanied by lament, which is the church's performative response to the so-called problem of evil.[89]

Finally, as we prepare to hear the Word proclaimed, a prayer for illumination positions and challenges our confidence in self-sufficient reason. Such a prayer stems from a consciousness that wisdom is not something simply available, ready at hand, and on the shelf to be picked up at our pleasure. Even if the Word is a gift, it is a gift that we can receive only if we are enabled by the Spirit (1 Cor. 2:6–16). If prayer is a performative ontology, then we might say the prayer for illumination is a performative epistemology. That's not to say that you even need to know the word *epistemology* to engage in such prayer; rather, it means that when we acquire the habit of praying for illumination—a habit that we pick up in gathered worship but that can then be extended to other areas of our life—we are training ourselves in a stance of reception and dependence, an epistemic humility. This position recognizes that in order to see things for what they really are—to understand the world as ordered to the Creator—we are dependent on a teacher outside of ourselves (1 John 2:27).

Scripture and Sermon: Renarrating the World

A prayer for illumination having been offered, we will now see those gathered attuned to listen to a reading and commentary (sermon) from an ancient book.[90] Once again, there is a certain strangeness to this from

89. See J. Richard Middleton, "Why the 'Greater Good' Isn't a Defense," *Koinonia* 9 (1997): 81–113; and David Burrell, *Deconstructing Theodicy: Why Job Has Nothing to Say to the Puzzle of Suffering* (Grand Rapids: Brazos, 2008).

90. Some liturgical traditions, including Jewish liturgies, include a rich array of very physical, embodied practices related to the Scriptures, including elevating and incensing the book, kissing the book, and having it read from different sites within the sanctuary. For an illuminating discussion, see Jim Fodor, "Reading the Scriptures: Rehearsing Identity, Practicing Character," in *The Blackwell Companion to Christian Ethics*, 142–45.

the perspective of our Martian anthropologists. When, for instance, they observed what looked like similar rituals at the university, it seemed that those with a book were concerned that it be as new as possible, that it represent the most recent advances in knowledge (there were a few exceptions, mainly in the philosophy department). But here, in this gathering of Christians, week after week they open themselves up to a strange edited collection of books that they take to be one book (the "canon" of Scripture), and they are attentive to it not merely as a historical document but also as a normative text. What's going on here? What function does this book have in the community? What role does it play? What does its public reading *do*?

The Scriptures function as the script of the worshiping community, the story that narrates the identity of the people of God, the constitution of this baptismal city, and the fuel of the Christian imagination. We have emphasized that humans are liturgical animals, whose desire is shaped by rituals of ultimacy that we described as liturgies. Implicit in such liturgies is a *story*; thus the claim that we are liturgical animals is a correlate of Alasdair MacIntyre's claim that "man [*sic*] is in his actions and practice, as well as in his fictions, essentially a story-telling animal."[91] We are essentially story-telling animals not because we just love a good yarn, or because we enjoy being entertained, but rather because we think narratively, as it were. "I can only answer the question 'What am I to do?' if I can answer the prior question 'Of what story or stories do I find myself a part?'"[92] I have been suggesting that, insofar as a story about the kingdom is implicit in all liturgies (both Christian and "secular"), we imbibe and absorb these stories without them necessarily being explicitly articulated as such. An entire narrative can be operative in and behind a thirty-second spot for either a new Volkswagen or Army recruitment. However, those implicit, liturgically conveyed stories can also be made more explicit in more recognizably narrative forms. Christian worship is deeply shaped by an explicit articulation of the story in the Scriptures.

When the Scriptures are read in the context of gathered worship, they are, in a sense, *enacted* at the same time. Though the entirety of Christian worship inscribes the story of God in Christ into our imaginations, the moment of Scripture reading and proclamation of the Word in preaching is the most intense or explicit moment for the articulation of this story. This is

91. Alasdair MacIntyre, *After Virtue*, 2nd ed. (Notre Dame, IN: University of Notre Dame Press, 1984), 216.
92. Ibid. For further reflection on the storied shape of our thinking, see Stanley Hauerwas, "A Story-Formed Community: Reflections on *Watership Down*," in *The Hauerwas Reader*, ed. John Berkman and Michael Cartwright (Durham, NC: Duke University Press, 2001), 171–99.

why "worship is Scripture's home, its native soil, its most congenial habitat. . . . It is in the liturgy . . . that Christians are schooled and exercised in the scriptural logic of the faith."[93] In particular, the Scriptures provide the story of which we find ourselves a part, and thus the narration and absorption of the story is crucial to give us resources for knowing what we ought to *do*.[94] The end of ingesting the story—"eating the book"—is in order to be and become a certain kind of person and a certain kind of people. Over time, when worship confronts us with the canonical range of Scripture,[95] coupled with its proclamation and elucidation in the sermon, we begin to absorb the story as a moral or ethical compass—not because it discloses to us abstract, ahistorical moral axioms, but because it narrates the *telos* of creation, the shape of the kingdom we're looking for, thus filling in the *telos* of our own action. We begin to absorb the plot of the story, begin to see ourselves as characters within it; the habits and practices of its heroes function as exemplars, providing guidance as we are trained in virtue, becoming a people with a disposition to "the good" as it's envisioned in the story. Because we are story-telling animals, imbibing the story of Scripture is the primary way that our desire gets aimed at the kingdom.

Scripture also functions as something like the constitution of the baptismal city.[96] If the church is a new *polis*—a new sociopolitical community constituted by God in baptism—then, like any good city, it will be defined and animated by a constitution. Aristotle argues that a constitution is the "formal cause" of a *polis*, though it need not be written. It constitutes the "way of life" of the citizens of the *polis*.[97] Indeed, "this community is the constitution; the virtue of the citizen must therefore be relative to the

93. Fodor, "Reading the Scriptures," in *The Blackwell Companion to Christian Ethics*, 141.

94. It is precisely this concern that organizes the helpful account of Scripture in Craig G. Bartholomew and Michael W. Goheen, *The Drama of Scripture: Finding Our Place in the Biblical Story* (Grand Rapids: Baker Academic, 2004). Compare also John W. Wright, *Telling God's Story: Narrative Preaching for Christian Formation* (Downers Grove, IL: InterVarsity, 2007).

95. Scripture's story can be easily domesticated in Christian worship when the selection of readings is left to the whim of the pastor or other intra-congregational decision making. This is why elsewhere I have suggested that something like the lectionary functions as a prompt for the worshiping community to hear the full range of the Scriptures over time (see James K. A. Smith, *Who's Afraid of Postmodernism? Taking Derrida, Lyotard, and Foucault to Church* [Grand Rapids: Baker Academic, 2006], 57, 76–79), though I recognize that this is not a sufficient guarantee. It also requires that the Word's proclamation be shaped by a canonical sense of redemptive history. Equipping preachers to proclaim the Scriptures in this way is precisely the burden of Wright's *Telling God's Story*.

96. Something analogous is suggested by Francis Schüssler Fiorenza, "The Crisis of Scriptural Authority: Interpretation and Reception," *Interpretation* 44 (October 1990): 353–68.

97. See Aristotle, *Politics* 3.1; 4.11.

constitution of which he is a member."[98] A constitution outlines the good of the *polis*, the end to which all its citizens are to be directed, thus specifying what counts as virtue, namely, habits and dispositions that make us the kind of people who "naturally" pursue the telos that the *polis* extols as the good life. The biblical story, situated in the context of the church's worship, does just this: it fills out and specifies what the kingdom (*telos*) of God's people looks like, and thus articulates the *telos* of virtue for citizens of the city of God. It shows us the kind of people we're called to be.

Finally, in the anthropology we sketched in chapter 1, we emphasized that as liturgical, affective animals, our construal and constitution of the world is shaped primarily by the imagination. With that in mind, we should emphasize that the narrative of Scripture is a primary fund for the Christian imagination. As Richard Hays puts it, learning to read Scripture well is a means for the "conversion of the imagination."[99] He is particularly interested in encouraging contemporary readers to follow the example of Paul's reading of Israel's Scripture: "If we do follow his example, the church's imagination will be converted to see both Scripture and the world in a radically new way." He points out that this is as old as Origen: "As a Christian interpreter living in a pagan world, Origen was able to see clearly that Gentile converts to the faith needed to have their minds re-made, and that instruction in how to read Scripture was at the heart of Paul's pastoral practice: Gentiles needed to be initiated into reading practices that enabled them to receive Israel's Scripture as their own."[100] This "conversion of the imagination" by reading Scripture happens primarily and affectively when Scripture is encountered liturgically (communally in worship). When we encounter Scripture in worship, we are invited into its performance and thus initiated into a way of reading the world.

Eucharist: Supper with the King

In some ways, Christian worship culminates in another sacrament that is a compacted microcosm of the whole of worship: the Eucharist, or Lord's

98. Ibid., 3.4.1276b.29–31. In this context, Aristotle is explaining how someone might be a virtuous citizen but not necessarily a virtuous "man" since virtue is relative. What counts as virtue in any particular *polis* (relative to its constitution) does not necessarily count as virtue elsewhere or as such; after all, it might be a bad *polis* with a bad constitution. This can also help to explain a tension that citizens of the "heavenly city" might also experience: with a certain kind of citizenship in two different cities (the heavenly city and, say, the United States), what counts as "virtue" in one *polis* might actually constitute "vice" in the other.

99. Richard B. Hays, *The Conversion of the Imagination: Paul as Interpreter of Israel's Scripture* (Grand Rapids: Eerdmans, 2005), viii.

100. Ibid.

Supper. This happens in many different ways across Christian traditions, but try to imagine one selective snapshot: Recapitulating much that has gone before (law, confession, absolution, Scripture, proclamation, prayer, and thanksgiving)—liturgical practices that have called upon our ears and our knees, our eyes and our tongues, our hands and our noses—now our mouths, with a sort of sanctified salivation, begin to anticipate a new role for taste. Inviting us to be stretched out of the comforts of immanence ("Lift up your hearts!"), the liturgy places us in the midst of the story, in an episode that compresses the gospel into an action:

> On the night he was handed over to suffering and death, our Lord Jesus Christ took bread; and when he had given thanks to you, he broke it, and gave it to his disciples, and said, "Take, eat: This is my Body, which is given for you. Do this for the remembrance of me."
>
> After supper he took the cup of wine; and when he had given thanks, he gave it to them, and said, "Drink this, all of you: This is my Blood of the new Covenant, which is shed for you and for many for the forgiveness of sins. Whenever you drink it, do this for the remembrance of me."[101]
>
> For as often as you eat this bread and drink the cup, you proclaim the Lord's death until he comes. (1 Cor. 11:26)

It's as if the story we've been hearing and rehearsing now comes with live illustrations. The bread that is his body is broken, its cracking perhaps reverberating through a tiny chapel. The wine that is his blood is poured with a flourish, even gusto, that makes it gurgle loudly among the few who are here gathered, its scent wafting across the space as our taste buds surprise us when, in an admittedly Pavlovian response, they begin to perk up at the thought of its bite on our tongue (and so early in the morning!). We join those proceeding to the front, helping one of the elderly widows to the rail as, with a grimace, she kneels at the altar. Hands outstretched, heads bowed, the wafer is placed in our cupped hands ("The body of Christ, the bread of heaven"), and we slip it onto our tongue in that weird moment of waiting for it to melt in our mouth. The cup follows, as we're still kneeling, and drinking from one chalice ("The blood of Christ, the cup of salvation"), we once again keep the feast.

The tangible display and performance of the gospel in the Lord's Supper is a deeply affecting practice. Its sights and smells, its rhythms and movements, are the sort of thing that seep into our imaginations and become second nature. Just as a song makes words stick in our memory, so the sights, smells, and rhythms of the Eucharist seem to make the story both come alive and wriggle into our imaginations in a way that it wouldn't

---

101. *The 1979 U. S. Book of Common Prayer*, 362–63. Available online at http://justus. anglican.org/resources/bcp/formatted_1979.htm.

otherwise.[102] But what's happening when that happens? What understanding of the world is implicit in this practice? What vision of the kingdom is carried in this ritual? Here we note just three themes.

First, lest we pass too quickly over the mundane and obvious, we should appreciate that the stuff of the Lord's Supper—the "elements" as they're sometimes called—are rather ho-hum stuff: bread and wine, staples of any daily diet in many parts of the world and across history. In instituting the feast, Jesus took up what was in hand, what would have been on any table at that time. And while these are rich with symbolism from Israel's history, they are also everyday items. So once again, in the very practices of Christian worship, we see a hallowing of the everyday, a sanctification of the domestic. It's as if God once again looks upon the table, laden with fruit of the earth, and proclaims, "It's all very good" (cf. Gen. 1:31). When Jesus takes up the bread, he blesses it, giving thanks for it. Embedded in this hallowing of the mundane staples of a meal is an echo of the creational affirmation of the stuff of the earth. Furthermore, in the institution of the Lord's Supper, God takes up as a sacrament one of the most essential and therefore most common of human activities: eating. Here we see a wonderful encapsulation of how the sacraments intensify the general sacramentality of the world: "The Eucharist is different from the common meals of daily life but it is also continuous with them. This suggests that the kingdom does not involve a cancellation of this-worldly concerns; it is not a wholly other world but rather *this* world transformed and transfigured."[103] Indeed, when Jesus celebrates the Last Supper, he actually intimates that it's not really the *last* supper, but the penultimate supper. Jesus doesn't announce that he'll never eat or drink again, in a final message before some gnostic escape from the body that needs nutrition and nourishment; rather, he announces, "I will never again drink of this fruit of the vine until that day when I drink it new with you in my Father's kingdom" (Matt. 26:29). The eucharistic feast itself is a blessing of our everyday eating, drinking, and all the habits and practices that are part and parcel of being dependent, finite creatures.

The Lord's Supper does not only hallow and sanctify nature's biological processes that bring forth grain and grapes and compel us to eat and drink. After all, it's not wheat and grapes that are on the table; it's bread and wine. These are not naturally occurring phenomena; they are the fruit of *culture*, the products of human making. In blessing the bread and giving thanks for it, Jesus not only hallows the stuff of the earth, but he also hallows the

102. I don't mean to suggest that the Lord's Supper is just an illustration of the gospel. It is a sacrament in which Christ is present. But again following Leithart, I will generally not be concerned here with "zoom lens" issues regarding "real presence," etc. In much that follows, I owe a debt to Leithart, "The Way Things Really Ought to Be."

103. Ibid., 166.

stuff of our hands. The affirmation of the goodness of creation includes not just the furniture of "nature" but also the whole panoply of cultural phenomena that humanity, by its cultural labor, teases out of creation. So "when bread is set on the table, an agricultural and culinary science and technology lies in the background. . . . Mankind is given the creation not only to use its products in their natural state but also to transform them for the enrichment of human life; not only as a guardian of what is but as creator of what is not yet; not only to eat but to bake."[104] Thus embedded in the very mundane practice of blessing bread and wine, Christian worship rehearses God's blessing of creation.

Second, as we've already seen, there's a certain sense in which the celebration of the Lord's Supper should be experienced as a kind of sanctified letdown. For every week that we celebrate the Eucharist is another week that the kingdom and its feast have not yet fully arrived. And every week the words of institution remind us of this fact, for we do it "until he comes." By this I don't mean to denigrate the peace, joy, and nourishment that is found in the Supper; rather, the point is to emphasize that the Eucharist is an *eschatological* supper. It's sort of a meal "to go," or at least a meal on the way. It's a table in the wilderness (Ps. 78:19) and in the presence of our enemies (Ps. 23:5), and so there's a certain sense in which we eat it "on the run"—not because of the frenetic pace of consumption and distraction that so often finds us in the drive-thru and eating fast food in the car, but rather because the Lord's Supper is an anticipatory meal that we eat while we sojourn in the earthly city, looking forward to the marriage supper of the Lamb (Rev. 19:9). So the Lord's Supper is a foretaste of the feast in the kingdom, which means that its meaning has to be situated within an eschatological horizon. It is a meal that constitutes us as an eschatological people: while it recalls and recapitulates Christ's death, burial, and resurrection, the Supper also looks ahead to the feast in the kingdom. As such, "the Eucharist should be understood as a sign of the renewed creation. The Eucharist is our model of the eschatological order, a microcosm of the way things really ought to be."[105] Thus it is a *normative* meal: by showing us a foretaste of how things ought to be, the practice of the Lord's Supper carries norms in it, and these norms constitute both a basis of critique for the present order, as well as hints as to how the church should order itself as a *polis* that is itself a foretaste of the coming community.

For instance, the bread and wine are freely distributed to all who are in communion; this itself anticipates the abundance of the kingdom, which is itself an answer to Israel's longing:

104. Ibid., 169.
105. Ibid., 165–66.

> Ho, everyone who thirsts,
> come to the waters;
> and you that have no money,
> come, buy and eat!
> Come, buy wine and milk
> without money and without price.
> Why do you spend your money for that which is not bread,
> and your labor for that which does not satisfy?
> Listen carefully to me, and eat what is good,
> and delight yourselves in rich food. (Isa. 55:1–2)

The eucharistic feast is a tiny normative picture of the justice that characterizes the coming kingdom of God, where none go hungry because of poverty or alienated labor (cf. Isa. 65:21–23). None will hoard a surplus, leaving others with a lack; as in the eucharistic meal, bread and wine are freely and equally distributed. The Lord's Supper constitutes practice for such a kingdom economics. And in *doing* it, we enact a foretaste of the way things really ought to be.

The third element is a particular instance of "the way things really ought to be": the Lord's Supper is a feast of forgiveness and reconciliation. If it is a table prepared in the presence of our enemies, it is also a table where God sits down with those who were once his enemies (Rom. 5:10; Col. 1:21). The Supper is a gracious communion with a forgiving God; but it is also a supper we eat *with one another*, and that too will require forgiveness. God's design for human flourishing cannot be satisfied in isolation. As dependent, social creatures, we are created for community. And unlike powerful narratives that shape political liberalism and consumer capitalism, competition and animosity between one another are not taken to be the natural state of affairs; rather, this "war of all with all" is taken to be an irruption of violence that befalls the created order. The reduction of all intersubjective relationships to competition—a war by other means—is a distortion and perversion of the creational ideal of collaboration and cooperation.

The church, as a body and *polis* that is a witness to the renewal of creation, is required to be a community of dependence—a body that can't possibly function, let alone flourish, without the collaborative contribution of each member (1 Cor. 12:12–26). But given the brokenness of our relationships, the abuses and violence and competition that fragment our communion, the body must be reknit together through practices of reconciliation and forgiveness. A kingdom-shaped community cannot be satisfied with private, isolated individuals only reconciled "vertically" to God, for the manifest witness of such reconciliation will be love of neighbor. This is one of the central themes of the First Epistle of John: "We love because he first loved us. Those who say, 'I love God,' and hate their brothers or sisters, are liars; for those who do not love a brother or sister whom they have seen, cannot love God whom they have not seen" (1 John 4:19–20). Indeed, "How does God's love abide in anyone who has the world's goods and sees a brother or sister in need and yet refuses help?" (1 John 3:17).

Hence, the Eucharist—the heart of the church's worship—is also the liturgical practice that requires and effects reconciliation. A table forces us to face up to reality, making the discomfort of fractured relationships starkly bubble up to the surface (think of those awkward dinner scenes in *The Gilmore Girls* where the family is silent and seething!). Marshaling the mundane and universal human practice of eating, and thus also taking up the common connection between food and fellowship, the table of the Lord is a catalyst for reconciliation on the "horizontal" level as well. This normal, everyday human activity of eating will be the occasion for undoing the abnormal but all-too-common reality of human enmity and discord.[106] Just as Jesus admonished us to be reconciled before leaving our gifts at the altar (Matt. 5:23–24), so too Paul admonishes the Corinthians to examine themselves before partaking of the Lord's Supper (1 Cor. 11:27–34). From the earliest practices of the church, the discipline of reconciliation has been tethered to the Eucharist. Thus in the *Didache*, the author warns, "Let no one who has a quarrel with a companion join you until they have been reconciled, so that your sacrifice may not be defiled."[107] The gracious invitation to the table is also a call to reconciliation, which is a reminder that the task of humanity is ineluctably *social*; we cannot image God in isolation ("in the image of God he created *them*").

In a broken, fragmented world, the church is called to be the first-fruits of a new creation by embodying a reconciled community; and the way we begin to learn that is at the communion table. The habits and practices of examination and reconciliation that are part of the Eucharist are like training wheels meant to let us "try out" forgiveness and reconciliation. And in this respect, the Eucharist is just a macrocosm of what the church is called to be as the new humanity: a community that gathers, irrespective of preferences, tastes, class, or ethnicity, in order to pursue a *common* good. I often tell my children that one of the reasons we go to church is to learn to love people we don't really like that much—people we find irritating, odd, and who grate on our nerves (the feeling's certainly mutual, I'm sure!). And sometimes we will even have

106. There is also a sense in which the Eucharist is a "feast for the plebs," opening up the table to all (contra the rigid structures of "commensality" in the first century, by which table fellowship was a means of imposing clear hierarchies of privilege and power). For discussion, see John Dominic Crossan, *Jesus: A Revolutionary Biography* (San Francisco: HarperSanFrancisco, 1994), 66–70.

107. *Didache* 14.2, in *The Apostolic Fathers: Greek Texts and English Translations*, ed. and trans. Michael W. Holmes, 3rd ed. (Grand Rapids: Baker Academic, 2007), 365–67.

to work through our frustrations and hurts when we fail one another and disappoint one another. The *communion* table is a historic catalyst for practices of reconciliation. In this sense, the Eucharist is yet another instance of Christian worship constituting a pedagogy of desire.[108]

As Pope John Paul II described it, the Eucharist is "the *school* of active love for neighbor." As a training in reconciliation, the "Eucharist educates us to this love in a deeper way; it shows us, in fact, what value each person, our brother or sister, has in God's eyes, if Christ offers Himself equally to each one, under the species of bread and wine."[109] This is not to claim that we accomplish perfect reconciliation, or that somehow the Eucharist magically undoes injustices we've experienced or committed in the past. Rather, the claim is that liturgical practices of reconciliation and forgiveness constitute a training ground for making a start—and they demand that we do so. Because "forgiveness and repentance are lifelong projects,"[110] and because we will almost always experience "this tension between the meal and longer processes of reconciliation,"[111] there will always be a sense in which we do so *in hope*. As a school for learning to love our neighbor, and thus becoming reconciled, it is also a school for learning to love our enemies—the most scandalous element of renewed community in the kingdom come.

Offering: Kingdom Economics of Gratitude

In some ways, we have come through the climax of the service and entered its denouement. But in another way, we are reaching its conclusion and *telos*. In response to all the graces bestowed in the service—in the sacraments of the Word, baptism, and the Lord's Supper, which have each included God's blessing, our confession, and God's assurance of pardon—we now respond in gratitude, in songs and hymns of praise, but also in that oddly awkward moment when people scramble for their purses on the floor or the wallets in their back pockets. The organ or piano or guitars muffle the sheepish sound of coins jingling, or the rustling of bills being folded and

108. I don't mean to suggest that the Supper is *just* "practice" and that reconciliation depends on what we can accomplish. In another sense, the Eucharist effects reconciliation. For discussion, see L. Gregory Jones, *Embodying Forgiveness: A Theological Analysis* (Grand Rapids: Eerdmans, 1995), 176–77.

109. John Paul II, *Dominicae Cenae*, Pastoral Letter on the Mystery and Worship of the Eucharist (1980), §6.

110. Jones, *Embodying Forgiveness*, 179.

111. Christopher Gundry, "A Table in the Midst of My Enemies? Power, Abuse, and the Possibilities for Reconciliation in Holy Communion," *Liturgy* 23 (2008): 27–34, at 32. Gundry provides an honest reflection on this tension that rightly questions idealized accounts of eucharistic reconciliation.

creased into the palm to be dropped into the basket in a sort of manual covert operation. Envelopes and notes are pressed into the hands of children, who are eager to place them in the plate as it passes by, giving what's not theirs for they know not what. To Martian anthropologists, this might look like people paying for the entertainment, settling accounts for the services rendered. But if we attend to the constructions of meaning given to the offering within the logic of worship, we see something different—and something suggested about the shape of the kingdom.

First, with apologies for repeating the obvious, it is worth noting that the practice of Christian worship takes up and involves something mundane, common, and even "dirty" (as in "filthy lucre"): the nitty-gritty reality of money. Just as worship touches our bellies, so it touches our pocketbooks. Once again we have an indication of how "worldly" worship is.

Second, contrary to the perception of our Martian anthropologists, this is not really an exchange. It certainly isn't a mutual or reciprocal gift exchange since there is a radical disproportion between the gifts we've received and the gifts we now offer "in return." Rather, the offering is an expression of gratitude. It is a symbolic but concrete indication that the "commerce" between God and humanity is not a contract but a covenant, which traffics not in commodities but gifts.

Third, following from this, the liturgical practice of the offering indicates that Christian worship—which is a foretaste of the new creation—embodies a new economy, an alternative economy. As we saw in baptism, the coming kingdom is not a collection of clean souls who have been washed in the waters of baptism in order to pursue an eternity of private devotion to God; rather, baptism is God's way of constituting a new *polis*, a new sociopolitical community. In short, the kingdom is political. And as we saw in the Eucharist, the coming kingdom is characterized not just by private individuals reconciled to God but by a human community reconciled to one another. In short, the kingdom is concerned with the stuff of sociology—with redeeming communities, institutions, and systems of human organization. And now, just as the eucharistic meal is continuous with other meals, the Sunday offering in gathered worship is not disconnected from other systems of commerce, distribution, and exchange. In other words, the kingdom is concerned with economics. This is not just a matter of individual acts of charity or discretionary giving from our so-called disposable income, but rather a reconfiguration of distribution and consumption.

The heritage of our Sunday offering, and the kingdom economics it points toward, can be seen in the practices of the early church. For instance, the miracle of the Spirit's descent at Pentecost did not just generate evangelism and conversions; it also spurred discipleship, and part and parcel of that discipleship was an economics: the same ones who were baptized and "devoted themselves to the apostles' teaching and fellowship, to the breaking of bread and the prayers" (Acts 2:42) also gathered together "and had all things in common; they would sell their possessions and goods and distribute the proceeds to all, as any had need" (Acts 2:44–45). This kingdom economics—"socialism by grace"[112]—becomes an important mark of the church and a central aspect of Christian practice. As the *ekklēsia* continues to grow, "the whole group of those who believed were of one heart and soul, and no one claimed private ownership of any possessions, but everything they owned was held in common" (Acts 4:32). One of the starkest instances of judgment in the narrative of Acts is occasioned by the failure of Ananias and Sapphira, who were judged not because they failed to continue in prayer or the apostles' teaching but precisely because they refused to participate honestly in the alternative economy of the church (Acts 5:1–11).

The reconciled and redeemed body of Christ is marked by cruciform practices that counter the liturgies of consumption, hoarding, and greed that characterize so much of our late modern culture. As a result, the *ekklēsia* is distinguished by very different procedures and criteria for the distribution of goods and wealth. In this sense, the church's mad economics anticipates a kingdom economics. As we saw in Isaiah 55:1–2, the kingdom is envisioned as an economy where we can buy wine and milk without money, where "rich food" is freely available to all.

Sadly, in many contexts of worship in North America, the offering in worship is little more than a parody of such an alternative economics. And yet the integration of a worship practice that is economic, tethered to the wider scope of Scripture, functions as a kind of haunting reminder of an economics that refuses the assumptions of the capitalist imagination.

Sending as Witnesses: The Cultural Mandate Meets the Great Commission

While we have been engaged with the triune God in the practices of worship, in a dialogic dance of gift and call, call and response, pleading and receiving, eating and drinking, we have also been practicing (for) the kingdom. We've gathered to do what we were made for—praise and worship—and in so doing, we have been learning a language, participating in a story, undergoing training to fulfill our mission as the communal *imago Dei*. Christian worship is an affective school, a pedagogy of desire in which we learn not how to be spiritual or religious, but how to be *human*, how to take up the vocation given to us at creation. And now we are sent from this practice arena—which is the *real* world—into the world to be witnesses *by* being God's image bearers, who cultivate the world in a way that exemplifies Jesus's perfect "cultural"

112. See John Milbank, *Being Reconciled* (London: Routledge, 2003), 162–86.

To Think About: Singing the End of Strangers

As I'm writing this, the words of Patty Griffin's song "No Bad News" have become newly illuminated for me, as if I just heard them for the first time. In a middle stanza, she sings of a social experiment not unlike the task of the church sent as witnesses to the kingdom of love:

> I'm gonna find me a man, love him so well, love him so strong, love him so slow.
> We're gonna go way beyond the walls of this fortress.
> And we won't be afraid, we won't be afraid, and though the darkness may come our way,
> We won't be afraid to be alive anymore.
> And we'll grow kindness in our hearts for all the strangers among us,
> Till there are no strangers anymore.

This, in a sense, is the vocation of the church as the new humanity, commissioned and sent to be God's image bearers and thus to provide a communal foretaste of the coming kingdom. Our love for one another should spill over the walls of our fortress, the built space of our worship, and without fear or shame, our love for the stranger and the enemy should be an invitation for all to become friends of God and friends of God's friends, "till there are no strangers anymore." This brings to mind Jeremiah's vision of a day when "no longer shall they teach one another, or say to each other, 'Know the LORD,' for they shall all know me, from the least of them to the greatest, says the LORD; for I will forgive their iniquity, and remember their sin no more" (Jer. 31:34).

---

labor. That now includes our cultural labor of being the church, the body of Christ, in a way that is hospitable and inviting—in a way that invites others to find their identity and vocation in Christ, to become "new creations" and thus become the humans they were called to be. In short, when we are sent as witnesses, we are sent as evangelists to proclaim the good news, to announce the story of God's redeeming and restoring a peculiar people, graced to bear his image. But in doing so, in carrying out this Great Commission, we are witnessing to the fact that God's action in the cross and resurrection has made it possible for humanity to be human, to take up their creational vocation as prince(sse)s and priests charged with cultivating creation. So the good news announced in the Great Commission is that God has made it possible for us to actually participate in the cultural mandate.

We are sent into the world to make disciples, which means we're being sent into the world to invite them to find their identity and vocation in Christ, the second Adam, the model of the new human. And they will do this by participating in the worship and practices of the called-out people that is the church. Thus the church is a cultural center, not just a spiritual filling station or a hospital for the soul. It is a cultural center of the baptismal city, the city of God. The cultural labors of disciples will look strange and scandalous because they are unfolded on the basis of the norms disclosed in the story of God in Christ. Thus Klaas Schilder notes, "It is in the *Church*, as the mother of believers brings forth the 'new' men [*sic*] who, also as far as cultural life is concerned, bear the burdens of the whole world. Only the *Church* joins them together into an unbreakable communion and teaches the norms for all the relationships of life, even outside the Church."[113] The church is elected to responsibility, called to be the church to and for the world—not in order to save it or conquer it or even transform it, but to serve it by showing what redeemed human community and culture look like, as modeled by the One whose cultural work led him to the cross. In short, we're sent out to be martyrs, witnesses of the Crucified One. In that way, we win by losing.[114]

Worship, like creation, ends as it began: with God's blessing. The minister raises her hands, we stretch out ours to receive, and God's blessing is proclaimed:

> The LORD bless you and keep you;
> the LORD make his face shine upon you
> and be gracious to you;
> The LORD turn his face toward you
> and give you peace. (Num. 6:24–26 NIV)

When we were called, we were blessed; now as we're sent, we're blessed. We are not sent out as orphans, nor are we sent out to prove ourselves. The blessing speaks of affirmation and conferral—that we go empowered for this mission, graced recipients of good gifts, filled with the Spirit, our imaginations fueled by the Word to imagine the world otherwise.

Worship, Discipleship, and Discipline: Practices beyond Sunday

All that we've just exegeted—the rhythms and practices of Christian worship—take place, in most cases, in about an hour and a half, one day a week. This is not much time to enact counter-measures to the secular liturgies in which we are immersed the rest of the week! Isn't it a bit of a naive overestimate to think that the practices of Christian worship, formative though they may be, could really function as sufficient counter-formation

---

113. Schilder, *Christ and Culture*, 106.

114. For a meditation on martyrdom, emphasizing that it not be "instrumentalized," see Craig Hovey, *To Share in the Body: A Theology of Martyrdom for Today's Church* (Grand Rapids: Brazos, 2008).

to the power and ubiquity of the secular liturgies we explored in chapter 3? Isn't this a bit of wishful thinking simply because of the simple quantification of time? And wouldn't this explain why Christian worship just doesn't seem to "work" the way I've been suggesting? Isn't it the case that, though many Christians in North America gather for worship week in and week out, we don't seem to look very peculiar? That is, we don't seem to be a people that looks very different from our neighbors, *except* that we go to church on Sunday mornings while they're home reading the paper.[115] These are important questions, and they press us to further expand our vision of Christian formation through Christian practices. As a start, I want to emphasize several things.

First, while the amount of time spent in Christian worship on Sunday mornings (or Saturday evenings, or what have you) is limited, it is nonetheless both dense and charged. Intentional Christian worship that includes the elements we've described above, and that draws upon a holistic tradition of worship that activates the whole body, is packed with formative power. In addition, we must remember that intentional Christian worship will always put us in the way of God's nourishing grace through the particularly charged practices of the sacraments: the Word, baptism, and the Lord's Supper.[116] Given the Spirit's unique presence in the sacraments, we ought not to underestimate the power of even a relatively brief encounter with the transforming triune God.[117]

This should be coupled with a second point: one of my claims in chapter 3 was that, to some extent, recognizing cultural practices and institutions *as* liturgies somewhat undercuts their formative force. My sense is that, seeing these cultural practices for what they are—formative liturgies bent

115. This is a critical line of questioning that I will address in volumes 2 and 3. Christian A. B. Scharen provides a helpful and provocative formulation of the issue in "'Judicious Narratives,' or Ethnography as Ecclesiology," *Scottish Journal of Theology* 58 (2005): 125–42. At this point, I suggest that my account of secular liturgies might be able to provide a framework for explaining why the practices of Christian worship don't seem to transform those who participate in them. For instance, I can think of a congregation gathering week in and week out for historic, intentional Christian worship that includes all the elements discussed here; and yet, from the perspective of *shalom*, some of its parishioners are unapologetic and public participants in some of the most egregious systemic injustices. Does that falsify my claims here? I don't think so, at least not necessarily. Rather, we will need a more nuanced account of how some liturgies *trump* others; in this case, we could suggest that though these parishioners participate in Christian worship, their participation in other secular liturgies effectively trumps the practices of Christian worship. Such a line of investigation might also require that we attend to empirical realities, drawing on a theologically informed psychology, sociology, and ethnography.

116. On the "sacramentalizing" of the Word in Calvin, see Dawn DeVries, "Calvin on the Word as Sacrament," in *Jesus Christ in the Preaching of Calvin and Schleiermacher* (Louisville: Westminster John Knox, 1996), 14–25.

117. On the Spirit in the sacraments, see Calvin, *Institutes*, 4.14.9, 12.

on shaping and aiming our desire—can effect a limited deactivation of them. Since their affective power thrives on bypassing our critical discernment, there is a sense in which, by rightly discerning them for what they are, we can, at least to some extent, minimize their effect. This is why I obviously don't mean to suggest that we should refrain from thinking or give up critical habits of mind. Indeed, the very project of this book is to engage our critical intellectual capacities in order to understand both cultural practices and Christian worship differently. If we can start to see cultural practices for what they are, it's as if we can then say to them, "I see what you're up to. . . ." So this recognition, coupled with intentional participation in Christian worship, can decrease (but not eliminate) the formative power of secular liturgies.

But such recognition cannot completely undo the formative power of cultural rituals that make competing visions of the kingdom seep into our imagination over time simply because of the sheer quantity of our immersion in them. For instance, even if we begin to see the mall as a rival liturgy, if we spent three nights a week there, coupled with hours and hours of absorbing television commercials (particularly since we usually watch TV to "veg out," to turn off our critical capacities), then the liturgy of the market has a cumulative force that can't help but be formative. Thus we need to consider a third piece of an answer to the questions above: monasticism.[118] By that I don't (necessarily) mean retreating to the desert to live on top of pillars. However, I think there are two elements of monastic life that should be considered as elements of Christian formation in our late-modern world: First, it may be the case, given the "quantity-of-immersion" challenge we've noted, that a Christian community that seeks to be a cultural force precisely by being a living example of a new humanity will have to consider *abstaining* from participation in some cultural practices that others consider normal.

Now, please note that I am not counseling abstention "from culture" *as such*, which would amount to pietist withdrawal from the goodness of creation. As Klaas Schilder rightly notes, because the cultural mandate is our creational vocation, "abstention from cultural labor is always a sin."[119] Rather, monastic abstention is abstention from participation in certain configurations of cultural institutions—abstaining from the *direction*, not the *structure*. It would be an abstention from participation in particular ("majority") cultural practices because of their liturgical formative power,

---

118. For Reformed folk who think that monasticism is simply incommensurate with a Reformed "world-and-life view," I commend Calvin's discussion of "a holy and lawful monasticism" in the *Institutes*, 4.13.10.

119. Schilder, *Christ and Culture*, 91. Compare the "ethic of secession" outlined in Brian J. Walsh and Sylvia C. Keesmaat, *Colossians Remixed: Subverting the Empire* (Downers Grove, IL: InterVarsity, 2004), 147–68.

but the abstention would not be primarily negative or protective: it would be undertaken in order to engage in cultural labor otherwise, to unfold cultural institutions that are ordered by love and aimed at the kingdom, cultural practices that are foretastes of the new creation and that, as such, would themselves function as winsome witness to God's redemptive love. Such a monastic[120] abstention *for* cultural labor sees itself as engaged in a struggle, but it forswears any pretension to a "culture war" because it doesn't think it's the job of the church to transform the world; rather, the ecclesial community, as witnesses and martyrs, is called to show the world that it is the world by living out an alternative embodiment of human community in concrete expressions of a kingdom economics, politics, and so forth. As Schilder claims,

> A Christian people maintaining their colleges, supporting missionaries, and caring for the needy who were left them by Christ, thus saving them from the clutches of state absolutism (that pioneer of the Antichrist!), doing a thousand other works of divine obligation, and primarily because of all this not able, for example, to set up an imposing Christian stage, supposing that such were possible, . . . such a people is indeed a heroic communion.[121]

Such a monasticism is not a retreat to the safety of a fortified isolated church (Augustine counseled the importance of urban monasteries right in the thick of things),[122] nor does it ensconce itself in a pietism of withdrawal. Abstention, in this case, is not a matter of seclusion. But neither does it see itself engaged in a triumphalist project of changing the world.[123] As a people called and gathered by the Crucified One, it sees Jesus as the second Adam, who has modeled what cultural labor looks like in a broken, hurting world; and so such a monasticism pursues a cultural labor that is not only creational but also cruciform. The abstention of such a monasticism is a retreat not to weakness but to a different kind of power, the weak power

120. Space does not permit full correction of the common denigration of monasticism, particularly in the Reformed tradition, as if it were just a pietistic withdrawal from culture *en tout*. Suffice it to say that the "holy and lawful monasticism" that Calvin hears in Augustine was very much a *cultural* project. It did not constitute a withdrawal from economics, politics, or labor, but rather it built cultural institutions that exhibited an alternative economics, politics, and concern with work.

121. Schilder, *Christ and Culture*, 93.

122. See Thomas F. Martin, OSA, "Augustine and the Politics of Monasticism," in *Augustine and Politics*, ed. John Doody, Kevin L. Hughes, and Kim Paffenroth (Lanham, MD: Lexington Books, 2005), 165–86.

123. As seen, for instance, in the confident triumphalism that is extolled by Michael Lindsay in *Faith in the Halls of Power: How Evangelicals Joined the American Elite* (New York: Oxford University Press, 2007), as well as the sort of "transformationist" program that animates a place like Patrick Henry College (see Hanna Rosin, *God's Harvard: A Christian College on a Mission to Save America* [New York: Harcourt, 2007]).

of witness, the sort of strange power exerted by martyrs.[124] "Blessed is my *wise* ward-elder," Schilder notes, "who does his home visiting in the right way. He is a *cultural* force, although he may not be aware of it."[125]

There is a second element of monasticism, beyond wise abstention, that commends itself to the "quantity-of-immersion" challenge: habits of *daily* worship. One of the features of monastic life is a rhythm of daily worship that might, when coupled with the abstention noted above, actually tip the scales regarding liturgical formation. Of course the Christian life is to be marked by daily prayer and devotional reading of Scripture, but this often occurs in private isolation. The monastic traditions (and other premodern configurations of society),[126] on the other hand, point to habits of daily worship that are communal and sacramental, including daily communion—practices of daily gathered worship that are holistic, activating the imagination through bodily participation. Who says that the shape of worship we've described above only has to happen on Sunday? A rich legacy in the history of the church suggests that this could be otherwise—that not just monks but also families and students, laborers and lawyers, could find ways to gather daily for worship that is nourishing and formative. For instance, many urban churches offer daily noontime communion, which makes it possible for those engaged in nonmonastic vocations to nonetheless gather with others for full-bodied worship. Often reflective of "intentional community" (which can take many forms), such daily gatherings can be fostered by geographical proximity.[127] You might say this is fighting quantity with quantity; Dietrich Bonhoeffer simply describes it as "life together."[128]

Finally, the "quantity challenge" is also countered by the fact that Christians engage in all kinds of formative practices and spiritual disciplines beyond the specifically liturgical practices of gathered worship.

124. See Marva J. Dawn, *Powers, Weakness, and the Tabernacling of God* (Grand Rapids: Eerdmans, 2001), 123–64.

125. Schilder, *Christ and Culture*, 114.

126. That is, such daily gathered worship was not only the routine of those who had taken vows of poverty, chastity, and obedience. It could also mark the life and routines of a whole community, including those engaged in the labors of family and trades. For an example, see Augustine Thompson, OP, *Cities of God: The Religion of the Italian Communes, 1125–1325* (University Park: Pennsylvania State University Press, 2005), 235–72.

127. This is why one of the "marks" of the new monasticism, which includes commitment to a rich life of gathered worship and spiritual discipline, includes "geographical proximity." See Jon Stock, "Mark 9: Geographical Proximity to Community Members Who Share a Common Rule of Life," in *School(s) for Conversion: 12 Marks of a New Monasticism*, ed. Rutba House (Eugene, OR: Cascade Books, 2005), 124–36. For the "12 Marks of a New Monasticism," see xii–xiii.

128. See Dietrich Bonhoeffer, *Life Together*, trans. John W. Doberstein (San Francisco: HarperSanFrancisco, 1954), esp. 40–75 ("The Day with Others").

Such communal practices happen at kitchen tables and in dorm rooms, in college chapels and cafeterias, in restaurants and on wooded trails. Families and friendships can be powerful incubators of desire for the kingdom.[129] When Christians engage in the practices of hospitality and Sabbath keeping, singing and forgiveness, simplicity and fasting, they are engaging in a way of life that is formative and constitutive of Christian discipleship.[130] These "practices beyond Sunday" are further opportunities to rehearse a way of life, to practice (for) the kingdom. For example, for several years now, my wife and I have gathered once a week with our best friends for a ritual we describe as "Wednesday Night Wine" (even if we sometimes have to push it to a Tuesday or a Thursday). After their little ones are in bed (our teenagers are left to fend for themselves), we make our way over to their place with a different bottle of wine each week, enjoyed with some cheese, crackers, and usually a little (Swiss) chocolate. We keep a journal of the wines, noting our tasting comments, rating them (rank amateurs that we are), and in the journal we also keep a little record of our topics of conversation, what's been happening with our kids, and significant events in the past week. We commiserate with one another about the burdens of parenting and share the joys of the same. We've mourned together, been frustrated together, worked through tensions with each other, confided in one another. When we were going through struggles "at church," in our community of gathered worship, this Wednesday night table was a refreshing and welcome "table in the wilderness." It has been nothing short of a shadow Eucharist, a veritable extension of the Lord's Supper.

I suggest that the range of Christian practices "beyond Sunday" are best understood as extensions of the liturgical practices of gathered worship; they are important and formative because (and insofar as) they draw on the formative power of specifically liturgical practices. Or, to put it conversely, the formative force of such extra-Sunday practices is diminished if they are unhooked from the liturgical practices of the

---

129. See David McCarthy's discussion, following *Lumen Gentium*, of the family as a "domestic church," situated in relation to the "first family" of the ecclesial community (*Sex and Love in the Home*, 113–14). In the Reformed tradition, consider the "Directory for Family Worship" approved by the Westminster divines (1647); see also Jacobus Koelman, *The Duties of Parents*, ed. M. Eugene Osterhaven, trans. John Vriend (Grand Rapids: Baker Academic, 2003).

130. Thus Craig Dykstra and Dorothy Bass simply define Christian practices as "things Christian people do together over time in response to and in the light of God's active presence for the life of the world." See Dykstra and Bass, "Times of Yearning, Practices of Faith," in *Practicing Our Faith*, ed. Dorothy Bass (San Francisco: Jossey-Bass, 1997), 5. This book provides a helpful compendium of Christian practices "beyond Sunday." For another discussion of specifically spiritual disciplines, see Richard Foster, *Celebration of Discipline*, 3rd ed. (San Francisco: Harper, 1988).

ecclesial community, particularly if they become ersatz substitutes for gathered worship. Instead, I think the sacramental intensity of liturgical practices (recalling that the sacraments are also *more* than practices) provides a center of gravity that then orients and nourishes other Christian practices, which are extensions of latent possibilities for practice in Christian worship.[131]

We might think of this by means of a metaphor: imagine the relationship between specifically liturgical practices and other Christian practices by picturing Christian formation as a cathedral. A cathedral is an intentional, complex space for the people of God to engage in worship and discipleship. The way it is organized (in the shape of a cross) not only *says* something; it also *does* something to those who frequent its spaces. At the heart of the cathedral, at the intersection of the cross, is the altar: This is the focal point of Christian worship that culminates in the celebration of the Eucharist. However, the cathedral is also home to all sorts of nooks and crannies that are devoted to other kinds of regular activity. All around the cathedral will be smaller chapels devoted to prayer and reflection that will be used for smaller gatherings, for daily communion, and will include icons and paintings for meditation and devotion.[132] There will be still other corners and spaces in the cathedral that host all sorts of activities. And sometimes these chapels and spaces will be bustling with activity even while worship is happening in the center of the cathedral.

This provides a visual metaphor for thinking about the relationship between the liturgical practices of gathered worship and other Christian practices outside of that. The practices of Christian worship function as the altar of Christian formation, the heart and soul, the center of gravity of the task of discipleship. But the energy and formative power of gathered worship is extended and amplified in the "chapels" around the cathedral— in the different gatherings and practices of Christian communities and friends who together intentionally pursue a life formed by the Spirit, engaged in formative practices that are bent on making us the kind of people who desire the kingdom. If, in a certain sense, the altar is not enough—a sense in which *just* liturgical practices are insufficient counter-measures to secular liturgies—there is also a sense in which extraliturgical practices

131. Dykstra and Bass suggest a different metaphor, which implies a slightly different relationship: "Worship is to daily life . . . as consommé is to broth. In liturgy at its best— in the common work of the people assembled to hear the Word of God and celebrate the sacraments—the meaning of all the practices appears in a form that is thick and tasty, darker and richer than what we get in most everyday situations" ("Times of Yearning," 9). Thus they see liturgical practices as a rehearsal for other Christian practices.

132. This is true not only of medieval cathedrals; the (postmodern) Cathedral of Our Lady of Angels in Los Angeles includes ten devotional chapels: five of them are reserved for fixed devotion; the others have flexible uses.

will have diminished formative power (or worse, could themselves become practices aimed at quite a distorted picture of the kingdom) if they are not tethered to and nourished by the practices of Christian worship. In the next chapter, we'll consider how this cathedral metaphor might help us to reenvision the relationship between the practices of Christian worship and the task of Christian education.

6

A Christian University Is for Lovers

The Education of Desire

In this final chapter, we return to the question that opened our adventure: What is education *for*? And more specifically, what is a distinctly Christian education for? But since we first asked the question, I hope we've come to appreciate three things: First, we humans are liturgical animals, whose fundamental orientation to the world is governed not primarily by what we think but by what we love, what we desire. Our being-in-the-world hinges fundamentally on the heart. Our loves and desires are aimed and directed by habits that dispose us to be the kind of people aimed at certain visions of the good life, particular visions of the kingdom (chapter 1). Those habits are formed through practices that train our desire by fueling our imagination through concrete, material rituals. Such formation is largely affective and precognitive, shaping our adaptive unconscious; but because we are affective, imaginative creatures, this makes such formation all the more powerful and effective (even if it might also be covert and subterranean).

Second, we argued that some practices are "thicker" than others—rituals of ultimate concern that are bent on shaping our most fundamental wants and desires, trying to make us the kind of people who desire a vision of the kingdom that is antithetical to the kingdom of God (chapter 2). Thus we described these thick practices as *liturgies* and considered examples of particular "secular" liturgies in North American culture (chapter 3).

The appreciation of human beings as liturgical, desiring animals, coupled with the exegesis of secular liturgies, then positioned us to take up a third theme: a reconsideration of what's at stake in Christian worship. Fundamentally, the concern was to emphasize that Christianity is not only (or even primarily) a set of cognitive, heady beliefs; Christianity is not fundamentally a worldview. Or, as so aptly put by Cardinal Ratzinger (now Pope Benedict XVI), "Christianity is not an intellectual system, a collection of dogmas, or a moralism. Christianity is instead an encounter, a love story; it is an event."[1] Rather, we sought to show that what Christians think and believe (and they *do* think and believe, and that's a good thing!) grows out of what Christians *do*. Christian practices, and particularly the practices of Christian worship, are the matrix for what can be articulated as a "Christian worldview" (chapter 4). Instead of articulating abstract formulas of a Christian worldview, we undertook an exegesis of the understanding implicit in the Christian social imaginary as it is carried in the practices of Christian worship (chapter 5). Christian worship was thus seen as its own pedagogy of desire, enacting a counter-formation to the secular liturgies in which we are otherwise immersed. Implicit and embedded in our full-bodied participation in Christian worship is a distinct, rich social imaginary.

Returning to our opening question, we can now formulate it with a little more nuance: First, how does this help us re-vision the end or goal of Christian education? Second, how does this help us re-vision the task of Christian education? In short: What is a Christian college for? And what makes it unique—what makes it "Christian"? In the space that remains, I will sketch what a Christian education could or should look like if we are liturgical animals. Before doing so, I make several provisos. First, my sketch of a distinctly Christian education will, I'm afraid, entail some critique

1. Ratzinger, "Homily for Msgr Luigi Giussani," *Communio: International Catholic Review* 31 (2004): 685, as cited by Tracey Rowland, *Ratzinger's Faith: The Theology of Pope Benedict XVI* (Oxford: Oxford University Press, 2008), 67. This was said in the context of a funeral eulogy for Luigi Giussani, who founded the Italian lay movement *Communione e liberazione* in 1969. Giussani also articulated influential reflections on the nature and task of Catholic education, including *The Risk of Education: Discovering Our Ultimate Destiny*, trans. Rosanna Frongia (New York: Crossroad, 2001), which could be read as a Catholic correlate to my project here. In an appreciative engagement with *The Risk of Education*, Stanley Hauerwas also criticizes such "intellectualization" of Christian faith, which seems a very apt description of certain tendencies in Christian higher education, particularly within the Reformed tradition. See Hauerwas, "How Risky Is *The Risk of Education*? Random Reflections from the American Context," in *The State of the University: Academic Knowledges and the Knowledge of God* (Oxford: Blackwell, 2007), 51. We'll return to this issue below.

of current practices in Christian education only because I think Christian colleges, universities, and schools have unwittingly bought into a stunted picture of the human person and a somewhat domesticated construal of Christian faith. Such criticisms do not constitute a wholesale critique or rejection of Christian higher education as it now stands; indeed, I hope that some of what we've considered to this point will help students at Christian colleges to understand something of what animates the existence of such institutions. So even if they involve some critique, these reflections are offered by a devotee, as the dreaming of a fellow laborer who is committed to the project of Christian education. Second, I am aware that, in some ways, the description of education that follows describes a university that doesn't exist.[2] Rather than seeing this as a description of a fiction, think of it as a description in hope. Third, you will not find here any tips or tricks, no nifty methods or alliterated formulas on handouts that you can take home and try out in your classrooms—at least not yet.[3] Nonetheless, I hope this brief sketch will suggest some concrete possibilities that can be taken up by others.

A New Monasticism for the University: Why Christian Colleges Should Corrupt the Youth

What is a Christian university[4] for? Or what is the end of a Christian education? Please note that this is not the same as asking, "What makes a university *Christian*?" As we noted in the introduction, the most com-

2. In this sense, I'm working in the spirit of Michael Budde's essay, "Assessing What Doesn't Exist: Reflections on the Impact of an Ecclesially Based University," in *Conflicting Allegiances: The Church-Based University in a Liberal Democratic Society*, ed. Michael Budde and John Wright (Grand Rapids: Brazos, 2004), 255–71.

3. With David Smith, I am currently co-directing an initiative entitled "From Christian Practices to Christian Pedagogy," funded by the Valparaiso Project on the Education and Formation of People in Faith. The initiative brings together an interdisciplinary team of scholars working in different sorts of church-related educational contexts in order to consider just how the "genius" of Christian formative practices—both liturgical and nonliturgical—could somehow be marshaled to contribute to education at Christian colleges and universities. We will host a conference on the theme in fall 2009 and produce a book that we hope will provide, not "tips and tricks," but at least some concrete examples from which others could extrapolate.

4. Perhaps it would be helpful to clarify that I will generally use the terms *university* and *college* interchangeably in this context, though I recognize there could be differences. Furthermore, in both cases, I have in mind something like a liberal arts college or a comprehensive university, schools that engage a wide range of disciplines (and perhaps even the professions). Thus I am *not* thinking of a "Bible college," which has a narrower task and identity. Finally, though I here focus on higher education, I think many of these issues and concerns extend to Christian K–12 education as well. I hope to address that context in more detail elsewhere.

mon answer to the latter question is that a Christian education provides "a Christian perspective" on the world, equipping young people to be successful but redemptive contributors to society precisely because they have been apprenticed in the disciplines and professions from the perspective of a Christian worldview. Such an answer to the latter question assumes an implicit answer to the former question, "What is the end of a Christian education?" According to this dominant paradigm, the goal of a Christian education is to produce professionals who do pretty much the same sorts of things that graduates of Ivy League and state universities do, but who do them "from a Christian perspective," and perhaps with the goal of transforming culture or redeeming society. So the Christian university graduates students equipped to take up vocations and careers that are largely the same as the graduates of the state university down the road: we graduate engineers and entrepreneurs, nurses and math teachers, museum curators and architects, social workers and audiologists, and a few philosophers to staff the local Starbucks. Our graduates have the requisite credentials[5] to become productive contributors to society, even leaders, exerting influence on culture. And on top of all this, they are graduating not only with the requisite knowledge, skills, and credentials, but also with a Christian worldview. They have been trained to think about and pursue their vocations "from a Christian perspective."

But what if that's not enough? Or worse, what if a Christian perspective turns out to be a way of domesticating the radicality of the gospel? What if the rather abstract formulas of a Christian worldview turn out to be a way to tame and blunt the radical call to be a disciple of the coming kingdom? Could it be the case that learning a Christian perspective doesn't actually touch my desire, and that while I might be able to *think* about the world from a Christian perspective, at the end of the day I *love* not the kingdom of God but rather the kingdom of the market? By reducing the genius of Christian faith to something like an intellectual framework—a "perspective" or a "worldview"—we can (perhaps unwittingly) unhook Christianity from the practices that constitute Christian discipleship. And when that happens, we end up thinking that being a Christian doesn't radically re-

5. John Wright rightly notes that accreditation is itself a matter of concern here: "Church-related colleges and universities ostensibly seek to initiate their church's young members into the society while simultaneously maintaining their loyalty to their church. Yet it is the society that measures an educational institution's quality, granting educational legitimacy by evaluating the church-related university's ability to recruit and train students who can best participate and govern within the liberal societal structures—i.e., producing those who, if they have Christian commitments and convictions, have learned to keep such convictions private and personal in service of the liberal nation-state." See Wright, "How Many Masters? From the Church-Related to an Ecclesially Based University," in Budde and Wright, *Conflicting Allegiances*, 23.

configure our desires and our wants, our practices and our habits. Sure, we might think that we're supposed to be moral, but we'll construe this in terms of personal integrity (e.g., "honest" business dealings) or instrumentalizing existing cultural systems for charitable ends (e.g., "redeeming" exploitative business practices by donating a portion of profits to charity; or generating philanthropy for non-profits that is fueled by the charity of the extremely wealthy). In too many cases, a Christian perspective doesn't seem to challenge the very configuration of these careers and vocations. To be blunt, our Christian colleges and universities generate an army of alumni who look pretty much like all the rest of their suburban neighbors, except that our graduates drive their SUVs, inhabit their executive homes, and pursue the frenetic life of the middle class and the corporate ladder "from a Christian perspective."

How does that happen? I'm suggesting that Christian education has, for too long, been concerned with *in*formation rather than *form*ation; thus Christian colleges have thought it sufficient to provide a Christian perspective, an intellectual framework, because they see themselves as fostering individual "minds in the making."[6] Hand in hand with that, such an approach reduces Christianity to a denuded intellectual framework that has diminished bite because such an intellectualized rendition of the faith doesn't touch our core passions. This is because such intellectualization of Christianity allows it to be unhooked from the thick practices of the church. When the Christianity of "Christian education" is reduced to the intellectual elements of a Christian worldview or a Christian perspective,

6. There are several other reasons why Christian colleges have been reticent to see themselves as engaged in Christian formation: for some, it is because such talk seems to come with the baggage of fundamentalist pietism. It seems to make the Christian college an extension of Sunday school. This is sometimes particularly amplified for institutions that were formerly Bible schools, or Bible colleges, and are now at pains to distinguish themselves as universities. For others, the reticence stems from a worry about making a distinction between the "sphere" of the college and the "sphere" of the church. And third, some are skittish about thinking of the Christian college as a site of formation because "spiritual formation" on campuses has often been configured as anti-intellectual—the sort of warm and fuzzy stuff that goes on in student life (and that can, admittedly, militate against the rigors of intellectual pursuit). Faculty who have these worries are usually concerned to emphasize that our task as faculty is to teach students to "think critically"—as if forming students in the fullness of discipleship wouldn't entail a place from which to engage in critique. In my book, none of these worries is sufficient to reject the centrality of Christian formation to the task of the Christian university. In contrast, I'm suggesting that if Christian colleges are not about Christian formation, there's really no reason for them to exist. There are much more efficient ways to pick up "a Christian perspective." At the end of the day, I think those who resist the notion of Christian formation as integral to the Christian college do so because of a commitment to liberal autonomy. Christian education for Christian formation is "illiberal," but that doesn't make it wrong; it might just make it *Christian*.

the result is that Christianity is turned "into a belief system available to the individual without mediation by the church."[7] "Such a strategy," Hauerwas notes, "assumes that what makes a Christian a Christian is holding certain beliefs that help us better understand the human condition, to make sense of our experience."[8] Such a transformation of Christian faith into a belief system unhooks Christianity from the practices of Christian worship, and thus keeps its distance from the radical revisioning of society that is implicit in Christian liturgy (see chapter 5). Christianity "is not beliefs about God plus behavior. We are Christians not because of what we believe but because we have been called to be disciples of Jesus. Becoming a disciple is not a matter of a new or changed self-understanding but of becoming part of a different community with a different set of practices."[9] But the domestication of Christianity as a *perspective* does little to disturb or reorient our practices; rather, it too often becomes a way of affirming the configurations of culture that we find around us—we just do what everyone else does "plus Jesus."[10] Or, to quote some favorite lingo, our Christian schools will be committed to "excellence"—which turns out to be what other schools value, but we add some Jesus-piety to the mix. And all the while the liturgies of the mall and the military-entertainment complex are making us the kind of people who desire *their* kingdoms, even though we might be *thinking* "from a Christian perspective."

What's the alternative? If Christian education is not merely about acquiring a Christian perspective or a Christian worldview, what is its goal? Its goal, I'm suggesting, is the same as the goal of Christian worship: to form radical disciples of Jesus and citizens of the baptismal city who, communally, take up the creational task of being God's image bearers, unfolding the cultural possibilities latent in creation—but doing so as empowered by the Spirit, following the example of Jesus's cruciform cultural labor. If the goal of Christian worship and discipleship is the formation of a peculiar people, then the goal of Christian education should be the same. If something like Christian universities are to exist, they should be configured as extensions of the mission of the church—as chapels that extend and amplify what's happening at the heart of the cathedral, at the altar of Christian worship. In short, the task of Christian education needs to be reconnected to the thick practices of the church.

7. Hauerwas, "How Risky?" 51.
8. Stanley Hauerwas, *After Christendom? How the Church Is to Behave If Freedom, Justice, and a Christian Nation Are Bad Ideas* (Nashville: Abingdon, 1991), 95.
9. Ibid., 107.
10. In addition, such unhooking of a Christian worldview from the thickness of the church's worship frees up this deracinated Christianity to then be hitched to other dominant visions of the good life, either conservative or liberal. This is why Christians on both the Right and the Left are prone to worldview-talk.

Instead of talking about "Christian colleges"—which makes it easier to traffic in the abstraction of "Christianity" as an intellectual system—perhaps we should instead speak of "ecclesial" colleges and "ecclesial" universities.[11] If Christian faith cannot be adequately distilled into the formulas of a Christian worldview, but rather is a social imaginary that is carried in the distinct practices of Christian worship, then any institution that would be meaningfully "Christian" would need to be a liturgical institution of sorts, animated by the specificity of Christian liturgical practices. If education is always a matter of formation, and the most profound formation happens in various liturgies, then a Christian education must draw deeply from the well of Christian liturgy. In short, the Christian university should not only be born but also nourished *ex corde ecclesiae*, "from the heart of the church."[12] In doing so, the Christian university should contribute to the formation of radical disciples of Jesus who, while exploring the properties of protons and the surrealism of Dali, will have our desires (and hence knowledge) configured by the practices of Christian worship that prime us to be a peculiar people whose thick vision of the kingdom of God has led us to make baptismal renunciations of what the surrounding culture might consider "excellence."

The ecclesial university will extend and amplify the formation that begins and continues in Christian worship, drawing on the liturgical formation of the imagination in order to be able to imagine the world otherwise, thus countering the liturgies of the status quo university, "the great institution of legitimation in modernity whose task is to convince us that the way things are is the way things have to be."[13] In this respect, the ecclesial university would be a counter-cultural institution without being an anticultural institution; rather, it would be an institution forming and equipping a peculiar people to unfold creation's cultural possibilities in a way that accords with the cruciform shape of the kingdom in the "not yet" of our sojourn.[14]

---

11. Compare discussions of the "ecclesially based university" in Budde and Wright, *Conflicting Allegiances*, passim.

12. Pope John Paul II, *Ex corde ecclesiae*, Apostolic Constitution on Catholic Universities, 1990. Speaking of "ecclesial" colleges presents both a challenge and an opportunity for existing "Christian" colleges. For those whose identity is nondenominational, it's hard to know just which church would constitute the heart from which they should be born and nourished. On the other hand, for colleges that are denominational, being an ecclesial university might make better sense of the relationship between the church and the college (though one hopes that the denomination or church sees itself as "catholic"). The model of an ecclesial college encourages a postmodern embrace of what I have elsewhere called "the scandal of particularity." See James K. A. Smith, *Who's Afraid of Postmodernism? Taking Derrida, Lyotard, and Foucault to Church* (Grand Rapids: Baker Academic, 2006), 122–27.

13. Hauerwas, introduction to *State of the University*, 6.

14. Hauerwas rightly perceives that the dream of an ecclesial university raises a challenging question: "The question for me is not whether the university can be Christian, but

Hence I would suggest that the ecclesial university—the Christian university that is nourished by the liturgical practices of the church—would represent a kind of "new monasticism" for the university.[15] While not being a church, or a substitute for the church, but rather an extension of it (a chapel connected to the nave of the cathedral), the new monastic university will be an institution of Christian formation, intentionally drawing on and incorporating the range of Christian practices that form desire and fuel the imagination. It will be an institution committed to the search for truth and advancing knowledge, concerned with "all things," but that doesn't necessarily mean it will look like a Christian knock-off of the state university. No realm of investigation will be out of bounds, but that doesn't necessarily mean it will invest resources in all the same things as the Ivy League.[16] It will be passionately concerned with the formation of cultural leaders, but the "culture" to which it hopes to provide leaders may not be the dominant culture it finds itself in. Because of the students' baptismal renunciations and select cultural abstention, the ecclesial university curriculum may not look like other "normal" universities but with a "Christian perspective." The new monastic university would be much stranger than many of our existing Christian colleges, but its strangeness would stem from the fact that it is a space for the formation of a peculiar people.

Now, in the interest of full disclosure, I should note that such a configuration of Christian education is likely to cause trouble. As Budde rightly observes, "To say that an ecclesially based university is concerned primarily with forming its students, faculty, and staff in determinate directions invites conflict with the dominant assumptions regarding education and formation in the U.S."[17] More to the point, it's likely that an ecclesial university would not lead to "success." As Hauerwas wryly observes, "to educate our children in such an alternative culture will mean that our children cannot presuppose that the education they receive will make it possible for them

whether a church exists sufficient to sustain a Christian university." Stanley Hauerwas, *With the Grain of the Universe: The Church's Witness and Natural Theology* (Grand Rapids: Brazos, 2001), 233.

15. On the "new monasticism," see *School(s) for Conversion: 12 Marks of a New Monasticism*, ed. Rutba House (Eugene, OR: Cascade Books, 2005). We would also do well to learn from "old" monasticism in this regard. For the classic study, see Jean LeClercq, OSB, *The Love of Learning and the Desire for God: A Study of Monastic Culture*, trans. Catharine Misrahi (Bronx, NY: Fordham University Press, 1961). My thanks to Bob Frazier for pointing me to this resource.

16. For some honest appraisals of related issues, see Therese Lysaught, "Love Your Enemies: The Life Sciences in the Ecclesially Based University," in Budde and Wright, *Conflicting Allegiances*, 109–27; and Robert Brimlow, "Who Invited Mammon? Professional Education in the Christian College and University," in ibid., 156–70.

17. Budde, "Assessing What Doesn't Exist," 258.

to be successful actors in a world shaped by a quite different culture."[18] Indeed, that is precisely the *risk* of an authentic Christian education. Is that a risk we're willing to take? I wonder. Most of the time I find myself agreeing with Hauerwas, who writes, "It is clear that those who support Christian universities would be quite upset if the qualifier came to mean that the education students received might put them at a disadvantage for being a success in America."[19] But at other times, I catch tiny glimpses that it could be otherwise: that perhaps a generation is coming that would see it as the calling and task of the Christian university to "corrupt the youth" precisely by making them citizens of the coming kingdom, thereby making them (thankfully) useless and unproductive for what currently passes for "society."

Christian Education Takes Practice: Three "Monastic" Opportunities

I have thus far suggested that Christian education ought to be specified as *ecclesial* education, more specifically tethered to the thick practices of Christian worship. If the Christian university's motto is, "I believe in order to understand," the ecclesial university's motto is, "I worship in order to understand." Indeed, the practice of Christian worship *is* understanding. So what would such liturgically informed learning look like? What would Christian education look like if the "Christian" were qualified and defined by Christian practices rather than just Christian beliefs or Christian ideas? I will briefly suggest three "monastic opportunities" for enacting this vision.

Reconnecting Church, Chapel, and Classroom: En-formed Learning

By now it is a truism that a chapel does not guarantee a Christian education. And nothing in my argument would want to suggest otherwise, for at least two reasons: First, a chapel could be part of an assumed rigid distinction between nature and grace, between the secular and the sacred. In such a scenario, the chapel might be ministering to students' "spiritual needs," while the real business of the university—the work of academic exploration and apprenticeship—is taken to be a wholly secular affair, a natural rather than a supernatural concern. As such, the chapel and the classroom would be partitioned by a towering wall of separation. Or, second, the shape of worship in the chapel might bear little if any resem-

18. Hauerwas, "How Risky?" 53.
19. Stanley Hauerwas, "How Universities Contribute to the Corruption of Youth," in *Christian Existence Today: Essays on Church, World, and Living in Between* (Durham, NC: Labyrinth, 1988), 240.

blance to the rich practices of Christian worship outlined in chapter 5, even if it might seem to be exuberantly concerned with praising Jesus. The chapel's worship might be little more than a "Jesufied" version of various secular liturgies, thus unwittingly reinforcing the liturgies of the mall and the market rather than contributing to any kind of counter-formation. In either case, the chapel would be doing nothing to make the educational project discernibly "Christian."

Because of these sorts of disconnects between campus worship and classroom learning, at some Christian colleges there can be a tension and even animosity between chapel/campus worship and what faculty take to be the mission of the university as expressed in the classroom. The suspicion can run both ways: on the one hand, faculty who are committed to intellectual formation and the rigors of developing "the life of the mind" worry that campus worship contributes to behaviors and dispositions that are "uncritical." They may find that some students who are heavily involved in campus worship express a piety that doesn't seem as interested in understanding the rigors of econometrics or Latin declensions. On the other hand, those involved with campus worship tend to see scholars and students who are devoted to the work of scholarship and the advancement of knowledge but are neglecting the life of worship, and they may even have little use for church. Their Christianity, if it finds any expression, seems to be expressed in theoretical constructs or progressive politics. From both sides, there is probably a combination of legitimate concern and biased misunderstanding. At its worst, the one side can't figure out why we have a chapel on campus, while the other side might sometimes find it hard to answer the question, "Why go to class?"

I think such disconnect and tension stems from the fact that both sides of this equation tend to work with an implicit philosophical anthropology that fails to appreciate that we are liturgical animals and thus fails to appreciate the central role of practices in formation. As a correlate to that, both sides will tend to either reduce Christianity to a belief system or an emotivist experience. But if we begin from the assumption that humans are liturgical animals, and that the Christian social imaginary is carried in the practices of Christian worship, then a very different picture should emerge: the role of the chapel is not to stir our emotions or merely fuel our "spiritual" needs; rather, it is the space in which the ecclesial university community gathers to practice (for) the kingdom by engaging in the liturgical practices that form the imagination. If Christian education is formation, and such formation happens in the full-bodied practices of worship, then worship is the sine qua non of Christian education. Worship, in other words, is the crucial incubator for hatching Christian accounts of the world.

Now, first and foremost, the liturgical nourishment of Christian education should happen in the context of the church proper; that is, Christian
students and teachers should be immersed in the gathered, sacramental
worship that happens in parishes on Sunday mornings.[20] It is only there
(at least in Protestant contexts) that the sacraments can be received. For
instance, one's imagination will not likely be shaped by baptism in campus
worship. In addition, there is something deeply formative about intergenerational worship that is crucial to the kind of people the church is called
to be. Thus students should resist the temptation to think of chapel or
campus worship as a substitute for church. However, what campus worship
does represent is precisely a sort of monastic opportunity, the opportunity to extend and amplify the church's Sunday worship in daily practices
of gathered liturgical observance. The chapel could be seen as a kind of
"mediating institution" between the university and the church.

Given that human beings are liturgical animals, and given that the Christian social imaginary is absorbed and formed in worship, I think campus
worship becomes an integral element of the *academic* project of the Christian university. Note, however, that this is not a matter of making the chapel
another classroom, the largest lecture hall on campus. The chapel needn't
"redeem" itself to suspicious faculty by becoming more academic. Rather,
the tasks of teaching, learning, and scholarship are always already fueled
by some social imaginary—some implicit understanding of the world.
Insofar as *Christian* teaching, learning, and scholarship are to be formed
by a *Christian* social imaginary, the rhythms and rituals of campus worship provide welcome opportunities to continue to form and reform our
imaginations. In addition, when faculty and students worship together, that
in itself is a mode of "life together" (Bonhoeffer) that further nourishes
the common tasks of teaching, learning, and cultural formation.

Reconnecting Classroom, Dorm Room, and Neighborhood: Environments for Learning

If the liturgical practices of the ecclesial university provide a rationale
for reconnecting the church, chapel, and classroom, they should equally
foster links between the classroom and the dorms, the sector on campus
that, from a faculty perspective, is a kind of netherworld. Neither the
classroom nor the chapel are vacuums or islands unto themselves; stu-

20. This is also why I think it is crucial for campus ministries at "secular" universities
to be connected with parishes and churches, lest students come to think of the selective
realities of campus worship as "church." This is not to denigrate campus worship or
campus ministry but only to invite it to find its fount and source in the church's gathered,
sacramental worship. In this respect, denominational campus ministries have an opportunity
where parachurch campus ministries may have a challenge.

dents and faculty enter them from other places. Generally, students make their way from dormitories, residence halls, apartments, or perhaps frat houses or sorority houses. Faculty are generally coming from somewhere else: surrounding neighborhoods or long commutes from elsewhere, from a condo shared with a roommate or a home bustling with kids. How do these environments prime us (or not) for the task of Christian teaching or learning?[21] Are these not also spaces of formation, for good or ill? How might the vision of an ecclesial university and liturgically shaped education invite us to rethink the relationship between living environments and learning? Here again, I think the task and vocation of a Christian university presents a monastic opportunity.

One of the most crucial things to appreciate about Christian formation is that it happens over time. It is not fostered by events or experiences; real formation cannot be effected by actions that are merely episodic. There must be a rhythm and a regularity to formative practices in order for them to sink in—in order for them to seep into our *kardia* and begin to be effectively inscribed in who we are, directing our passion to the kingdom of God and thus disposing us to action that reflects such a desire. As we saw at the end of chapter 5, Sunday morning worship is crucial but insufficient in this regard; thus we noted that what is required are daily Christian practices, including liturgical practices of communal worship. But here even a half hour of chapel each day, while crucial and formative, seems a bare minimum. What if we saw the wider environment of the university as also a space for fostering Christian practices, including liturgical practices? The unique nature of residential higher education provides an opportunity to create intentional communities within the dorms that not only gather for Bible study and prayer but also engage in a range of full-bodied Christian practices, including liturgical practices such as prayerful observance of the Daily Office or "Divine Hours."[22] Such intentional community could also include commitments to common meals; Sabbath observance; works of mercy in the neighborhood; weekly acts of hospitality for students, faculty, or those outside the university community; fasting together once a week; worship together at a local parish; a yearly service project; and more. Together these practices would constitute a rich fabric of formation

21. Urie Bronfenbrenner provides a fascinating analysis of the various layers of a learning environment in terms of ecology, noting the effects of microsystems, mesosystems, and macrosystems. See Bronfenbrenner, "The Ecology of Cognitive Development," in *Development in Context: Acting and Thinking in Specific Environments*, ed. R. H. Wozniak and K. W. Fisher (Hillsdale, NJ: Lawrence Erlbaum Associates, 1993), 3–44. This framework is ripe for thinking further about the issues being briefly explored here. My thanks to David Smith for the reference.

22. For an accessible introduction to the practice of fixed hour prayer, see Phyllis Tickle, *The Divine Hours*, pocket ed. (New York: Oxford University Press, 2007).

that would nourish the imagination and prime the community for thinking Christianly in their learning and scholarship.

Two related opportunities in this regard should be noted. First, there is no reason why such intentional communities should be limited to on-campus dormitories. Off-campus intentional communities would provide a unique monastic opportunity for students to be the *ekklēsia* for the world simply by being a community in and for a neighborhood, enacting Augustine's vision of "urban monasticism." Being situated in a neighborhood would provide opportunities for formation not available in a dormitory context, including learning to be a good neighbor in a very concrete way, disciplining one's rhythms by the bus schedule, walking to get groceries and actually getting to know one's neighbors.[23] Such off-campus community would provide an occasion for adopting rhythms of inhabiting the built environment that are reflective of a people who are looking for a city (Rev. 21:2) and who are enjoined to "seek the welfare of the city" (Jer. 29:7). Or conversely, students may intentionally live on a nearby farm, contributing to the work of community-supported agriculture, committing to local food and economies, inhabiting space in a way that witnesses to our creational charge to care for a now broken and groaning creation.[24]

Second, and related to what we've just mentioned, there is also no reason why such intentional communities should be comprised of just students. The richness of "life together" would be deepened and extended if such communities brought together students, faculty, staff, and their families to pursue a common regimen of Christian practices.[25] This could either happen by creating on-campus living arrangements that can include faculty/staff families in a meaningful environment; or it can happen by having students live in homes in geographical proximity to faculty families, building a neighborhood nexus of friendship and common practice. The intergenerational mix provides opportunities for those who are older to mentor those who are younger, partly by example and partly by discussion—including students mentoring faculty and staff children—as together the community pursues a life of discipleship that includes intentional concern for learning and scholarship as the unique "apostolate" of these communities. This

23. For further discussion, see James K. A. Smith, "The Architecture of Urban Altruism: Learning to Love Our Neighbor(hood)s," *Comment* (September 2007): 60–64; and Nicholas Wolterstorff, "A City of Delight," in *Until Justice and Peace Embrace* (Grand Rapids: Eerdmans, 1983), 124–40.

24. They might begin by tackling the work of Wendell Berry with the help of J. Matthew Bonzo and Michael R. Stevens, *Wendell Berry and the Cultivation of Life: A Reader's Guide* (Grand Rapids: Brazos, 2008).

25. My thanks to the students who joined us for the Semester in Britain program in York in spring 2008. The experience of becoming friends helped me to see that this might actually be possible.

is not a covert way of having faculty function *in loco parentis*; rather, it would be an opportunity for faculty and their families to function *in loco amici*—as "wise friends" who are sisters and brothers of our students, engaged in the common project of trying to be the people of God.[26]

Reconnecting Body and Mind: Embodied Learning

Finally, how might actual pedagogy be transformed in an ecclesial university? Drawing on the anthropology that is implicit in Christian worship—which performatively affirms that we are embodied, material creatures whose orientation to the world is governed by the imagination—the pedagogy of the ecclesial university will extend and amplify the pedagogical genius that is implicit in the practices of Christian worship as well as other Christian practices. It will not be sufficient (or effective) to deliver Christian content in pedagogies that are designed for thinking things. If the practices of Christian worship attest to the fact that we are embodied, liturgical animals whose desire is shaped by material practices, how odd it would be to think a distinctly Christian education could be effected by what Bradford Hadaway calls "read and talk" courses.[27] Rather, a liturgically informed pedagogy, assuming and drawing upon the "education" that already takes place in the liturgy, will also seek ways to extend and improvise upon Christian practices in order to create a learning environment that is animated by intentional practices that form the imagination and shape character. Consider just a few examples:

- An advanced seminar in continental philosophy investigates a key theme in contemporary French thought—the shape of hospitality, particularly as explored in the work of Emmanuel Lévinas and Jacques Derrida. As a way of concretizing the issues in practice, the instructor requires students in the seminar to adopt intentional practices of hospitality throughout the semester, working through the Service-Learning Center. Some work at a homeless shelter in the inner city; others work in restorative justice programs for ex-convicts at the county jail; others work with a refugee ministry at a local church.

26. See Michael Cartwright, "Moving beyond Muddled Missions and Misleading Metaphors: Formation and Vocation of Students within an Ecclesial Based University," in Budde and Wright, *Conflicting Allegiances*, 197–201. Cartwright rightly cautions, "At the end of the day, if we no longer believe that faculty at church-related colleges and universities should aspire to cultivate 'wise friendships' with their students, then perhaps church-related higher education in American culture doesn't deserve to survive at all" (201).

27. Bradford S. Hadaway, "Preparing the Way for Justice: Strategic Dispositional Formation through the Spiritual Disciplines," *Spirituality, Justice, and Pedagogy*, ed. David I. Smith, John Shortt, and John Sullivan, special issue of the *Journal of Education and Christian Belief* 10 (2006): 143.

While undertaking practices of hospitality, students are reading arduous philosophical texts discussing hospitality, which are then discussed in the seminar. Throughout the semester, students keep a journal of their experiences and their readings. Many are surprised to find that though they went to the poor, homeless, and needy to "show hospitality," *they* were the ones who were welcomed. The concrete exercise of hospitality—and being welcomed—also gives them a critical perspective on the texts under consideration that they would not have had otherwise.[28]

- A class in German literature adopts the Christian practice of *lectio divina* as a way of inculcating a hermeneutics of charity and humility in the reading of literature. In addition to fostering a more loving, attentive approach to texts (rather than the usual consumptive, chew-it-up and spit-it-out voracious reading that our syllabi encourage), student journals indicate that the dispositions and habits formed by the practice of *lectio divina* are beginning to spill over into a general hermeneutic, a general stance toward the world, as one of the students finds herself "reading" a problematic stranger in the coffee shop differently than she would have before engaging in the practices of *lectio divina*.[29]

- Or finally, consider a version of a course on "Poverty and Wealth: Issues in Economic Justice" that, rather than adopting the standard "read and talk" approach to various readings, incorporates required practices intended to foster "dispositional formation" to justice. The syllabus requires students to select from a range of "moral exercises," practices directly relevant to issues of poverty, drawing on spiritual disciplines of voluntary simplicity, fasting, and so on. What would have otherwise been rather abstract readings on hunger, poverty, and the distribution of wealth—particularly for mainly middle-class students—takes on a new life, even urgency, because they are being read by students engaged in relevant bodily practices and spiritual disciplines.[30]

These are just a few concrete examples of ecclesial pedagogies that incorporate embodied learning, both assuming and extending a network of liturgical practices and spiritual disciplines. This is not teaching that is

28. Consider also the exploration of hospitality to the stranger as a way to reframe practices of foreign-language education in David I. Smith and Barbara Carvill, *The Gift of the Stranger: Faith, Hospitality, and Foreign Language Learning* (Grand Rapids: Eerdmans, 2000).
29. Thanks to my colleague David Smith for sharing this vignette.
30. This example is recounted in Hadaway, "Preparing the Way," 143–65.

content to disseminate ideas or remain at the level of providing *in*formation; it is teaching that is committed to a thick vision of Christian education as *form*ation. In doing so, it takes seriously our nature as liturgical animals and the *telos* of a robustly Christian education.

Christian Worship as Faculty Development: From Christian Scholars to Ecclesial Scholars

These (albeit brief) reflections on the shape of liturgically informed Christian teaching and learning invite correlate reflections on the shape of liturgically informed Christian scholarship. Unfortunately, space does not permit articulation of that here.[31] Suffice it to say that if Christian education "takes practice," so too does Christian scholarship, which is itself a practice. If our theorizing and scholarship are going to be informed by Christian accounts of the world, our imaginations must first be fueled by a vision of the kingdom, and such formation of the imagination takes place in the practices of Christian worship, which carry a unique understanding of the world ("I worship in order to understand"). Such understanding—a Christian social imaginary that, really, *precedes* a Christian worldview—is absorbed through participation in the liturgy. Thus any Christian scholarship worth the name must emerge from the matrix of worship. In short, Christian scholarship must be ecclesial scholarship.

31. I hope to develop this in a small book for faculty development programs at church-related universities; the book will focus on both the importance of "Scriptural reasoning" and "liturgical reasoning" for the task of Christian scholarship and Christian teaching in higher education.

Name Index

Subject Index